CONTENTS

Eating & Drinking 105

Living 135

Frommer's

NYC FREE

& DIRT CHEAP

1st Edition

by Ethan Wolff

Wiley Publishing, Inc.

Published by:

Wiley Publishing, Inc.

111 River St.

Hoboken, NJ 07030-5774

ISBN 0-7645-5932-X

Editor: John Vorwald
Production Editor: Tammy Ahrens
Cartographer: Nick Trotter
Production by Wiley Indianapolis Composition Services
Interior design by Melissa Auciello-Brogan
Front cover cartography courtesy of Mapquest
Photos on p. x, 4, 16, 134, 170, 208, 256, and 292 by John Vorwald
Photo on p. 104 by Ethan Wolff

For information on our other products and services or to obtain technical support, please contact our Customer Care Department within the U.S. at 800/762-2974, outside the U.S. at 317/572-3993 or fax 317/572-4002.

Wiley also publishes its books in a variety of electronic formats. Some content that appears in print may not be available in electronic formats.

Manufactured in the United States of America

5   4   3   2   1

LIST OF MAPS

About the Author

Ethan Wolff left Virginia 10 years ago to take advantage of Manhattan's low, low cost of living. He now lives in the heart of the Bargain District, on the Lower East Side. Ethan is also the author of *Frommer's Irreverent Guide to Manhattan*, 5th Edition.

Acknowledgments

Thanks especially to John Vorwald, who thought up this idea and did the dirty work of development, not to mention editing the damn thing. Thanks also to Johanna Lee, Evelyn Grollman, Anna Sandler, Karen Quarles, Elroy Wolff, and everyone else whose contributions made this book possible; and to anyone who has had to put up with my cheapness over the years. It was all just research.

—Ethan Wolff

Many thanks to Ethan for being a great cheapskate and an even better writer; to Daniel Felsenfeld for his notable contribution to the Entertainment chapter; to Gene Cawley for lending his design prowess; to Nick Trotter for his excellent maps, and Alan Buchnam for advising on the inside front cover; to AE Kessel for being our model consumer; to Aliyah Vinikoor and Erin Weaver for helping out in a pinch; to Tammy Ahrens for her patience, input, and attention to detail; and to Kelly Regan and Brice Gosnell for, among many other things, supporting the idea of this book in the first place.

—John Vorwald

An Invitation to the Reader

In researching this book, we discovered many wonderful places—hotels, restaurants, shops, and more. We're sure you'll find others. Please tell us about them, so we can share the information with your fellow travelers in upcoming editions. If you were disappointed with a recommendation, we'd love to know that, too. Please write to:

Frommer's NYC Free & Dirt Cheap, 1st Edition
Wiley Publishing, Inc. ● 111 River St. ● Hoboken, NJ 07030-5774

An Additional Note

Please be advised that travel information is subject to change at any time—and this is especially true of prices. We therefore suggest that you write or call ahead for confirmation when making your travel plans. The authors, editors, and publisher cannot be held responsible for the experiences of readers while traveling. Your safety is important to us, however, so we encourage you to stay alert and be aware of your surroundings. Keep a close eye on cameras, purses, and wallets, all favorite targets of thieves and pickpockets.

Free & Dirt Cheap Icons & Abbreviations

We also use **four feature icons** that point you to the great deals, in-the-know advice, and unique experiences that separate urban adventurers from tourists. Throughout the book, look for:

FREE Events, attractions, or experiences that cost no more than your time and a swipe of your Metrocard.

FINE PRINT The unspoken conditions or necessary prepartations to experience certain free and dirt cheap events.

☆ The best free and dirt cheap events, dining, shopping, living, and exploring in the city.

OVERRATED Places or experiences, free or otherwise, not worth your time or money.

Frommers.com

Now that you have the guidebook to a great trip, visit our website at **www.frommers.com** for travel information on more than 3,000 destinations. With features updated regularly, we give you instant access to the most current trip-planning information available. At Frommers.com, you'll also find the best prices on airfares, accommodations, and car rentals—and you can even book travel online through our travel booking partners. At Frommers.com, you'll also find the following:

- Online updates to our most popular guidebooks
- Vacation sweepstakes and contest giveaways
- Newsletter highlighting the hottest travel trends
- Online travel message boards with featured travel discussions

Other Great Guides for Your Trip:

Frommer's New York City

Frommer's New York City from $90 a Day

Frommer's Portable New York City

Frommer's Memorable Walks in New York City

Frommer's Irreverent Guide to Manhattan

The Unofficial Guide to Manhattan

For more information about the deals you can find at City Opera and other great thrift stores in NYC, see p. 177 in chapter 5.

THE BEST THINGS IN LIFE ARE FREE

t's no secret that NYC prices are out of control. Take the city's recent hamburger arms race. Were restaurants knocking themselves out to see who could serve up the tastiest, least-expensive patty? Not in New York. This was a contest to see who could post the most absurd price on a hamburger and still get somebody to buy one. DB Bistro Moderne's entry was a $29 burger, made with ground short ribs, foie gras, and shaved black truffles. The Old Homestead restaurant fired right back with the winner, $41 for 20 ounces of Kobe beef and a side of fries.

In May 2004, Norma's at the Parker Meridian unveiled an omelet recipe that put both those burgers to shame. A quick breakfast pick-me-up of six eggs, one lobster, and 10 ounces of sevruga caviar could be had for a cool $1,000. $1,000. For a plate of eggs. Insider bargain tip for *Free & Dirt Cheap* readers: You can get a $100 version made with only 1 ounce of caviar.

It's not just luxury goods like hamburgers and omelets that have gone through the roof lately. The morning *Times* is up to a buck. Cab rides just went up 26%, and a subway ride is up 33%. The sale price of Manhattan apartments leapt almost 30% in just the last year. Want to invest in an "average" place? It's a hair under a million now.

So, in a town with a $50 hamburger and a $1,000 plate of eggs, where an apartment that would make a convict feel claustrophobic sells for a million, a book on living on the cheap must be a pretty slim volume, right?

Wrong.

New York takes a lot of pride in being the cultural capital of the world, and to maintain that reputation we let a lot of the goods go for free. Art, music, dance, drama, and history can all be found for simply the price of showing up. Many of our top-tier museums set aside several hours a week where you pay what you wish to enter. The best work of the world's emerging artists hangs in our galleries, which never charge a fee. TV shows tape all over Midtown and with a little planning you can join the audience for free. New York's libraries circulate thousands of books, videos, and albums, in addition to offering us free films, classes, and lectures.

Attending a big free New York event also entitles you to complementary camaraderie. There's no better feeling than knowing you're in on something amazing, like a band playing its heart out in front of sunset on the Hudson, or a movie flickering beneath the lights of the Brooklyn Bridge, or wending your way out of Central Park with fellow theatergoers after another world-class Shakespearean production. Our legendary festivals and parades kindle that same group spirit. Even little everyday moments can be inspiring. How many years has it been since Hollywood made a movie half as entertaining as a couple of hours sitting on the steps of the New York Public Library, or Federal Hall, or the Met?

In the post-9/11 era we're all appreciating the city in new ways, but it's easy enough to forget that New York is not an inevitability, it's a rare phenomenon. Taking advantage of all the amazing resources here is practically a civic duty. You don't have to be a millionaire to get the most out of the Big Apple. The city's great charm is that it's available to anybody, at any time. You can experience it on your own terms whenever you want. This book will show you the hundreds of ways to get the most for the least in New York City.

After all, the best things in life are free.

Not NYC's most famous freebie, but with a jaw-dropping view and great flicks, the *Brooklyn Bridge Film Series* is one of the city's treasures. See p. 55.

BEST OF THE FREE & DIRT CHEAP APPLE

A lot of great bargains in this world don't withstand close scrutiny. Anyone who's ever "won" a free weekend at a North Carolina timeshare can attest to that. New Yorkers are lucky, however, in having a menu of freebies and cheapies that aren't just discards or traps. From Shakespeare in the Park, to carless drive-in movies, to kayaking along the Hudson, there's a host of remarkable activities here that can't be had in other cities for any price. In the dirt cheap realm, the Big Apple's big volume creates bargain opportunities left and right. From cheap ethnic food to cheap avant-garde theater, an urban adventurer can go far on very little. What follows is the best of the best.

1 Best Entertainment Bets

● **Best Manhattan Parade:** New Yorkers are pros at assembling en masse, especially when it comes time to celebrate the ethnic accidents of birth. My favorite pageant is one of the city's most inclusive, the **Greenwich Village Halloween Parade** `FREE`, where elaborate costumes and a healthy dose of gallows humor make the festive spirit infectious. See p. 26.

● **Best Outer-Borough Parade:** As New York events become more and more commercialized, it's nice to have one occasion that's defiantly do-it-yourself. Coney Island's **Mermaid Parade** `FREE` brings low-budget finery to the Atlantic shore. Classic cars serve as the chariots for a procession of mermaids and Neptunes who will never be accused of being overdressed. See p. 23.

● **Best Festival: Harlem Week** `FREE` began as a single day 30 years ago and now stretches across the entire month of August. Film, jazz, and food festivals are among the highlights to be found along lovely brownstone blocks Uptown. See p. 24.

● **Best DIY Rock Show:** Why trek out to the Nassau Coliseum to watch some aging monsters of rock, when the Lower East Side offers up the same three chords for free? **Punk Rock Heavy Metal Karaoke at Arlene's Grocery** `FREE` (95 Stanton St.; ℂ 212/358-1633) is the tri-state's best place to play rock star, with a real-live band standing in for a soulless laser disc. See p. 30.

● **Best Cultural Center with Beer: Pete's Candy Store** `FREE` (709 Lorimer St.; (ℂ 718/302-3770) does its part to keep Williamsburg elevated and enlightened, bringing in a bushel of live music and poetry and prose readings. Backgammon, quiz, and Scrabble nights round out a full schedule of free diversions. See p. 33.

● **Best New-York-Studio-Sized Music Venue:** The stage is tiny and the seats are few, but the back room of **The Lakeside Lounge** `FREE` (162 Ave. B; ℂ 212/529-8463), brings in improbably big acts. Rock and rock tributaries can be found on most nights and there's never a cover. See p. 31.

- **Best Jazzy Venue:** Upper West Siders can enjoy cover-free jazz on the weeknights at **Smoke** (2751 Broadway; © **212/864-6662**). Retro and nouveau bebop, Hammond B-3 organs, and even a little funk fill out the diverse schedule. Drink minimums apply, but they're not too onerous, especially midweek. See p. 36.

- **Best Concerts for Skipping Out on the Office:** The worker bees of the Financial District have long taken advantage of the great classical performances heard during the **"Concerts at One"** series at **Trinity Church** (74 Trinity Place; © **212/602-0747**) and **St. Paul's Chapel** (Broadway and Fulton St.). St. Paul's hosts lunchtime Mondays and Trinity on Thursdays. The acoustics are great in both churches and the $2 suggested donation doesn't begin to reflect the caliber of talent. See p. 39.

- **Best Summer Music Festival:** Every year **SummerStage** **FREE** (© 212/360-2777) seems to get even better organized, efficiently channeling music fans into a stage area just off the Rumsey Playfield in the middle of Central Park. Though several shows a

year are benefit performances with steep ticket prices, the calendar is still littered with huge names playing for free. See p. 47.

- **Best Summer Music Festival That's Not Summerstage:** The massive **Lincoln Center Out of Doors** **FREE** (70 Lincoln Center Plaza; © **212/546-2656**) festival presents hundreds of acts every August. The range is staggering, covering jazz and dance and opera and everything in between. See p. 46.

- **Best Movie Screenings with a Roof:** Every Sunday night guest curators put together intriguing mini-film festivals for **Ocularis at Galapagos** (70 N. 6th St.; © **718/388-8713**). The films are usually shorts and a long way away from anything you'll find in a multiplex. See p. 50.

- **Best Movie Screenings without a Roof:** Forty-second Street welcomes movie fans with an eclectic selection of classics during the **HBO/Bryant Park Summer Film Festival** **FREE** (© **212/512-5700**). The lawn crowds up quickly, but that only enhances the festive atmosphere. See p. 54.

● **Best Outdoor Summer Theater:** Forsooth, New York's greatest summer asset is no secret. **Shakespeare in the Park** FREE (✆ 212/539-8750) hooks up tens of thousands of bard hounds with the best in Elizabethan drama (using some of today's best actors and directors). The Delacorte Theater's site in the middle of Central Park is well nigh enchanted. See p. 63.

● **Best Outdoor Summer Theater That Isn't Shakespeare in the Park:** Energetic performances substitute for big names and big budgets in downtown's alternative **Shakespeare in the Park(ing) Lot** FREE (✆ 212/253-1813). The setting couldn't be less formal, but somehow the troupe manages to cast its spell. See p. 64.

● **Best Dinner Theater:** A mere $10 investment will get you in to the **Monthly Spaghetti Dinner Series,** put on by Great Small Works at P.S. 122 (150 First Ave.; ✆ 212/477-5288). While forks wrap noodles the stage resounds with dance, drama, film, and sometimes even a little puppeteering. See p. 69.

● **Best Free Dance:** Modern and experimental dance has a home during **Movement Research at the Judson Church** FREE (55 Washington Sq. South; ✆ 212/539-2611). Dancers and choreographers vary from week to week, but the talent level stays consistently high. See p. 73.

● **Best Comedy Troupe:** The founders of **The Upright Citizens Brigade Theatre** (307 W. 26th St.; ✆ 212/366-9176) have gone on to movie and television fortune and fame, but the institution's classes continue to crank out rapier wits. Improv nights here are cheap when they're not free, and the legendary ASSSCAT 3000 is not to be missed. See p. 77.

● **Best Readings:** The great writerly look of **KGB Bar** FREE (85 E. 4th St.; ✆ 212/505-3360) is well matched by the great writers who come through here almost every night of the week. Enough quality words have been spilled beneath the Soviet-kitsch furnishings to justify the publishing of KGB anthologies. See p. 91.

● **Best Readings in a Bookstore:** New York has many great literary events at its mom and pop shops, but the little players don't have quite the juice to bring in huge names every time. The Union Square branch of **Barnes & Noble** `FREE` (33 E. 17th St.; © 212/ 253-0810) has no difficulty booking the literati glitterati— check out their calendar for a steady stream of famous scribblers. See p. 86.

2 Best Cheap Eats

- **Best Investment of 65¢ (Bagel):** New York exported the bagel to the four corners of America, but after the indignities that have been performed (piña colada bagels?) we should ask for them back. Fortunately, New York still has the best, and 65¢ will let you sample one at **Kossar's Bialys** (367 Grand St.; © 212/ 473-4810). With flavor and texture honed to perfection, you can't make a better carb investment. See p. 118.

- **Best Investment of $1 (Pizza Bread):** The pizza bianca at the **Sullivan St. Bakery** (73 Sullivan St.; © 212/334- 9435) is more a piece of bread than a *Noo Yawk* slice, but it's long on old-world charm. Subtly flavored with rosemary and olive oil (no tomato or cheese), the dough manages to be simultaneously fluffy and chewy. A single greenback scores a nice big piece. See p. 117.

- **Best Investment of $1.50 (Sandwich):** Though not technically a sandwich (a big wedge of sesame pancake stands in for bread), the sliced beef item at the **Eldridge Street Dumpling House** (118a Eldridge St.; © 212/625- 8008) is the city's best buck and a half purchase. The pancake is big on taste, as is the fresh cilantro and carrot that dresses up the meat. See p. 106.

- **New York Slice:** On a Harlem block that might charitably be called unprepossessing, **Patsy's** (2287 First Ave.; © 212/534-9783) serves up the legendary slices they've spent the last 7 decades perfecting. The crust is chewy and thin, with a lot of character, a perfect complement for the tangy sauce. The two elements combine to make the best slice in the city, still available for the price of a circa-2002 subway ride ($1.50).

- **Best Investment of $2 (Tacos):** Served in a huge corn tortilla and garnished with fresh pico de gallo and guacamole, the tacos at **Del Valle Restaurant & Deli** (655

Tenth Ave.; ✆ **212/262-5510**) burst with flavor. Starting at $2 for standouts like chicken and carne asada, they're the cheapest way to pay a visit south of the border without leaving NYC. See p. 282.

● **Best Investment of $3 (Falafel):** I wouldn't put any New York falafel over **Rainbow Falafel & Shawarma** (26 E. 17th St.; ✆ **212/691-8641**). A big fresh pita holds marinated onions and crisp, flavorful falafel balls. The rest of the Syrian menu here isn't too shabby, either. See p. 121.

● **Best Investment of $3.25 (Hot Dogs & a Drink):** The best dogs in the East Village are impounded at **Crif Dog** (113 St. Marks Place; ✆ **212/ 614-2728**). The house special gets you a pair with a soda kicker. Protein cravings are

accommodated well into the wee hours—4am on the weekends. See p. 113.

● **Best Dirt Cheap Sit-Down Meal with Atmosphere: Lovely Day** (196 Elizabeth St.; ✆ **212/925-3310**) has the feel of an upscaled diner, but the chic NoLita crowd grazes for decidedly downscale prices. Japanese and Thai inflected entrees, including delicious noodle plates, come in under $10. See p. 116.

● **Best Burger:** New Yorkers have voted with their palates by keeping the **Corner Bistro** (331 W. 4th St.; ✆ **212/242- 9502**) busy at every hour. With the succulent, unpretentious $5 burgers here, it's no wonder. The city's expense-account $15 rivals at the fancy-shmancy places don't even come close. See p. 114.

3 Best Living & Shopping Bets

LIVING

● **Best Free School:** With college tuitions spiking endlessly upward, **Cooper Union** `FREE` (Cooper Sq.; ✆ **212/ 353-4120**) is a definite anomaly: The 1,000 students here get their education for exactly $0 and 0 cents. The rest of us are invited in for exhibitions,

readings, and a great series of lectures. See p. 136.

● **Best Free Smarts: The Graduate Center at the City University of New York** `FREE` (365 Fifth Ave.; ✆ **212/817- 8215**) keeps adults educated with a terrific selection of lectures, seminars, and panel discussions. Fees are reasonable and big chunks of the program are on the house. See p. 137.

● **Best Cheap Bed:** Who needs a mint on his pillow and a $250 bill, when **Big Apple Hostel** (119 W. 45th St.; ℂ **212/302-2603**) can provide a good night's sleep for under $30? You'll get a high-rent location, too: right in the heart of the Theater District. See p. 149.

● **Best Gyms:** Stay thin without a fat wallet. For less than 14¢ a day, 36 gyms and rec centers can belong to you. The facilities of the **Department of Parks and Recreation** (ℂ **212/360-8222**) include tracks, weight rooms, dance studios, and boxing rings. For $75 a year ($25 more), you get access to the swimming pools, too. See p. 158.

● **Best Grooming:** Style-conscious New Yorkers flock to Bumble and bumble salon for the latest looks. Savvier souls sign up for the model calls at their school, **Bumble and bumble.University** FREE (415 W. 13th St.; ℂ **866/7-BUMBLE**). If you're selected for the stylist training program, you'll get a free cut, a head full of styling products, and an invitation to call back

in 8 to 10 weeks to do it all over again. See p. 152.

● **Best Cultural Center Without Beer: Three Jewels Refuge and Free Internet Cafe** FREE (211 E. 5th St.; ℂ **212/475-6650**) is an East Village Buddhist center that doesn't let its small square footage limit its options. The long list of communal services includes free jazz, film, meditation, and workshops. See p. 161.

SHOPPING

● **Best Thrift Shopping: Housing Works Thrift Shop** (143 W. 17th St.; ℂ **212/366-0820,** plus other locations) brings the prices of fashionable clothes and furniture down to levels real people can afford. The inventory is lightly used and quick to turn over, and the money you spend goes to support a great cause (housing, services, and advocacy for people living with HIV and AIDS). See p. 177.

● **Best Department Store: Century 21** (22 Cortlandt St.; ℂ **212/227-9092**) is the Shakespeare in the Park of shopping—everybody knows about it, it's in great demand, and despite New Yorkers' high expectations it rarely comes up short. Amazing selection

New York's Top-Five Best-Kept Free Secrets

1 As far as New York vistas go, it's hard to beat the Brooklyn Bridge at night with the Manhattan skyline twinkling in the background. The **Brooklyn Bridge Park Summer Film Series** `FREE` (☎ 718/802-0603) does its best to enhance the view by projecting Brooklyn-angled fare against the epic scenery. Compared to its Manhattan competitors, this event is much more under control. The friendly, low-key crowd is perfect for watching a flick with. See p. 55.

2 Though the **National Museum of the American Indian** (1 Bowling Green; ☎ 212/514-3700) has seen the bulk of its collection moved to the Mall in D.C., the three gallery spaces here still put on great exhibits of contemporary and historic Native American art. The building itself, a magnificent Beaux Arts customs house, is worthy of a visit of its own. See p. 215.

3 In addition to free Internet, 5,000 videos, 8,500 films, and 35,000 CDs, the **Donnell Library Center** `FREE` (20 W.

and equally amazing prices draw in the crowds 7 days a week. See p. 186.

● **Best Gourmet Food Shop for Tightwads:** Tracking down fancy *fromage* is not a difficult task in NYC, but to actually purchase a wedge without emptying your purse is another issue. Thank the cheese gods then for the **East Village Cheese Store** (40 Third Ave.; ☎ 212/477-2601), which has a gigantic selection at humble prices. This is the ideal place for cocktail party hosts to fortify themselves. See p. 191.

4 Best Exploring Bets

● **Best Exhibits:** The main branch of the public library, formally known as the **Humanities and Social Sciences** Library `FREE` (Fifth Ave. and 42nd St.; ☎ 212/869-8089), puts on terrific shows in the hushed interiors behind the

53rd St.; ℂ 212/621-0618) is also the place Winnie-the-Pooh calls home. The original Winnie and his pals Piglet, Eeyore, Kanga, and Tigger have lived in Manhattan for 50 years now, most recently in a glass case in the Central Children's Room at the Donnell. Oh yeah, they've got some books here, too. See p. 229.

④ The **New York Earth Room** `FREE` (141 Wooster St.; ℂ 212/989-5566) is just that: 140 tons of soil hidden away in a SoHo loft. Even after multiple visits it's a completely unexpected sight, and a few whiffs of the earthy scent can be oddly rejuvenating. See p. 234.

⑤ Malcolm Forbes' affection for his idiosyncratic collections is obvious from the well-crafted displays at the **Forbes Magazine Galleries** `FREE` (62 Fifth Ave.; ℂ 212/206-5548). As you wind through model boats, toy soldiers, Monopoly boards, and trophies, you just may find Forbes' enthusiasm rubbing off on you. See p. 213.

lions. Rare editions and manuscripts are often on display, accompanied by thoughtful captions that make equally illuminating reading. See p. 229.

● **Best Use of a Former Factory Space in Queens:** The perfunctory design of MoMA QNS couldn't touch Long Island City's **SculptureCenter** `FREE` (44-19 Purves St.; ℂ 718/361-1750). Maya Lin left a lot of rough edges, but the overall effect is reminiscent of a cathedral, complete with a catacomblike basement. The intriguing sculptures and installation art shown here further justify the trip to Queens. See p. 217.

● **Best Art Center in Queens:** The **P.S. 1 Contemporary Art Center** (22–25 Jackson Ave.; ℂ 718/784-2084) puts on great art shows just a stop away from Manhattan in Long Island City. The museum is a beautiful conversion of a Renaissance revival public school, and the interior spaces have been inventively redone to complement the cutting-edge art displayed here. See p. 226.

● **Best Dirt Cheap Date Night:** First Saturdays `FREE` at the **Brooklyn Museum of Art** (200 Eastern Pkwy.; © **718/ 638-5000**) are among the best parties of the year. You can generate conversation fodder at exhibits, films, and lectures. You'll also find plenty of live music, should all that talk lead to a little dancing. See p. 220.

● **Best Natural Oasis:** Visions of rhododendron valleys, waterfalls, and wetlands conjure up only one place in New York: the Bronx. If you've never seen the **New York Botanical Garden** `FREE` (200th St. and Southern Blvd.; © **718/817- 8700**), you'll be amazed at the biological diversity here. It's arguably the country's greatest public garden. See p. 244.

● **Best Elephant Procession:** Forget Republican conventions—the best **elephant show** `FREE` occurs when the circus (Ringling Brothers; © **212/ 465-6741**) comes to town. Once a year, around midnight, the elephants (sometimes accompanied by their zebra and camel comrades) stroll up the Queens-Midtown Tunnel and across town to Madison Square Garden. As far as New York wildlife goes, this spectacle is hard to beat. See p. 246.

● **Best Boat Ride:** Transform yourself into river traffic through the programs at the **Downtown Boathouse** `FREE` (Pier 26, 66a, and 72nd St.; © **646/613-0375**). They'll loan you a kayak and let you paddle around their west side piers. If you get your strength up, you'll be eligible for a longer ride into New York Harbor. See p. 162.

Every summer, the Joseph Papp Public Theater hands out tickets to Shakespeare in the Park, one of New York's best free events. *See p. 63 for a full review.*

ENTERTAINMENT

2

For a little while in the boom years, it looked like dot.com zillionaires would be the only folks able to afford New York entertainment. Taverns upped cover charges, cigar and champagne bars came into fashion, and Broadway tickets went through the roof. But that was a whole different city. With the economy still unsettled, entertainment for the people has made a major comeback. It's easy to find top-tier dance, drama, film, and comedy for no more than the price of showing up. Shakespeare in the Park, the Metropolitan Opera, and the Upright Citizens Brigade are among the New York legends that give it up for free. Big-time wits can be found at TV-show tapings, and big-name scribes make themselves accessible at complimentary literary readings. Meanwhile, music seeps up from the subway platforms and fills our parks and bars. Everything from jazz to classical to country to rock can be heard in NYC, and a surprising amount of it comes without cost. For those attractions that do charge, discerning patrons can easily keep the cost down in the $5 range. New York is a magnet for talent and even the performances on the cheap end of the entertainment spectrum can be spectacular. In short, money is no longer the barrier to experiencing great New York entertainment. Now it's an issue of time management.

FREE & DIRT CHEAP CALENDAR OF EVENTS

New York knows how to throw a party. Throughout the year, you can find massive celebrations of ancient tribal affiliations, sexual orientations, and pagan holidays. Money isn't an object, either, as most of these celebrations are free. Of course, event quality is in direct proportion to audience size. The Big Apple's big events draw huge crowds, and if you want a decent view, you'll have to stake out your spot hours early. Lesser events may be more spur-of-the-moment accessible, but four or five listless floats later you may find yourself fully sated with the rites of Zemblan Independence Day.

In addition to the numbers listed below, **NYC Visit,** the city's convention and visitor's bureau, has the lowdown on most events (© **212/484-1222; www.nycvisit. com).**

JANUARY

New Year's Eve in Times Square FREE OVERRATED The calendar year begins and ends with a gathering of thousands of non–New Yorkers, most of whose primary motivation in life is to get on television. All the good sideline spots in Times Square are long gone by dusk. Add the extra buzz kills of high security, crushing crowds, brutal cold, and a ban on booze, and that's all the excuse you need to stay at home with the remote control, marveling at how much younger Dick Clark looks now than he did in his '50s heyday. 1 Times Square. © **212/768-1560** or 212/484-1222. www.timessquarebid.org. Subway: N/Q/R/S/W/1/2/3/7/9 to Times Square. December 31.

5K Midnight Run in Central Park Spending New Year's in a New York saloon is not a lot more attractive as a New Year's alternative; do you really need to drop $100 on an open bar, a complimentary champagne toast, and a couple of hunks of 6-foot-long cold-cut party sub? A healthier option is to hook up with the New York Road Runner's Club's, which hosts a 5K Midnight Run that takes racers from 72nd Street to the Central Park East Drive, north to 102nd, and back around. The registration fee will set you back between $25 and $35, but if you don't feel an absolute need to get winded in the small hours, you can enjoy the prerun costume show and the fireworks display for free. The parade begins at 11pm. Gather near the Central Park Bandshell, just south of the 72nd Street Transverse. ☎ **212/860-4455.** www.nyrrc.org. Subway: B/C to 72nd St.; 6 to 68th St. December 31.

Brooklyn New Year's Prospect `FREE`   There's no borough envy in Brooklyn as rival pyrotechnics welcome the new year above Prospect Park. Enjoy the fresh air as the embers cascade above the Grand Army Plaza at the stroke of midnight. Prime viewing areas include West Drive and along Prospect Park West between Grand Army Plaza and 9th St. ☎ **718/965-8999.** www.prospectpark.org. Subway: 2/3 to Grand Army Plaza; B/Q to 7th Ave. December 31.

New Year's Concert for Peace at the Cathedral of St. John the Divine `FREE`   Leonard Bernstein inaugurated this event, and in the subsequent decades, it's become a beautifully honed candlelit legend. St. John's is the largest Gothic cathedral in the world (possibly the whole universe) and can seat 6,000, though the best spots are reserved and come with steep price tags. For the rest of us, however, the concert is free. General seating is open to all comers, who sit in wide rows in the back of the church. Between the great acoustics and the soft glow of candlelight, you may not even realize there's not a bad seat in the house. Cathedral of St. John the Divine. 1047 Amsterdam Ave., at 112th St. ☎ **212/316-7540.** www.stjohndivine.org. Subway: B/C to Cathedral Parkway/110th St. December 31.

FEBRUARY

Chinese New Year `FREE`   Come February Chinatown will be partying like it's 4703, in honor of the lunar new year. The omnipresent firecrackers of Chinese new years past are no more (yup, Giuliani), but there's still plenty of noise and chaos to go around. The parade route traverses Mott, Canal, Bayard, and East Broadway, with dragon and lion dancers winding through the squares and streets of Chinatown. At the Asian American Business Development Center. ✆ **212/966-0100.** Subway: N/R to Prince St.; 6 to Spring St. Early February.

MARCH

Saint Patrick's Day Parade `FREE`   The free entertainment on St. Patrick's Day starts on the subway ride. In years past I've ridden in cars that local teens have magically transformed into mini–Irish pubs, complete with energetic gossip, Guinness cans rattling down the aisles, and clouds of cigarette smoke. And then there's the parade. The green wave gathers momentum through Midtown and converges on Fifth Avenue, where 150,000 marchers (and at least that many spectators) celebrate Ireland's patron Saint. Much of the crowd arrives well before the 11am start time. The entertainment continues with live music and drunken shenanigans at New York's thousand-plus Irish pubs. Wear green or risk pinchery. The parade runs from 86th to 44th streets, right past Patrick's own cathedral. ✆ **212/484-1222.** www.saintpatricksdayparade.com. Subway: N/R/W or E/V to Fifth Ave. March 17.

Easter Parade `FREE`   With the return of spring nature is reborn from the small deaths of winter, and what better way to symbolize new life than by showing off your new threads? That's been the thinking behind New York's Easter Parade for almost a century and a half. More an informal procession than a parade, people join and leave as they please. Expect amazing hats and plenty of pastels. The stroll runs from 10am until 3 or 4pm, along Fifth Avenue between 48th and 57th streets. ✆ **212/484-1222.** Subway: E/V to Fifth Ave.; B/D/F/V to 47-50 sts.–Rockefeller Center. Easter Sunday.

APRIL

NYC's Public Tax Deadline Party `FREE`   If procrastinators make up only 1% of New York's population, that's still 80,000 people pushing their tax returns to the last possible minute. You can find them converging on the main post office for the city's most unlikely party. Tax day ends at midnight on April 15, but all evening long you'll see people rollerblading by with forms, filers pulling up in limos rented for the occasion, and citizens with headphones blasting, filling out their 1040s while waiting in line. In addition to the great free party, you can usually pick up some swag—marketers know a captive audience eager for condoms or Snapples when they see one. Just ask the friendly out-of-work actor in the gorilla suit for that free sample. Eighth Ave., between 33rd and 34th sts. Subway: A/C/E to 34th St./Penn Station. April 15.

Dachshund Friendship Festival FREE Twice a year New York's dachshunds gather with their humans in Washington Square Park to mix, mingle, and wear diabolically adorable little wiener outfits. Watch dachshund brides samba with dachshund cowboys before the whole herd runs in circles around the center of the park. The festival ends with a chorus of "The Dachs Song." With the hounds lifted overhead and the spring air filled with the refrain of "Dachsie, meine dachsie," there's nary a dry eye to be found. Washington Square Park is bounded by Waverly Place, 4th Street, University Place, and Mac-Dougal Street. ✆ **212/ 475-5512.** www.dachshund friendshipclub.com. Subway: A/C/E/F/S/V to W. 4th St.–Washington Sq. Noon, the last Saturday in April, and again the first Saturday in October. Rain date Sunday.

> **Pieces of April 1st**
>
> The press releases for Fifth Avenue's **April Fool's Day Parade** promise elaborate floats with budgets in the billions and throngs of costumed celebrities, but the most action you can hope to see at this event is the occasional irritated news crew standing around watching the traffic flow. Fox News and CNN have showed up for the parade in years past only to discover that they've been played for April fools.

MAY

Ninth Avenue International Food Festival FREE If some human in some obscure corner of the globe will shove it in his mouth and call it a comestible, odds are you can find it at this festival. Come mid-May, you'll find booths vending street fair stand-bys like Italian sausages and pad Thai, in addition to stands operated by local restaurants, which have more adventurous offerings. My taste favors the Peruvian, Brazilian, and Afghani, but other options abound, many served in affordable sample sizes. In 2004, mini crab cakes were available for just a buck, and the prices for everything else topped out at $5. Musicians and sock retailers add to (or detract from, depending on your biases) the scene. Ninth Ave., from W. 37th to 57th sts. ✆ **212/581-7217.**

OVERRATED **The Street Fair Sham**

It takes less than a New York minute for a newcomer's excitement about "street fairs" and "block parties" to fizzle into the reality of another traffic-clogged exercise in low-end commerce. Each fair has the exact same CDs, massage stands, and three-for-a-buck socks (open the package and it smells like you've just bought a wedge of Swiss cheese.) The deep-fried corn can be tasty if you're in a certain mood, and occasionally a band will play live, but generally it's hard to fill more than a couple of minutes at one of these affairs.

Subway: A/C/E to 42nd St. From 9am until 7pm, Saturday and Sunday in mid-May.

Fleet Week For 1 week, New Yorkers get nostalgic at the sight of thousands of sailors on the make in the port of Manhattan. Squint and pretend it's V-E Day. Along the west side piers you can get a closer look. Navy, Coast Guard, and Marine reps will let you tour some of the floating behemoths you spent all those tax dollars on. ℂ **212/245-0072.** www. fleetweek.com or www.intrepid museum.org. Last week in May.

JUNE

Museum Mile Festival FREE The classiest fair in New York sees Fifth Avenue closed to car traffic so 50,000 culture vultures can take in the white marble architecture of Manhattan's Gold Coast to the sounds of string quartets. Kids get live performances and special arts and crafts opportunities. Nine of the museums that give the mile its moniker offer free admissions. This is one street fair where low-rent commerce doesn't predominate: No vendors are allowed. Fifth Ave., from 82nd to 104th sts. ℂ **212/606-2296.** www.museum milefestival.org. Subway: 4/5/6 to 86th St.; 6 to 77th, 96th, or 103rd sts. From 6pm to 9pm, usually the second Tuesday in June.

Lesbian and Gay Pride Week and March FREE The city bursts with Pride every June in a week that begins with rallies and protests and ends in a dance, fireworks, and a parade. Pride commemorates the June 27, 1969, Stonewall Rebellion, where gay men first stood against police harassment outside the Stonewall Inn in the West Village. Thirty-five years later seeing Fifth Avenue overtaken by rainbows is a heartening sight, as the Sunday Gay Pride

March wends its way from 52nd Street down into the Village. Just standing on a street corner downtown can be almost as entertaining as the parade, especially the spectacle of drag queens teetering on high heels as they rush across multiple lanes of traffic. © **212/807-7433.** www. nycpride.org. Mid- to late June.

Puerto Rico Day Parade
FREE Fifth Avenue's staid character goes into remission for the Puerto Rico Day parade. There's salsa music and festive floats and millions of spectators lining the way. The parade has been running annually since 1958, and despite some ugly incidents, it remains a quality spectacle. Fifth Ave., from 44th to 86th sts. © **718/401-0404.** From 11am to 6pm, the second Sunday in June.

Body Work

Fans of gay cars should check out **Empire Autorama's** free car show the Saturday of Pride Week. Some 60 cars show off their hard bodies in Dag Hammarskjold Plaza, 47th Street between First and Second avenues. Check the website, www.empireautorama.com, for details.

☆ **Mermaid Parade** FREE Old-time New Yorkers had one destination for the best in tattoos, sideshows, and amusement parks. In its '20s heyday, Coney Island saw over a million visitors a day. Now only a lone roller coaster remains, but there is still some continuity with the glorious and tawdry past, especially during the eclectic freak show that is the Mermaid Parade. With body paint and beads—plus a few strategic scraps of fabric to keep things legal—the avatars of New York's retro-culture scene transform themselves into mermaids and Neptunes. Classic cars join the procession as it works its way up Surf Avenue, dispersing when the participants dash down the beach to the ageless Atlantic. Surf Ave., from W. 15th to W. 10th sts. © **718/372-5159.** www.coney island.com/mermaid.shtml. Subway: D to Coney Island/Stillwell Ave., then walk toward the Atlantic. First Saturday after the summer solstice, 2 to 6pm.

JULY

Fourth of July Fireworks FREE In New York's previous incarnation, you knew July 4th was coming because starting mid-June your sleep was interrupted by nightly amateur firework shows. With recent quality-of-life crackdowns, however, firepower is hard to come by and The Man has a monopoly on the summer eye-candy. Fortunately, The Man does a nice job of blowing up stuff for our entertainment. Locations can shift, but generally Macy's explodes 80,000 shells into the air over the East River in the 20s and 30s. At 7:30pm the FDR closes to traffic between 14th and 42nd streets and folks start to grab seats on the guardrails. If you're not totally Manhattancentric, the other side of the river has decent views. Try Hunter's Point in Long Island City, Queens, and Greenpoint in Brooklyn. ✆ **212/494-2922.** www.macys.com. July 4.

Battery Park 4th of July Concert FREE New York also puts the free back in freedom with an outdoor concert in Battery Park. Past performers have ranged from legend Emmylou Harris to alleged entertainer Ryan Adams. Either way, there's a festive, laidback vibe, with blankets spread on the grass and New York Harbor in the background. Gates open at 2pm and the show is at 4pm. ✆ **212/835-2789.** www.downtownny.com. Subway: A/C or 1/2/3/9 to Chambers St. July 4.

AUGUST

☆ **Harlem Week** FREE Harlem Day was first celebrated in 1975, and over the subsequent 3 decades it has grown from a day to a week to an entire month of cultural celebration. Harlem Week now includes the **Black Film Festival,** the **Harlem Jazz and Music Festival,** and the **Taste of Harlem Food Festival.** The two biggest days come in the middle, with **Uptown Saturday Nite** taking over West 135th Street between Malcolm X Boulevard and St. Nicholas Avenue. Sunday is **Harlem Day,** from 10am to 9pm. W. 135th, between Fifth and St. Nicholas aves. ✆ **212/862-8477.** www. harlemdiscover.com. Subway: B/C to 135th St.; 1/9 to 137th St. From noon to 9pm, the month of August.

Howl! Festival of East Village Arts Though the East Village's legendary artistic past is increasingly obscured by layers of gentrifying paint, 1 week in late August brings back the old contrarian spirit. The Howl! Festival serves up theater, live music, and art. Although there's an admission charge for many events (usually reasonable, in the $7 range), the Allen Ginsberg Poetry Festival in Tompkins Square Park is free. Ave. A, between 7th and 10th sts.

ⓒ **212/502-1225.** www.howlfestival.com. Subway: L to 1st Ave.; 6 to Astor Place; N/R to 8th St. Third or fourth week in August.

SEPTEMBER

Tugboat Festival `FREE`   One day a year New York's attention-starved tugs get some play at the Intrepid Museum's annual Tugboat Festival. The rites begin with a tug parade down the Hudson, continue with nose-to-nose tug-pushing-tug contests, races, and line-throwing competitions, and conclude with prizes for best crew and best tattoo. Pier 86. Twelfth Ave., at 46th St. *ⓒ* **212/245-0072.** www.intrepidmuseum.org. Subway: N/Q/R/Q/1/2/3/7/9 to Times Square; A/C/E to 42nd St./Port Authority. From 12:30 to 4pm, the Sunday before Labor Day.

West Indian–American Day Parade `FREE`   New York's biggest parade takes place a long way from Fifth Avenue, along Eastern Parkway in Brooklyn. Two million revelers (yup, *2,000,000*) come together on Labor Day for the West Indian–American Day Parade. The Caribbean rhythms are infectious and the costumes out of control, and the food's not a bad t'ing either. Jerk chicken ($6), oxtail ($5–$8), and veggie roti ($4) are among the delicacies that make the trip worthwhile. The route varies, but generally follows Eastern Parkway at Utica Avenue in Crown Heights down to the arch at Grand Army Plaza in Prospect Heights. *ⓒ* **718/625-1515.** www.wiadca.com. Subway: 2/3 to Grand Army Plaza. From 11am to 6pm, Labor Day.

September Concert `FREE`   In any other circumstances, a day bringing hundreds of performers to dozens of venues across all five boroughs would be cause for upbeat excitement, but the context of the September Concert is a somber one. To commemorate the World Trade Center attacks, the city's stages are filled with the healing sounds of music. Throughout the day, find the free sounds in the city's cafes, bars, libraries, squares, and parks. It's a perfect excuse for people to be together. *ⓒ* **212/333-3399.** www.septemberconcert.org. Multiple venues, check the website. From noon to 10pm, September 11.

Germanic-American Steuben Parade `FREE`   According to the U.S. Census more Americans consider themselves to be of German descent than any other ethnicity, but German-Americans tend to keep a low profile. New York sees an exception to that rule every September when 12,000 marchers show off their Old Europe pride at the Germanic-American Steuben Parade. The parade is considered one of New York's best organized (the germanparadenyc.com website notes without irony the mayor's office's appraisal of the parade as being "clean and very orderly"). German food is served starting at 2pm at the Friendship Party in Central Park, at East 72nd Street. Bratwursts are $3 to $4, big spenders can have a big pork dinner for $9. The accompanying beverage of choice is no mystery; beers run $3 to $5. The parade begins at noon and runs along Fifth Avenue from 63rd to 86th streets. ✆ 516/239-0741. The third Saturday in September.

The Feast of San Gennaro **FREE**   This is New York's oldest and biggest street fair—11 days of zeppoles, pork braciole, and deep-fried Oreos in honor of the patron saint of Naples. Little Italy main drag Mulberry Street becomes an extremely narrow small-town carnival. There are rides for the kids, cannoli-eating contests for the adults, and an abusive clown in a dunking booth that's discomfiting for everybody. With the heavy emphasis on commerce and the beer-addled crowds, the fair gets old fairly quickly. Mulberry St., between Canal and Houston, with runoff on Hester and Grand. ✆ 212/226-6427. www.sangennaro.org. Subway: N/R to Prince St.; 6 to Spring St. or Canal. Starts the second Thursday in September, from 11:30am to 11:30pm, midnight on Friday and Saturday.

OCTOBER

☆ **Greenwich Village Halloween Parade** **FREE**   For many New Yorkers, every day feels like Halloween. Come late October, the last thing we need to wade through is another crowd of costumed freaks. Fight this instinct, however, and you will enjoy New York's most underrated holiday. The central event is the annual Halloween parade. Running up Sixth Avenue from Spring to 23rd, the parade shows off New Yorkers' legendary gallows humor. If you're feeling restless, the neighborhood's surrealistic collisions—javelin-toting African warriors kibitzing with drag-queen astronauts—are entertainment enough. *Note:* This parade is one of New York's most participatory events; no one will think any less of you for not being covered in body paint or latex, but you run the risk of feeling like you're in a wet-blanket minority. *Village Voice* Parade hot line: ✆ 212/475-3333, ext. 4044. www.halloween-nyc.com. Subway: C/E to Spring St.; A/B/C/D/F/V to W. 4th St.; F/V/L to 14th St. October 31, with the coming of night.

New York's Great Halloween Party `FREE`   Goblins hobnob across 40 of the city's back acres when this party fills Central Park with haunted sites and throngs of excitable costumed children. Some 7,500 pumpkins get scattered among the straw at the Bethesda Fountain. Once the little demons have made their incisions they take the resulting jack-o'-lanterns north, to the Charles A. Dana Discovery Center, midpark at 110th Street. A parade is followed by an annual pumpkin sail, where the jack-o'-lanterns glow on the Harlem Meer as they gently float away. ✆ **212/860-1370.** www.central parknyc.org. Subway: C to 110th St. Generally from 3:30 to 6:30pm. Saturday, a few days before Halloween (date varies).

November

The New York Marathon `FREE`   As much fun as it looks to completely deplete your body while forming manhole-sized blisters from pounding 26.2 miles of hard pavement, I'm happy to leave the marathoning to the pros. There are five boroughs' worth of prime viewing territory, and the steady stream of runners, with their varied looks of determination and exhaustion, has an unexpected poetry. The race ends in Central Park near Tavern on the Green, where you can watch the survivors, adorned in the glory of heat-retaining silver blankets, as they walk it off. The race begins in the morning, with the elite runners getting off around 11am. ✆ **212/423-2249** or 212/860-4455. www.nyrrc.org. Subway (to Central Park): B/C to 72nd St. First Sunday in November.

Macy's Thanksgiving Day Parade `FREE`   New York's favorite excuse for dragging bloated floating cartoon characters down the west side of the city comes with the Macy's Thanksgiving Day Parade. Rocky, Bullwinkle, and Garfield join slightly-less-inflated celebrities to march down Central Park West from 77th Street to Columbus Circle, where they turn onto Broadway and head straight for the Mothership (Macy's in Herald Square). The wee ones love this event and crowds are thick, with a lot of prime viewing territory reserved for VIP's, so arrive well before the scheduled start time. *Tip:* Balloon fanatics can get a head start on the action the night before, when the balloons get their helium fixes on the broad sidewalks around the Natural History Museum. ✆ **212/494-2922.** www.macysparade.com. Subway: B/C to 72nd St.; A/B/C/D/1/9 to Columbus Circle. From 9am to noon, Thanksgiving morning.

DECEMBER

Lighting of the Christmas Tree at Rockefeller Center

FREE   The week after Thanksgiving marks the first major "Grid-lock Alert" of the holiday shopping season. Traffic comes to a near stop on the blocks around Rockefeller Center. Down on the rink professional ice-skaters make graceful turns, live music plays, and Hizzonner throws the switch on 30,000 bulbs strung along 5 miles of wire. Rock Center's overflow crowd, many of whom have been waiting in the cold for 4 or 5 hours, cheer with relief. Even for grinches like myself, watching the tree come alive is a pretty cool moment, but they'd have to make the spruce levitate while spouting a fountain of $50 bills for me to want to weather that crowd twice. Better to come back at a more mellow time, especially if you can visit at dusk, when the tree is at its most quietly dramatic. ✆ **212/332-6868.** www.rockefellercenter. com. B/D/F/Q to Rockefeller Center. At 9pm, the Wednesday after Thanksgiving.

Free Radical Theater

New York supplements its famous parades with other festive mass gatherings: protest marches and rallies. Whether you're standing up to be counted or just on the sidelines digging the specta-cle, you won't find yourself shorted on stimuli. New York-ers have sharp senses of humor and the creative plac-ards alone are worth a look. The confluence of political relevance and cutting cultural commentary recurs often, as in this gem from 2003:

BEN AFFLECK IS A TERRIBLE ACTOR.

NO WAR IN IRAQ.

There's no argument on at least one of those points.

Alternatives to the Rocke-feller Tree Lighting FREE

It's not like Rock Center has the only Christmas tree in New York City. The Tuesday after Thanks-giving sees 100,000 lights softly glowing in the **Winter Garden** at the **World Financial Center.** On the same day on the Upper West Side, **Lincoln Center** hosts its own Christmas celebration. A tree lighting supplements crafts booths and live music along Broadway and Columbus from 61st to 68th streets. You'll find plenty for the kids and the crowds are a fraction of Rock Center's. World Financial Center: ✆ **212/945-0505.** www.worldfinancial center.com. Subway: 1/2/3/9/A/C to Chambers St. Lincoln Center

BID: ✆ **212/581-3774.** www.lincolnbid.org. Subway: 1/9 to 66th St./Lincoln Center. The Tuesday after Thanksgiving.

Festival of Lights `FREE`   If you want to celebrate the other half of the Judeo-Christian cultural tradition, you can attend the lighting of Midtown's menorah. This skyscraping candle-holder (at 32 ft., it's the world's largest) shines at sunset on the first night of Hanukkah, gaining another light on each of the following 7 days. Grand Army Plaza on Fifth Ave., at 59th St. Subway: N/R to Fifth Ave.; F to 57th St. During Hanukkah.

A Brooklyn Christmas `FREE`   The big department stores offer the sidewalks plenty of entertainment with elaborate window displays, but for my money, New York's best free Christmas show is in Brooklyn. Homeowners from Bay Ridge to Bensonhurst run up the Keyspan bills to bring bulb envy to their neighbors. Dyker Heights is "Christmas Central," with 100,000 tourists drawn every year to the blocks around 83rd and 84th streets, between Tenth and Thirteenth avenues. Choruses of mechanical Santas and snowmen compete to prove the lights are always brighter on the other side of the fence. Take the D/M to 79th St., or the R to 86th St. Then walk toward the lines of wide-eyed-munchkin-packed minivans. Between Thanksgiving and New Year's.

1 Music Uncovered

New York is in the midst of yet another great rock-'n'-roll scare. A slew of young bands have rediscovered the jittery energy of New York's '70s and '80s heyday, and they're threatening to become a movement. The jury is still out on how much of this is hype (and how much of the sound is anything more than derivative), but in the immediate a surplus of live music bangs away across the city. It's not just rock, either. Classical performances, acoustic acts, salsa bands, jazz quartets, even alt-country make a stand in Yankee confines. The only fly in this ointment is capitalism; the bars have to pay rent. Most places try to keep the booze flowing, although with a few exceptions New York is not superuptight about enforcing its drink minimums. The musicians certainly don't care—most of the time they're just happy you're there to listen. You'll find free music waiting 7 nights a week. You may as well embrace the cacophony because Lord knows it's hard to find a quiet hour in New York City.

FOR THOSE ABOUT TO ROCK

Arlene's Grocery From the outside, this popular music hall still resembles the humble bodega it replaced. Inside the bands are polished, but a little too obviously courting major label attention. Their confidence won't dim as long as no one minds that they all sound exactly the same. Cover charges vary, generally $7 or so. Some of the best nights are free (see "Sing, Sing: Karaoke," on p. 75). Beers and well drinks are $3 during happy hour, which covers Monday through Friday, 4 to 7pm, and noon to 7pm on the weekends. Otherwise drinks range from a $3 Pabst Blue Ribbon to a $12 fancy-pants martini.

95 Stanton St., between Orchard and Ludlow sts. ℂ 212/358-1633. www.arlene-grocery.com. Subway: F/V to Second Ave. or Delancey St.; J/M/Z to Essex St.

Free & E-Zeens

With a city in endless flux and so much stuff going on, it's hard to stay abreast of the best in free and cheap events. My favorite means of keeping up is via electronic newsletters, conveniently e-mailed right to my inbox. Of the e-lists, **Nonsensenyc's** (www.nonsensenyc.com) is my favorite, specializing in the cheap and offbeat, and providing a comprehensive rundown of the city's many hipster events. A few other newsletters worth reading can be found at **www.dailycandy.com**, **www.flavorpill.net**, and **www.manhattanusersguide.com**.

The Baggot Inn Nestled in a cozy basement beneath street level, the Baggot Inn brings in a mix of rock and old-timey music. Wednesday nights feature a Bluegrass and Good Times Jam, where the folks on stage have the most fun. The sound is good and generally there's no cover Sunday through Wednesday nights. Happy hour is 11am to 7pm with $3 for a beer or a nightly special cocktail. At other times, the cheapest drink is a $3 Pabst. FINE PRINT There's a two-drink minimum.

82 W. 3rd St., between Thompson and Sullivan sts. ℂ 212/477-0622. www.thebaggotinn.com. Subway: A/C/E/F/S/V to W. 4th St.-Washington Sq.

Continental FREE Proximity to St. Marks Place assures a young, semipunk demographic at the Continental. Bands tend to err on the side of loudness and aggression, although the talent level is fairly high. Classic rock tribute bands fill out the rest of the schedule. Most weeknights are free. If there's a cover it'll be $5, or maybe $10 on Saturday night.

25 Third Ave., between St. Marks Place and 9th St. ☎ 212/529-6924. www. continentalnyc.com. Subway: 6 to Astor Place; N/R to 8th St.

Hank's Saloon FREE The painted flames on Hank's wall identify the place as prime rockabilly territory. Live music plays most nights, with a little country and rock thrown in with the '50s stylings. It's all no cover, no minimum, and on Sunday night you can even eat for free. The adventurous can enjoy the fruits of the grill during Sean and Daria's Country BBQ and Jamboree. Delicacies vary, but tend to the hot dog and hamburger side of things. Pabsts are $2, as are Schaeffers (the ones to have if you're having more than one).

46 Third Ave., at Atlantic Ave. ☎ 718/625-8003. www.hankstavern.com. Subway: 2/3/4/5/Q to Atlantic Ave.; M/N/R/W to Pacific St.

Hogs & Heifers Uptown FREE There's no cover, no minimum, plus live music most every night at this rural outpost at the edge of overcultivated Uptown. Upper East Siders who don't mind scuffing their Bally loafers come here for tribute bands, blues jams, and other staples of white-bread culture. Pabsts are $2, and the most expensive drink in the house is a $6 shot of Patron.

1843 First Ave., between 95th and 96th sts. ☎ 212/722-8635. www.hogs andheifers.com. Subway: 6 to 96th St.

☆ The Lakeside Lounge FREE The Lakeside may lack in lake views, but it has no shortage of great music. Steve Earle, Amy Allison, and Freddy Johnson have all played here. The back room that holds the stage is tiny, so you're guaranteed an intimate experience. If you arrive late, there's extra standing room off to the side. Never a cover, or a minimum, and during set breaks you can get a souvenir from the notorious black-and-white photo booth. Cans of Tecate are $3.50, and if you identify yourself as a cheapskate to the bartender, he or she may cut you a better deal on a lesser can. During happy hour from 4 to 8pm daily, it's two for one.

162 Ave. B, between 10th and 11th sts. ☎ 212/529-8463. www.lakeside lounge.com. Subway: L to First Ave.

The Living Room A mellow music mecca, The Living Room hosts a slate of live performances every night, biased toward acoustic and otherwise low-key up-and-comers. I find the musical taste here to be decent, if a tad bland. The new space 1 block over is less intimate than the old, but the sounds are still clean. Buds runs only $3. Other bottles and drafts go from $5 to $6, and wine is $6. Happy hour happens on weekends only, from 2 to 7pm, when you get $2.50 World Select bottles (Anheuser-Bush), $3 drafts, and $3 well drinks. FINE PRINT No cover, but one-drink minimum per set, casually enforced.

154 Ludlow St., between Stanton and Rivington sts. ✆ 212/533-7235. www. livingroomny.com. Subway: F/V to Second Ave.; J/M/Z to Essex St.

Luna Lounge FREE Come for the foosball table in front, stay for the rock in the back. The area facing the stage is tight so show up at a reasonable hour if you want decent sightlines. Though the bands won't be anyone you've heard of, they're often surprisingly good. No cover and no minimum makes them sound even better. Luna Lounge has no happy hour; bottles of Rolling Rock are $4, draft beer pints are $5, and the most expensive drink is $9.

171 Ludlow St., between Houston and Stanton sts. ✆ 212/260-2323. www. lunalounge.com. Subway: F/V to Second Ave.; J/M/Z to Essex St.

Paddy Reilly's FREE Here's an odd innovation: an Irish pub with live music. Most nights there's someone strumming or picking in here, whether it's bluegrass, folk, or a traditional Irish session. With regular Joes from the street invited to sit in, earnestness often trumps professionalism, but the results are no less enjoyable. Happy hour eye-openers begin at 11am every weekday and run until 7pm, with Guinness pints $4 and bottles of beer $3. Otherwise, it's $6 for a pint, $5 for a bottle, and $7.50 for the most expensive drink in the house (single-malt scotch, naturally).

519 Second Ave., at 29th St. ✆ 212/686-1210. www.paddyreillys.com. Subway: 6 to 28th St.

Parkside Lounge Nestled between projects and East Village tenements, this former brothel brings in an eclectic crowd. Being too far east for most trendroids helps, too. The back room brings in rock shows and electric Friday-night salsa. Happy hour is from 1pm to 8pm, 7 days a week, with all well drinks and domestic beers only $3. During unhappy hours, drinks range from a $3 can of Pabst all the way up to an $8 Grey Goose. FINE PRINT If there's a cover it'll be $5 for the band, and there's often a loosely enforced two-drink minimum in the back room.

317 E. Houston St., at Attorney St. ℭ 212/673-6270. www.parksidelounge. com. Subway: F/V to Second Ave.

★ **Pete's Candy Store** FREE   So much good music comes through this Brooklyn gem that you'll feel like a kid in a great music venue. Housed in a friendly former fountain shop on a quiet Williamsburg block, the small stage area brings in surprisingly big acts. There's also a rotating selection of nonmusical entertainment, from readings to backgammon to quiz night (check out "Word Up: Readings" and "Game Night," on p. 86 and 79, respectively). FINE PRINT No cover or drink minimum, but the staff encourages contributions to the musicians' tip jar.

709 Lorimer St., between Frost and Richardson sts., Williamsburg, Brooklyn. ℭ 718/302-3770. www. petescandystore.com. Subway: L to Lorimer St.; G to Metropolitan Ave.

Rodeo Bar FREE   This is as country as Manhattan gets, which isn't saying much. The sprawling space doesn't have the feel of an intimate honky-tonk, but the stage area is segregated and more or less self-contained. The cream of the local crop rounds up here, as do a host of great national acts. Mostly Americana and alt country (whatever that is). There's no cover and no minimum. Happy hour is Monday through Friday, 4 to 7pm, with $3 beer and free wings and nachos. At other times, Buds are $4 and margaritas $5.

Avoid the "Rock Bars" Around NYU

Close to NYU in the West Village sit a cluster of "rock bars" that purport to offer "no cover" entertainment. This is as pure a tourist trap as New York offers, as the various clubs try to cash in on their West Village cache. Although the joints may boast Bleecker or Macdougal addresses, there is little of the neighborhood's old rock-'n'-roll spirit here. The patrons are almost exclusively bridge and tunnel burbsters, drinks are overpriced, and the best you can hope for music-wise is an earnest cover band. If you want to hear at least one original thought per set, better to avoid this zone altogether.

375 Third Ave., at 27th St. ℂ 212/683-6500. www.rodeobar.com. Subway: 6 to 28th St.

Sidewalk Café   Having outlived the other live-music spots on Avenue A, the Sidewalk Café maintains a loyal following. The Café serves as a home base for East Village singer-songwriters, and a little comedy gets thrown in as well. Each night sees a big bunch of acts. Buds and Rolling Rocks are $4, and during happy hour (2–8pm daily) every other drink is free. FINE PRINT No cover, but a two-drink minimum during performances.

94 Ave. A, at the corner of 6th St. ℂ 212/473-7373. http://antifolk.net/ sidewalk.html. Subway: F/V to Second Ave.

JAZZ IT UP

Arthur's Tavern   A West Village relic, Arthur's would be eligible for social security if it was a person and not an amiable, low-rent jazz joint. The music runs the Dixieland-to-trio gamut and the quality can be spotty, but something's on stage 7 nights a week. Drink prices start at $6 for a beer and top out at $10.50. FINE PRINT No cover, but a one-drink per set minimum.

57 Grove St., between Bleeker and W. 4th sts. ℂ 212/675-6879. www. arthurstavernnyc.com. Subway: 1/9 to Christopher St.

The C-Note   Noteworthy for its eclectic acts, this narrow Avenue C spot keeps the bands rotating across its stage. Several groups appear each night, often performing for free. Although the club's original emphasis was on jazz, the mix has been expanded to include singer-songwriters, rock, and even alt country. A bottle of Bud is $4 and the top shelf comes in at $9. Look for drink specials on Sunday nights. FINE PRINT Cover generally $5 or less, one-drink minimum per set, casually enforced.

157 Ave. C, between 9th and 10th sts. ℂ 212/677-8142. www.thecnote.com. Subway: L to First Ave.

Cleopatra's Needle   Organ trios, quartets, and jam sessions highlight the calendar at this new, neighborhoody club. Beers run $5 to $7, wine $5 to $10, and drinks are between $7 and $12. Happy hour is Monday through Saturday from 4:30 to 7:30pm, with $2 off any drink, but a decent Mediterranean menu provides an alternative to boozing the night away. Shows start at 8pm. FINE PRINT There's never a cover, although there is a $10 minimum per set, which can be spent on food, drinks, or a combo of both.

2485 Broadway, between 92nd and 93rd sts. ℂ 212/769-6969. www.
cleaopatrasneedleny.com. Subway: 1/2/3/9 to 96th St.

55 Bar   Still not entirely recovered from its Prohibition days, 55
Bar has been entertaining the Village on the sly since 1919. The
cluttered room brings in top-shelf acts. The cover charges reflect
it on some nights, but other times you can slip in for a pittance.
Tuesday and Sunday nights are your best bets for inexpensive
jazz. For all nights, covers range from as low as $3 up to $15,
depending on the act. During happy hour (5–7pm daily), you can
get two Buds or two Yuenglings for $5. FINE PRINT Officially, there's
a two-drink minimum, but the laid-back staff enforces it loosely.
55 Christopher St., between Seventh Ave. and Waverly Place. ℂ 212/929-
9883. www.55bar.com. Subway: 1/9 to Christopher St.

Freddy's Bar FREE   The much ballyhooed Brooklyn Nets development threatens to displace beloved local dive Freddy's. The
neighborhood is putting up resistance, but it's hard to fight City
Hall. In the meantime, we should all enjoy the scene before
Freddy's dead. There's never a cover or minimum for the back-room
acts, which include jazz, blues, old-time, and the monthly Kings
County Opry. Stimuli freaks should check out Rev-99, a collective
that makes live audio and video mixes on select Tuesday nights.
Call it jazz channel-surfing, clips of which can be watched nightly
on the front-room monitors. Bud nips (8 oz.) are $1.75, Pabst is
$2.50, pints of Bud are $3, and a mixed drink is $4.75, all the time.
485 Dean St., at Sixth Ave., Brooklyn. ℂ 718/622-7035. www.freddysback
room.com. Subway: 2/3 to Bergen St.

Jazz Detour   Jazz Detour waylays music fans with a full
schedule of no-cover acts. Trios and quartets make up the majority of the acts, although Wednesday provides an intriguing departure. "The Intimate Room" is a torch-song evening, with the likes
of Bacharach and Gershwin providing the tunage, and a different
singer every week to provide the mellow vibe. (The dimmed
lights don't hurt either.) Happy hour is 4 to 7pm, 7 days a week,
with occasional live performances. Drafts, bottles, and house
liquor are $3 each. Otherwise, Rheingolds and Buds cost $4 and
mixed drinks run between $5 and $9. Sunday through Thursday
live music from 9:30pm to 12:30am, Friday and Saturday from
10pm to 1:30am. FINE PRINT There's a two-drink minimum, and
patrons are asked to tip the musicians.

349 E. 13th St., between First and Second aves. ℭ 212/533-6212. www.jazz atdetour.com Subway: L to First Ave.

K'av'h'az   An art gallery slash coffee house, the accent-happy K'av'h'az has recently moved to bigger digs in Chelsea. You can hear live jazz most every night, usually for no cover. From 5 to 7pm nightly, happy-hour beers are $3.50. Otherwise prices range from $5 beers to $11 superpremium mixed drinks. FINE PRINT There can be an $8 minimum for food and drink.

37 W. 26th St., between Broadway and Sixth Ave. ℭ 212/343-0612. www. kavehaz.com. Subway: F/V to 23rd St.

Knitting Factory   The Knitting Factory is the elder statesman of the downtown avant-garde. Filling the multiple levels of an old schoolhouse, all forms of cutting-edge music are represented here. There are fewer free shows than there used to be, but at least one night a week you can find something in either the Old Office Space or the Tap Bar. If they're not free, the covers keep to the $5 to $7 range, though the bands won't have the profile of the higher-priced main space.

74 Leonard St., between Broadway and Chruch St. ℭ 212/219-3055. www. knittingfactory.com. Subway: 1/9 to Franklin St.

The Slipper Room   When burlesque and other theatrics aren't afoot at the Slipper, hip-hop, alternative, rock, and everything in between fill the bills. The evenings are usually loaded up with four to five bands. Though the names won't be familiar, booking here encourages a little ambition in terms of sound. Cover usually $5.

167 Orchard St., at Stanton St. ℭ 212/253-7246. www.slipperroom.com. Subway: F/V to Second Ave.

☆ Smoke   A quintessential old-fashioned jazz classic except for the Bloomberg-era pristine air, Smoke offers cover-free music on the weeknights. There's bebop of both the retro and nouveau varieties, funk on Wednesdays, and Latin jazz on Sundays. Tuesday nights vibrate with Hammond B-3 Organ Grooves. Best of all, your eyes aren't red and burning when you leave. Libations will run you from $5 to $10. FINE PRINT Weekend covers, weeknights free with $10 drink minimum (Tues–Thurs only a one-drink minimum).

2751 Broadway, between 105th and 106th sts. ℭ 212/864-6662. www. smokejazz.com. Subway: 1/9 to 103rd St.

FREE **The Underground Scene**

In this modern world it's hard to find a spontaneous public expression that can't be codified and regulated. Even street performers in New York get caught up in bureaucracy's net (the MTA's underground music Web address is a good indicator of the situation: www.mta.nyc.ny.us/mta/aft/muny.htm). The New York Metropolitan Transit Authority's program is called "Music Under New York," and it allows preselected performers to legally play at preselected stations. Illegally stationed musicians are often more melodically challenged—the quality level varies wildly beneath the streets. Times Square, Penn Station, Union Square, and Columbus Circle are the most heavily trafficked in the system, and it takes very little to draw an audience. In addition to the ubiquitous pan-flute Andean bands and tumbling demonstrations, you can hear amplified funk bands, jazz quartets, weird Chinese bow work, Brazilian drumming, blues, gospel, Calypso, and rock. The quality often competes with the music played aboveground on gel-lit stages. Not bad for the price of a swipe.

CLASSICAL ACTS
by Daniel Felsenfeld

New York City is the home of the greatest classical music community in the country, if not the world, boasting everything from the most opulent to the most cutting edge to the downright recherché, and with three major conservatories (not to mention the universities and colleges with music programs) guiding the future generations to expected technical excellence, it's hard to find a bad concert in town. Seeing great classical music on a shoestring is pretty easy to do in NYC. Like anything, you roll the dice on quality when you venture below the $20 ticket, but with the quality of young players in this town, your risk will most often pay off.

THE BIG THREE
Note: Every summer, music-loving New Yorkers get to hear the best of the best in Classical music perform for free in Central Park.

The **New York Philharmonic** and the **Metropolitan Opera** each present two separate programs of summer concerts on the Great Lawn every year. For more information, check out "High Culture for Free," in the Outdoor Summer Concerts section below.

Carnegie Hall For those not in need of planning in advance, it is not impossible to go see the best in classical music play at Carnegie Hall on the cheap. At noon on the day of a show, the hall box office often releases a number of partial-view tickets for $10. For select events, $10 student/senior rush tickets are also sold in the lobby beginning at noon until 1 hour before concert time. Check the website for a calendar of events. FINE PRINT Cash only for student/senior rush tickets; bring a valid ID.

154 W. 57th St., at Seventh Ave. ℂ 212/247-7800. www.carnegie hall.org. Subway: Q to 57th St./Seventh Ave.; F to 57th St.; E/B/D to Seventh Ave.

New York City Opera (Lincoln Center) If you're a full-time student under the age of 29 (or if you know one), New York City Opera's Student Coalition for the Arts offers $10 tickets to students just before each show. The low-cost tickets are available at the State Theater Box Office on the day of the performance. The price alone should make you forget you're sitting in the third of four rings of the theater. If not, the music will. FINE PRINT Three tickets per person. You'll need your student ID and a completed voucher. Check the website to fill one out online.

New York State Theater at Lincoln Center, between W. 62nd and 65th sts. and Columbus and Amsterdam aves. ℂ 212/870-5630 or 212/870-5570 (State Theater Box Office). www.nyopera.com. Subway: 1/9 to 66th St./Lincoln Center.

> **FREE VOX: Showcasing American Composers**
>
> If you happen to be in town in the spring, City Opera, now in collaboration with American Opera Projects, presents its annual VOX: Showcasing American Composers, a wall-to-wall couple of days wherein readings of new operas by America's best and brightest composers are presented in varying locations annually. Check the website for schedule and concert locations (www.nycopera.com/www/hide3/about/vox/index.html).

FREE Divine Inspiration: Concerts at the Churches

With spectacular acoustics and an often rather charitable rental fee, churches are the site of some of the best music making in the city. From the ed opera aspirants who make their living rolling into church choirs every Sunday morning to the wide array of organ concerts, vocal recitals, amateur choirs (though don't let that fool you, they can really be something), new music concerts, piano recitals, and semistaged operas, you are likely to stumble onto some genuinely impressive performances. There are hundreds of churches in Manhattan alone, but here are some of the more prominent ecclesiastical stages in town:

St. John the Divine   1047 Amsterdam Ave., at 112th St. © 212/316-7540. www.stjohndivine.org. Subway: B/C to Cathedral Parkway/110th St.

St. Ignatius Loyola   980 Park Ave. at 84th St. © 212/721-6500. www.saintignatiusloyola.org. Subway: 4/5/6 to 86th St.

St. Bartholomew   109 E. 50th St., between Park and Lexington aves. © 212/378-0248. www.stbarts.org. Subway: 6 to 51st St.

☆ **St. Paul's Chapel/Trinity Church**   For more information about the "Concerts at One" series, see p. 288, in chapter 7. 209 Broadway, at Fulton St. © 212/233-4164. www.saint paulschapel.org. Subway: 2/3/4/5 and A to Fulton St.-Broadway Nassau; 6 to Brooklyn Bridge-City Hall; E to Chambers St.; R to Cortlandt St.

Call or check the church websites for concert schedules you'll find both afternoon and evening concerts available. And, of course, donations are *always* accepted, though there will be no collection plate passed.

Metropolitan Opera (Lincoln Center)   You can get standing-room tickets at slightly more than $10—more like $12 or $16—but well worth it for the die-hardest of budget-minded opera fans. Don't try this for big stars (either in fame *or* girth—Pavarotti, should he return, would sell out within minutes) or fancy opening nights, but do chance it if you dare. Tickets go on sale at the box office on Saturday mornings at 10am for Saturday through the following Friday performances, but the line starts much earlier than 10am, so grab the morning java and try to get there no later than 9am. FINE PRINT Cash only and only one ticket allowed per person.

Metropolitan Opera at Lincoln Center, between W. 62nd and 65th sts. and Columbus and Amsterdam aves. ℂ 212/362-6000. www.met opera.org. Subway: 1/9 to 66th St./Lincoln Center.

Sources

In addition to *Time Out* and *The New Yorker*, another excellent source for information on the occasional free or cheap concert is WNYC's radio program **Soundcheck** (available at 93.9 FM, 820 AM, or on the Web at www.wnyc.org), hosted by John Schaeffer, where music personalities of all types join the imminently knowledgeable host, often to plug something they've got going on in town that week.

AMATEURS OF NOTE

Jupiter Symphony   The Jupiter Symphony performs both at the Good Shepherd Presbyterian Church during the year and at venues like the beautiful Ethical Cultural Society during the summer. A delightful, if not terribly progressive group, the Jupiter presents lovely, nonthreatening concerts of oldies but goodies at $15 a ticket. Check the website for a calendar of performances. *Note:* The summer concert series venue may change from year to year. Check the website for locations.

Good Shepherd Presbyterian Church, 152 W. 66th St., between Broadway and Amsterdam Ave. ℂ 212/799-1259. www.jupitersymphony.com. Subway: 1/9 to 66th St./Lincoln Center.

New York Repertory Orchestra FREE   Also performing at Good Shepherd, the NYRO tends to be a little more adventurous than the Jupiters in its programming. Better yet: The concerts cost no more than a swipe of your Metrocard.

Good Shepherd Presbyterian Church, 152 W. 66th St., between Broadway and Amsterdam Ave. ℂ 212/662-8383. www.nyro.org. Subway: 1/9 to 66th St./Lincoln Center 83.

Concerts in the Heights FREE   This series offers chamber music, one concert per month, at the Fort Washington Collegiate

Church. As high rents drive most of the cities musicians farther north, these free concerts are likely to be excellent offerings from the less-than-famous leading lights of the city—No Yo-Yo here, but good music making to be sure.

Collegiate Church of Washington Heights, 181st St., at Fort Washington Ave. ℭ 212/740-5923. Subway: A to 181st St.

OUTDOOR SUMMER CONCERTS

The high season for free music is summer, when cool sounds seem to be coming from every corner. You would think that with so many events the crowds would spread thin, but concerts tend to be consistently well attended. If you're going primarily to see the band, better allow at least an hour to carve out some space. For particularly big names you'll have to get there even earlier. If the scene is more interesting than the sound, however, New York concerts are laid back enough that you can just wander in and out as the mood strikes you. With concerts at so many spectacular sites, a sunset on the Hudson or late afternoon light on the Brooklyn skyline often come with your metaphorical price of admission (pretty much everything is free).

Battery Park FREE   Battery Park has the city's most spectacular gardens and shoreline, but its corner-pocket location causes it to be overlooked. Much of the working crowd rushes off to subway cars and ferries come quitting time, leaving the rest of us more space to enjoy the cultural resources. The River to River festival cosponsors several summer concerts down here, many of which are underattended by New York standards. There's no better way to watch dusk settle over the island. My favorite spot is **Robert F. Wagner, Jr. Park,** at the south end of the park. Boat traffic in New York Harbor and the Statue of Liberty provide the backdrop. The **River and Blues** series presents blues bigs like Shemekia Copeland over four Thursdays in July at 7pm. A little ways north is the **World Financial Center Plaza.** Nestled between the Winter Garden and the North Cove Yacht Harbor, the space rings into life on Tuesday nights in summer when live bands play. Recent booking has brought in some solid indie rockers like Fountains of Wayne. Shows also begin at 7pm. Wednesday nights the place to be is Rockefeller Park, on the northernmost end of Battery Park, for another series of 7 o'clock concerts. Indie rock

Free Outdoor Summer Concerts

Monday	Tuesday	Wednesday	Thursday	Saturday	Sunday
Martin Luther King Jr. Concert Series	Washington Square Music Festival, 8pm	Rockefeller Park, 7pm	BAM R&B Festival at MetroTech, noon	East River Park Amphitheater, 1pm	Harlem Meer Peformance Festival, 4pm
	World Financial Center Plaza, 7pm		Castle Clinton, 7pm		
			River and Blues, Battery Park, 7pm		
			Summer Nights at El Museo del Barrio, 6pm		

and alt-country are favored here, with bigish names like the Old 97's making the scene. Check www.rivertorivernyc.org for full schedules.

Robert F. Wagner, Jr. Park, between Battery Place and New York Harbor. ✆ 212/267-9700. www.bpcparks.org. Subway: 1/9 to Rector St. or South Ferry; 4/5 to Bowling Green.; World Financial Center Plaza, due east of the North Cove Yacht Harbor. ✆ 212/528-2733. www.worldfinancialcenter.com. Subway: E to World Trade Center; R/W to Cortlandt St.; Rockefeller Park, at the west end of Chambers and Warren Sts. ✆ 212/528-2733. www.battery parkcity.org. Subway: 1/2/3/9 or A/C to Chambers St.

BAM Rhythm & Blues Festival at MetroTech `FREE`
MetroTech Commons is as close to a municipal center as Brooklyn gets, and in the summer it's the site of a free lunchtime concert series. As the name suggests, R&B is the focus, though the definition stretches to include blues, reggae, and funk as well. Surprisingly big names like the Neville Brothers and Ohio Players come through. Ten shows are held in all, Thursdays from noon to 2pm, mid-June to mid-August.

MetroTech Commons, at Flatbush and Myrtle aves. ✆ 718/636-4100. www. bam.org. Subway: 2/3 to Hoyt St.; M/R to Lawrence St.; A/C/F to Jay St./ Borough Hall.

Bryant Park `FREE`   Every year, Bryant Park seems to pack its live music schedule a little tighter. There's a big range of genres and the park's central location makes it a convenient place to catch some sounds. Broadway's brightest croon on selected summer afternoons (see p. 65), while the Good Morning America Summer Concert Series (see p. 82) brings out beats at 7am. Every June, the JVC Jazz Fest (*(C)* **212/501-1393;** www.festival productions.net) takes over the stage. Expect three concerts on 3 separate days, with musicians you may even have heard of. On a less-elaborate note, you can also hear pianists every weekday in summer. The songs are old-timey, popularized by the likes of Fats Waller, Scott Joplin, and the Gershwins. Piano in the Park can be heard Mondays, Wednesdays and Fridays from noon to 2:30pm, and Tuesdays and Thursdays from 4:30pm to 7pm.

Bryant Park, between W. 40th and 42nd sts., along Sixth Ave. www.bryant park.org. Subway: B/D/F/V to 42nd St.; 7 to Fifth Ave.

Castle Clinton `FREE`   This old defensive battery took a turn as a fashionable concert hall in the first half of the 1800s, and it recalls those former duties on Thursday nights in summer. Indie favorites like Cat Power, The Magnetic Fields, and Del McCoury have done the honors in the past. The series kicks off with a July 4th show in Battery Park. All shows are free, although you need to pick up tickets for Thursday nights. Distribution begins at Castle Clinton at 5pm, but people start lining up a good couple of hours before.

Battery Park, on the west side at New York Harbor. *(C)* **212/566-6700.** www.downtownny.com. Subway: 1/9 to South Ferry; 4/5 Bowling Green.

Celebrate Brooklyn! `FREE`   The Prospect Park Bandshell is a perfect place for a concert, with a festive and friendly crowd. The audio selections are as eclectic as Brooklyn, with acts like Rufus Wainwright, the Spanish Harlem Orchestra, and the Brooklyn Philharmonic. Shows are generally well attended, so show up early if you want a decent view. Check the website for schedules. FINE PRINT A $3 donation is suggested.

The Prospect Park Bandshell, Park Slope, Brooklyn. *(C)* **718/855-7882.** www. celebratebrooklyn.org. Subway: F to Seventh Ave.; B/Q to Seventh Ave.; 2/3 to Grand Army Plaza. Enter at Prospect Park West and 9th St.

Chamber Music at the Frick `FREE`   Inside the Gilded Age confines of this elegant art museum, you can catch regular Sunday afternoon performances. The tickets are a little hard to score, however. Send a SASE and a written request for a specific show a little over 3 weeks in advance. If you do get tickets, don't arrive more than half an hour in advance of the concert, lest they hit you up for the $12 admission fee. Check the website for the updated calendar. Send ticket requests to The Frick Collection, Concert Department, 1 E. 70th St., New York, NY 10021-4967. FINE PRINT You can only request one show at a time, and there's a two-ticket maximum.

1 E. 70th St., between Madison and Fifth aves. ℂ 212/288-0700. www.frick. org. Subway: 6 to 68th St./Hunter College.

City Parks Foundation FREE   This group is a major player in New York's free music scene, putting on some 900 performances every year. Shows take place in parks across the boroughs; check online to see what's playing and when. One event to keep an eye out for is late **August's Charlie Parker Jazz Festival.** Bird gets honored with shows in two of his home neighborhoods, Harlem and the East Village. The Harlem show is Saturday afternoon in Marcus Garvey Park. Tompkins Square Park takes over on Sunday.

Marcus Garvey Park, 18 Mount Morris Park West, at Fifth Ave. ℂ 212/860-1373. www.cityparksfoundation.org. Subway: 2/3 or 4/5/6 to 125th St. Tompkins Sq., between 7th and 10th sts. and aves. A and B. Subway: 6 to Astor Place; F/V to Second Ave.

East River Park Amphitheater FREE   This newly renovated spot on the East River, with beautiful Brooklyn and bridge views, hosts free music programs on summer Saturday. Proximity to the LES and EV ensure that the hipness readings are off the charts. The **East River Music Project** puts on three Saturday shows featuring the likes of Cat Power and Ted Leo. You can usually hear four acts over the afternoon. Check the website for scheduling, www.ermp. org. Arlene's Grocery is the force behind **Three Farms,** a second festival that brings in four to five acts over a couple of Saturdays in June. David Johansen and Laura Cantrell were the big names in '04. Shows run all afternoon. The amphitheater's capacity is around 1,000, so you may even be able to wander in late and snag a seat. Check online for the schedule.

600 Grand St., at the East River. ℂ 212/358-1633. www.arlene-grocery. com. Subway: F to Delancey St.; J/M/Z to Essex St. Walk along the south side of the Williamsburg Bridge and take the pedestrian bridge over the FDR. Turn left and follow the river down to the amphitheater.

Harlem Meer Performance Festival FREE   Latino and African sounds predominate at this meer-front festival. The scene

High Culture for Free

New York Philharmonic Concerts in the Parks `FREE`   The New York Philharmonic, one of the world's premier symphonies, gives away a week's worth of shows every summer. The covered composers range from Mendelssohn to Strauss to Ives. While the atmosphere is more hackey sack than Harnancourt—more background for a group picnic than an event for the serious music lover—the performances by guest conductors and musicians are often inspired. If the classical music doesn't lure you in, you might stop by just for the free fireworks show afterwards. Performance locations vary, but generally all five boroughs and Long Island are included. Check the website (www.newyorkphilharmonic.org) for exact locations. Shows start at 8pm, no tickets required. ✆ 212/875-5709.

Met in the Parks `FREE`   Critics may sniff that the Metropolitan Opera rests on its laurels, but this spectacular institution maintains extremely high standards. Tickets can approach $300 for shows at the Opera House, but for 2 weeks every summer the fat lady sings for free. Shows are held in parks in all five boroughs, with a couple of Jersey visits thrown in as well. Two different operas are performed, usually six performances of each. Check the website for exact locations and times; no tickets are required. ✆ 212/362-6000. www.metopera.org.

The classic summer Met and Phil shows are performed on the Great Lawn in Central Park (midpark, just below 86th St.; Subway: B/C or 4/5/6 to 86th St.). There are two different programs for each institution each year, and they're wildly popular, with the picnic blankets spread out hours before the music begins. The leafy setting is ideal, but if you want a closer view and a shorter waiting time, I recommend checking out the less-crowded shows in Queens and the Bronx.

is as upbeat as the music, which is usually very danceable. Blankets and picnics are not discouraged. Concerts are Sunday afternoons from 4 to 6pm, Memorial Day weekend through late August, near the Charles A. Dana Discovery Center.

Central Park, at 110th St., between Fifth and Lenox aves. © 212/860-1370. www.centralparknyc.org. Subway: 2/3 to Central Park North.

☆ **Lincoln Center Out of Doors** FREE   Lincoln Center is a veritable city of performing arts, and every summer for over 30 years now, the great public square has been home to a diverse series of shows. The breadth is breathtaking, from Chinese opera to Greek dance to cutting-edge jazz to children's story time. Incredibly, it's all free. Check online for exact schedules, covering 4 weeks in August. *Note:* Look for several shows that take place in the nearby Damrosch Park Bandshell, at W. 62nd St. and Amsterdam Avenue.

70 Lincoln Center Plaza, at Broadway and 64th St. © 212/546-2656. www. lincolncenter.org. Subway: 1/9 to 66th St.

Martin Luther King Jr. Concert Series FREE   Jazz, soul, gospel, and old school are some of the genres that can be heard on the Monday night program here. Seating is limited, so you might want to bring your own chair. In case of rain, concerts are postponed to Tuesday.

Wingate Field, Winthrop St., between Brooklyn and Kingston aves., Brooklyn. © 718/469-1912. www.brooklynconcerts.com. Subway: 2/5 to Winthrop St.

Naumburg Orchestral Concerts FREE   The Naumburg Bandshell in Central Park hosts this concert series, which varies from classical orchestral presentations to brass to flamenco. The series is one of the oldest in the country, with a century's worth of experience in entertaining New Yorkers. Shows are Tuesday nights at 7:30pm, with no rain dates.

Midpark, just below 72nd St. Subway: B/C to 72nd St.; 6 to 68th St./ Hunter College.

RiverRocks FREE   I love the festive atmosphere of this concert series. The crowd is friendly and sunset over the Hudson and the Jersey skyline is inspiring. Roomy Pier 54 does the hosting. If you show up late you won't get very close to the band, but you will find plenty of space for hanging out, or even dancing. Music varies, from up-and-comers, to groups in slow decline. Check the website for time and dates, and also check for other concerts on the same pier.

Pier 54 on the Hudson, at 13th St. © 212/533-PARK. www.hudsonriver park.org. Subway: A/C/E to 14th St.; L to Eighth Ave.

Siren Music Festival `FREE`   The best in below-the-radar rock can be found at the *Village Voice*'s annual Siren Music Festival. Over a hundred thousand fans assemble near the Coney Island boardwalk for music on two stages. The bands tend to be high-quality performers, on the cusp of breakthroughs, or not too far removed from indie-rock triumphs. See p. 265 in chapter 7 for more information.

Main stage: 10th St., at the boardwalk. Second stage: Stillwell Ave., at the boardwalk. © 212/475-3333. www.villagevoice.com/siren. Saturday in mid-July, noon–9pm. Subway: D/F/Q/W to Stillwell Avenue/Coney Island.

Summer Nights at El Museo del Barrio `FREE`   Latin flavors are on the bill on summer Thursdays at this Harlem institution. Shows are performed outdoors in the courtyard, with music ranging from Cuban son to modern Latino rock. In case of rain, shows move indoors. Select Thursday nights from 6 to 9pm, from June through August.

1230 Fifth Ave. at 104th St. © 212/831-7272. www.elmuseo.org. Subway: 6 to 103rd St.

★ **SummerStage** `FREE`   Words like *summer* and *music* and *free* conjure an idyllic picture, especially in the context of Central Park. SummerStage is a crack outfit that brings big-name performers to a stage just off the Rumsey Playfield. To get a seat in the bleachers, better show up a couple of hours before start time. If you're not that patient you can just wander in at any time, and you should be able to find a spot to stand and/or dance. Since no tickets are required, it's easy to come and go freely unless it's a superpopular show. Acts as varied as James Brown, Sonic Youth, and Hugh Masekela have played here. `FINE PRINT` Every summer it seems more and more of the concerts are pricey benefit shows, with tickets going for about $40. To further support the series, donations are solicited as you enter. (No contribution is required.)

Central Park, at the Rumsey Playfield, near E. 72nd St. © 212-360-2777 or 212/360-2756. www.summerstage.org. Subway: 6 to 68th or 77th sts.: 1/2/3/9/B/C to 72nd St. Enter the park at 69th St. and Fifth Ave.

Seaport Music Festival `FREE`   The South Street Seaport isn't much more than a glorified mall, which is cause enough for most locals to give it a wide berth. In the summer, however, Pier 17 is loaded with great free music. The scene is still a little commercial, but recently the bills have been laden with bands a person really wants to hear. Selections are diverse, from salsa to alternative rock to zydeco. A couple of afternoons are set aside for music and dance demonstrations, showing off a single country's traditions. Events are held just about every Wednesday through Friday night from 6 to 9pm. Tuesday afternoons from 1 to 3pm also have live music. The festival runs late June through August. Limited seating is available.

Pier 17, between Beekman and Fulton sts., just east of South St. ℂ 212/SEA-PORT. www.seaportmusicfestival.com. Subway: A/C/J/M/Z/2/3/4/5 to Fulton St./Broadway Nassau.

Washington Square Music Festival `FREE`   One of the city's oldest festivals brings classical music (and a little jazz) to the heart of the Village. Three pieces, connected by an overall theme, are played every Tuesday night in July from 8 to 10pm. The last Tuesday of the month is often set aside for jazz or swing tunes. The festival is held in the southeast corner of Washington Square Park. Limited seating is available.

Near the intersection of Washington Sq. South and Washington Sq. East. ℂ 212/252-3621. www.washingtonsquaremusicfestival.org. Subway: A/B/C/D/E/F/V to W. 4th St.

2 The Reel Cheap World

The movies love New York. Blithely ignoring our existing congestion, productions flock to the city to steal our parking spaces and tie up our sidewalks. Gotham-themed films line the video store shelves. Is it because we're a convenient symbol of urban glamour? Or is it simply because New York is the greatest goddamn city in the history of the world? Either way, NYC has a lot of cinematic pride, which allows New Yorkers to be extorted with $10 movie tickets, a dearth of cheap afternoon matinees, and new releases sold out by 4pm even on gorgeous sunny days. Fortunately in New York there are always alternatives. Our libraries are stocked with videos, our bars screen in their backrooms, and in the summer we get spectacular film al fresco. Most events are on the house, and those that aren't won't break the bank.

INDIES, CULTS, CLASSICS & MORE

Arlene's Grocery Picture Show   Even at $10 a ticket or more, it's tough to get into a show at most of the city's slick corporate-sponsored film fests. One exception remains, on the Lower East Side, of course, where Arlene's Grocery puts on an annual Picture Show. The fest is growing exponentially with up to 400 shorts now. The submission fee is a democratic $5, and all the showings are free, including the Monday night awards ceremony ("The Groceries," with mounted cans of pigeon peas instead of Oscars). The series takes place in late April.

95 Stanton St., between Orchard and Ludlow sts. ℂ 212/358-1633. www. arlene-grocery.com. Subway: F/V to Second Ave.; J/M/Z to Essex St. Other screenings at additional neighborhood venues.

Barbès FREE   In the international spirit of its namesake Parisian neighborhood, Barbès presents **Traveling Cinéma,** a film series that veers from *Nosferatu* to *Bringing Up Baby.* More movies show on Sundays in the film and video series, and every night after 11pm films play silently on the newly upgraded Barbès digital system. Traveling Cinéma happens on Monday at 8pm, all films in 16mm and free as the air. Check out See the Film and Video series Sundays at 7pm. They don't have a happy hour, but a can of Pabst Blue Ribbon is only $3.

376 9th St., at Sixth Ave. Park Slope, Brooklyn. ℂ 718/965-9177. www. barbesbrooklyn.com. Subway: F to Seventh Ave. Take the southwest exit and make a U-turn when you get out, walking downhill on 9th St. toward Sixth Ave.

Coney Island Museum   On Saturday nights in summer, the museum drags its carny relics to the side and lays in rows of chairs so it can show off Coney Island's sideshow heritage, or at least movies made in the same spirit. In addition to explorations of burlesque, expect uplifting cinematic triumphs with the words *bikini* or *bandit* in the title. The low-budget productions beget budget prices: just $5. Saturdays at 8:30pm.

1208 Surf Ave., 2nd floor. ℂ 718/372-5159. www.indiefilmpage.com. Subway: D to Coney Island/Stillwell Ave.

Millennium Film   Despite the Y2K-sounding name, Millennium Film has been providing a home for experimental and cutting-edge film since 1966. The regular calendar of movies often

The Film Forum Membership

Does Hollywood still make movies that aren't just flimsy remakes of second-rate television shows? Just when we're ready to give up forever on the medium, the marquee of the Film Forum draws us in with some irresistible nugget and we're hooked again. Three screens rotate between revivals, retrospectives, and indies that can't be found elsewhere. The crowd is just as interesting, with big-shot actors and directors often in the house, upping their avant-garde cinematic cred. A 1-year membership to Film Forum is one of the city's best steals. Sixty-five bucks buys you half-price movie tickets for all three screens 365¼ days a year. That's $5 instead of $10. The next membership level up is an even sweeter deal: $95 entitles you to two half-price tickets for every show. Imagine: cheap date opportunities every single day. Membership is good for 1 year from the date of purchase. But wait, there's more. It's also 100% tax deductible. Now if only they could make the seats a little more comfortable. 209 W. Houston St. between Sixth Ave., at Varick. ℂ 212/727-8110. www.filmforum.com. Subway: 1/9 to Houston St.

highlights unfairly forgotten flicks and directors. Open film nights come around on Fridays, with filmmakers allowed to contribute anything they want as long as it's finished and not more than 20 minutes, first come, first served. Most shows are $7; open films and selected other nights are admission by contribution. 66 E. 4th St., between Second Ave. and Bowery. ℂ 212/673-0090. www. millennuiumfilm.org. Subway: F/V to Second Ave.; 66 E. 4th St. F/V to Second Ave.

☆ **Ocularis at Galapagos**   Ocularis ("of eyes" in Latin) began its Brooklyn run with rooftop screenings before finding a permanent home at Galapagos, the Williamsburg mayonnaise factory turned cultural center. Every Sunday at 7pm guest curators present a series of shorts on themes like failure, or "Exotica from the MoMA Collection." Tickets are $6.

70 N. 6th St., Williamsburg, Brooklyn. ℂ 718/388-8713. www.ocularis.net or www.galapagosartspace.com. Subway: L to Bedford Ave., walk west on 6th St., toward the East River.

Pioneer Theater   As a hedge against poets displacing film-makers in the public imagination, the Pioneer Theater holds a weekly film "slam." Films compete for audience adulations, and the winners get a chance to be shown on other slates. It's free to submit, and if you're the director, there's no cost to watch. Everyone else has to pay $5 to get in—not too bad for a couple of hours of shorts. Every Sunday at 5pm.

155 E. 3rd St., at Ave. A. ℂ 212/254-3300. www.twoboots.com/pioneer. Subway: F/V to Second Ave.

RaFiFi/Cinema Classics This shabby-chic bar put itself on the East Village cultural map with weekly screenings of *The Wizard of Oz,* creepily synched to Pink Floyd's "The Dark Side of the Moon." Burlesque and comedy nights have encroached on the original cinematic focus, but there are still screenings in the back room. Cover is $6 for films ($5 for burlesque). Check the website for a calendar of events.

332 E. 11th St., between First and Second aves. ℂ 212/677-6309. www.cinemaclassics.com. Subway: 332 E. 11th St., between 1st and 2nd aves.; L to First Ave.; N/R to 8th St.

> ### The Pioneer Theater Membership
>
> For just $20 a year you can pick up a membership at the Pioneer Theater. Regular tickets will only cost you $6.50, compared to $9, for a savings of $2.50 a shot. With only $20 invested, your membership will pay for itself in eight screenings. The Pioneer is only a uniplex so the options are a lot more limited than a Film Forum membership (p. 50), but on Monday nights members can get two tickets for just $6.50 total, making for a very cheap date.

Rooftop Films   Rooftops. Brooklyn's got 'em in spades. Rooftop Films has a lovely one on top of the American Can Factory. This sprawling industrial compound dates back at least as far as the Civil War. On Friday nights in summer, God dims the overheads and indie shorts play. Despite perennially low budgets, Rooftop

Current Releases for Little Currency

"That $3 theater" became "that $4 theater" and then closed altogether. The uptown bargain-matinee place got torn down to make way for million-dollar condos. It's becoming harder and harder to find a current release for anything less than the usurious $10 charged for prime-time viewing. If you're in the right neighborhood, though, there are still a couple of options left.

Brooklyn Heights Pavilion   Bargain days (and nights) come to the Heights on Tuesdays and Thursdays, where all seats are $6. On the weekends the first show of the day is also $6. 70 Henry St., at Orange St., Brooklyn Heights, Brooklyn. ✆ **718/596-7070.** Subway: 2/3 to Clark St.; A/C to High St.

Cobble Hill Cinema   Monday through Friday all shows before 5pm are only $5, as are the first shows of the day on the weekend (as long as they start before 2pm). If matinees don't do it for you, there are also two bargain days, Tuesdays and Thursdays, when all seats for all shows all day and all night are a humble $5. FINE PRINT No discounts for the first 2 weeks of any Sony Pictures run. 265 Court St. at Butler, Boerum Hill, Brooklyn. ✆ **718/596-9113.** Subway: F/G to Bergen St.

Kew Gardens Cinemas   First-run films play here, with several bargain showtimes. Monday, Wednesday, and Friday, all seats are $5 until 5pm, as are seats for the first show before 2pm on Saturdays and Sundays. Tuesdays and Thursdays are bargain

Films does a good filtering job and quality is surprisingly high. Film themes run along the lines of "Home Movies" or "Scenes from Texas." Screenings cost $7, a bargain if you value films made by actual human beings and not Hollywood-studio automatons. Fridays at 9pm, May to September. Live music for some showings at 8pm.

232 3rd St., Bldg. B, between Third and Fourth aves., Brooklyn. ✆ **877/ 786-1912.** www.rooftopfilms.com. Subway: F/G to Carroll Gardens; N/R to Union St./Fourth Ave. When it rains, screenings are held indoors at the same location.

days, with all shows day and night going for $5. Holidays and special engagements are excepted for the cheap seats. ℂ 718/441-9835. 81-05 Lefferts Blvd., at Austin St., Kew Gardens, Queens. Subway: E/F to Kew Gardens/Union Turnpike.

Loews Cineplex State   Second-run Hollywood flicks can be found at this small theater in the basement of the Virgin Megastore. The bad news is that the films are often clunkers, but at least the seats are only $5.50. The theater also presents imports from Bollywood, but for those sweet Indian harmonies you'll have to pay the full $10.25. ℂ 212/50-LOEWS (express code #901). 1540 Broadway, between 45th and 46th sts. Subway: 1/2/3/9/N/Q/R/S/W to 42nd St./Times Square.

Magic Johnson Harlem USA   Magic offers the first performance of every show on weekends and holidays at a discounted rate of $6.75. On the weekdays the same deal goes for any show before 2pm. 2309 Frederick Douglass Blvd., at 124th St. ℂ 212/665-8742. www.enjoytheshow.com. Subway: A/B/C/D to 125th St.

UA Kaufman Astoria 14   Right across the street from the legendary Kaufman Astoria Studios, this Queens megaplex has bargain matinees on the weekdays. Every show before 6pm is only $6. 35-30 38th St., off Steinway. Astoria, Queens. ℂ 718/786-2020. Subway: G/R/V to Steinway St.

Screeners Club `FREE`   The average bar keeps a camera or two around just for safety, but the Remote Lounge goes nuts, with 60 electronic eyes studding the club. Control is ceded to patrons, who gleefully spy on one another from specially rigged consoles. This technophilic scene creates a perfect atmosphere for the Screeners Club, a series that shows off shorts by independent filmmakers. It's free to submit and free to watch, in the downstairs lounge on the first Wednesday of every month, from 8 to 10pm.

327 Bowery, between 2nd and 3rd sts. www.screenersclub.com. Subway: 6 to Bleecker St.; B/D/F/V to Broadway/Lafayette.

Sony Wonder Technology Lab `FREE`   Sony goes to bat for high-def technology by hosting weekly free films in its 73-seat theater. The flicks tend to be well-known Hollywood products of recent vintage. Sprinkled throughout the year are additional afternoon screenings for the kiddies. Thursday at 6pm. Weekly in summer, otherwise every other week. Reservations recommended.

550 Madison Ave., at 56th St. ℂ **212/833-7858.** www.sonywondertechlab. com. Subway: 4/5/6 to 59th St.; N/R to Lexington Ave.

Telephone Bar & Grill `FREE`   Anglophile cinephiles and the people who love them gather at Gene's Backroom British Cinema Club for Brit flicks on a big screen. Free films are shown every week, conforming to monthly themes that favor British obsessions like psychedelic spies. Tuesdays at 8pm.

149 Second Ave., between 9th and 10th sts. ℂ **212/529-5000.** www.telebar. com. Subway: 6 to Astor Place; L to Third Ave.

NYC'S DRIVE-IN: OUTDOOR SUMMER SCREENINGS

We may be too cheap for insurance, garages, tickets, tolls, and all the other joys of car ownership, but New Yorkers do know how to enjoy their very own brand of drive-in movie. Come summer, the parks roll out the big screens and the locals trundle in with blankets and picnic dinners. Each festival has its own identity, with movies ranging across the decades and the genres, assuring something for every cineaste's taste. As dusk settles over the city, around 8 or 8:30pm, the crowd hushes and the reels spin. Lay back and be transported by the magic of the movies under the starry skies. Well, skies.

☆ **HBO/Bryant Park Summer Film Festival** `FREE`   Bryant Park is the most famous and most popular of New York's outdoor talkies. A huge screen goes up along Sixth Avenue across from the library, and the lawn fills with friendly movie fanatics. Film selections run from kitsch like *Jailhouse Rock* to classics like *The Philadelphia Story* to tripped-out wonders like *2001: A Space Odyssey*. Watching the latter from the grass brings a creepy resonance: Bryant Park was once a potter's field. The gates open for blanket spreading at 5pm, and if you want a decent view you should be on-site by then. Bring a crossword puzzle and a picnic

Free Outdoor Summer Movies
Note: All movies begin at dusk.

Monday	Wednesday	Thursday	Friday
HBO/Bryant Park Summer Film Festival	On the Waterfront at Socrates Sculpture Park	Brooklyn Bridge Park Summer Film Series	RiverFlicks-Pier 25
	RiverFlicks-Pier 54	Crotona Park Hip Hop Film Festival	
		Prospect Park Film Series Celebrate Brooklyn!	

dinner and pretend you're just sitting in the park and not waiting for a show. Latecomers have to watch from way back or the wings. It's not untenable, it's just not as much fun as dancing through the HBO trailer from the heart of the crowd. If you time things right, and the director's done his work, this event is totally worth its logistical impositions. Monday nights June through August.

W. 40th to 41st, on the Sixth Ave. side of Bryant Park. ℂ **212/512-5700.** www.hbobryantparkfilm.com. Rain date Tues. Subway: B/D/F/V to 42nd St.; 7 to Fifth Ave.

RiverFlicks FREE   The waters of the Hudson and the Jersey skyline provide the backdrop for RiverFlicks. It's a viewer-friendly scene, with chairs laid out on the pier, free popcorn, and filmic fare tending toward crowd-pleasing recent hits. *Legally Blonde, 8 Mile,* and *Gladiator* have all made the cut. If you're too late to garner a seat, there's space aplenty for blanket spreading. Pier 54 hosts Wednesday nights and Pier 25 takes Fridays in July and August. Pier 25 also gets called upon for the **Tribeca Film Fest Drive-In** (www.tribecafilmfest.org). Usually three big-name films play during the festival. Entry is free but tickets are required; check online for the specifics.

Pier 25, at North Moore and the Hudson. ℂ **212/533-7275.** www.hudson riverpark.org. Subway: 1/2 to Franklin St.; A/C/E to Chambers St. Walk toward the river. Pier 54, at W. 13th St. and the river. Subway: A/C/E to 14th St. Walk toward the river.

☆ **Brooklyn Bridge Park Summer Film Series** FREE   What could be better than the spectacular sight of downtown lights shimmering behind the Gothic span of the Brooklyn Bridge? A

The New Committee: The *Voice*'s Ticket Giveaways

Before the Internet ruled our lives, the *Village Voice* sponsored weekly movie ticket giveaways. You'd queue up somewhere near the NYU campus with a great crowd of fellow-scroungers known as "The Committee." Anything the city offered up for free would attract them. If you showed up early enough at the location, you'd be guaranteed a ticket for you and a guest. With the Internet's ascendance, however, promoters have a more direct way of getting your butts in the seats. Scroll down the left side of the *Voice*'s homepage (www.village voice.com) and you'll see a selection of giveaways that almost always includes a movie premiere. *Time Out New York* (www. timeoutny.com) has contests and giveaways, too, though usually it's for theater, and they only offer a couple of seats, making for some long odds. In these new lottery systems, they get your name, address, e-mail, and other invasive disclosures, which the old Committee members wouldn't have given up for anything less than a T-shirt. Oh well—at least it's still free.

free movie flickering in front, that's what. Every summer, Brooklyn Bridge Park, a DUMBO oasis on the former site of the Fulton Ferry Landing, shows Brooklyn features—movies shot in the scrappy underdog borough or bearing the stamps of Brooklyn-born biggies like Woody Allen and Richard Dreyfuss. This program is the anti–Bryant Park—it's low key, with no hassles, and you don't have to be überorganized to carve out a decent spot to watch. Thursday nights at dusk, in July and August.

Empire-Fulton Ferry Park, just west of Water St. ⊘ 718/802-0603. www. bbpc.net/filmseries.html. Subway: F to York St.; A/C to High St.; Water Taxi to Fulton Ferry Landing.

On the Waterfront at Socrates Sculpture Park Queens is the most culturally diverse spot on the planet, so it makes sense that a Queens film festival would show off movies from around the world. You'll even find culture-appropriate food vendors, so you can eat Italian during *The Bicycle Thief* or Indian while *Monsoon Wedding* plays. The movies flicker at Socrates Sculpture Park in Long Island City, a former dump site resuscitated as an artistic gem along the East River. There's great skyline sightlines, along with slightly less uplifting Costco parking lot views. Music, dancing, and food at 7pm, movies at dusk. Wednesday nights in July and August.

32-01 Vernon Blvd. at Broadway, Astoria, Queens. ℰ 718/784-4520. www. socratessculpturepark.org. Subway: N/W to Broadway. Walk 8 blocks along Broadway toward the East River. *Note:* Rain site is the American Museum of the Moving Image, 8pm. ℰ 718/784-0077. www.ammi.org. Subway: R to Steinway St.; N to Broadway.

Crotona Park Hip Hop Film Festival `FREE`   The Bronx celebrates hip-hop culture with free movies, dancing, and, of course, a surfeit of spinning DJs. The jam runs from 7pm to 8:30pm and then gives way to the films, which vary from hip-hop docs to camp classics like *Krush Groove*. Every Thursday in July.

Crotona Park East and Charlotte St. ℰ 718/378-2061. Subway: 2/5 to 174th St. Walk south on Boston Rd. to Suburban Place, take a right on Crotona Park East and then a left onto Charlotte St., where you'll see Indian Lake and the festival.

Prospect Park Film Series Celebrate Brooklyn!   Celebrate Brooklyn! earns superfluous exclamation points with an amazing program of music and film. At times the two are combined, like last year's showing of *The Creature from the Black Lagoon!* in 3-D! with a live performance from The Jazz Passengers. The series runs Thursdays at 8pm, June to August. `FINE PRINT` A $3 donation is suggested.

The Prospect Park Bandshell. Enter at Prospect Park West and 9th St. Park Slope, Brooklyn. ℰ 718/855-7882. www.celebratebrooklyn.org. Subway: F to Seventh Ave.; B/Q to Seventh Ave.; 2/3 to Grand Army Plaza.

SCREENINGS AT THE NEW YORK PUBLIC LIBRARY `FREE`

New York's book repositories bear no hard feelings for the many indignities the movies have imposed over the years. Our libraries are so forgiving, in fact, that dozens of branches offer free film screenings every week. Check the NYPL website (www. nypl.org) for showings besides the ones listed below. The fare is

For Real Culture Vultures

Our allies across the globe maintain cultural outposts throughout the city. With the support of universities and embassies, these organizations are able to offer a swath of free readings, lectures, and films. Though the material can be esoteric if you're not from the nation in question, and pick the right events you'll find plenty of accessible entertainment.

Austrian Cultural Forum `FREE` See "Donau, Dunak, Duna, Dunav, Dunarea" along with the rest of your favorite new Austrian flicks. Generally two showings, 6 and 8pm, day of the week varies. Admission is free; no reservations necessary. 11 E. 52nd St., between Fifth and Madison aves. ℂ 212/319-5300. www.acfny.org. Subway: E/V to 53rd St.

Czech Center `FREE` The only Czech center outside of Europe, our Czech mates offer Video Thursdays. Screenings are generally at 7pm, but not every Thursday. Check the Czech Center schedule. 1109 Madison Ave., at 83rd St. ℂ 212/288-0830. www.czechcenter.com. Subway: 4/5/6 to 86th St.

Deutsches Haus `FREE` This NYU-related institution bridges old and new worlds. Regular screenings of German-language films. Check the website for a calendar of events. 42 Washington Mews, between Fifth Ave. and University Place. ℂ 212/958-8660. www.nyu.edu/deutscheshaus. Subway: N/R to 8th St.; 6 to Astor Place.

French Institute Fans of French film (or freedom flicks, as they're called these days) enjoy screenings of contemporaries and classics every Tuesday at the Florence Gould Hall. English subtitles come at no additional charge. Other film nights can be found scattered through the schedule. 55 E. 59th St., between Madison and Park aves. ℂ 212/355-6160. www.fiaf.org. Showings at 12:30, 3:30, 6:30, and 9pm. Regular tickets are $8, but admission is free to French Institute members. Membership costs $75 per year. Subway: N/R/W or 4/5/6 to 59th St.

all over the map, from classics to avant-garde to recent Hollywood hits. There's even a few adaptations mixed in.

In Manhattan

58th Street Library Films for adults, Fridays at 2pm. 127 E. 58th St., between Lexington and Park aves. ℂ **212/759-7358.** Subway: 4/5/6 to 59th St.

96th Street Regional Branch Films for adults Wednesdays at 4pm, for kids from 3pm to 6pm. 112 E. 96th St., near Lexington Ave. ℂ **212/289-0908.** Subway: 6 to 96th St.

Bloomingdale Library Films for adults Thursdays at 2pm. 150 W. 100th St., between Columbus and Amsterdam aves. ℂ **212/222-8030.** Subway: B/C to 96th St.

Donnell Library Center Movies for adults at various times, generally Wednesday and Thursday at 2:30pm, again on Thursday at 6pm, and Saturday at 1pm. 20 W. 53rd St., between Fifth and Sixth aves. ℂ **212/621-0618.** Subway: E/V to 53rd St.; F to 57th St.

The Early Childhood Resource and Information Center (ECRIC) Wednesdays at 3:30pm, classic shorts for kids ages 3 to 8. On the first Wednesday of each month, a full-length feature for kids plays. On the second floor of the Hudson Park Branch Library. 66 Leroy St., off Seventh Ave. ℂ **212/929-0815.** Subway: 1/9 to Houston St.

Epiphany Branch Films for adults Mondays at 5:30pm. 228 E. 23rd St., near Second Ave. ℂ **212/679-2645.** Subway: 6 to 23rd St.

> **FREE Let's Go to the Videotape**
>
> New York's libraries have extensive video collections. They're like Blockbuster, only less censorship and you don't have to pay for anything. The Donnell Library Center has some 3,000 popular movies, on top of 2,200 unpopular arty movies. Plus, if you still haven't gotten around to upgrading to DVD, they've got 8,500 16mm films. The collection is predominantly circulating. (While you're there, you can skip a trip to Tower by checking out their 35,000 CDs, too.) 20 W. 53rd St., between Fifth and Sixth aves. ℂ 212/621-0609. www.nypl.org. Subway: E/V to 53rd St.; F to 57th St.

Fort Washington Branch   Films for kids ages 4 to 8 on Tuesdays at 3:30pm. 535 W. 179th St., between St. Nicholas and Audubon aves. ☎ **212/927-3533.** Subway: 1/9 to 181st St.; A to 175th St.

Jefferson Market Library   Mondays at 3:30pm, for kids ages 4 to 8. Films for adults Tuesdays at 3:30pm. 425 Sixth Ave., at 10th St. ☎ **212/243-4334.** Subway: F/V to 14th St.; A/B/C/D/E to W. 4th St.

St. Agnes Library   Wednesday at 2pm, for kids ages 3 to 8 years old, adults on Thursdays at 4pm. 444 Amsterdam Ave., between 80th and 81st sts. ☎ **212/877-4380.** Subway: 1/9 to 79th St.; B/C to 81st St.

Yorkville   Films for adults Fridays at 1pm. Wednesday at 4pm for kids 3 and up. 222 E. 79th St., between Second and Third aves. ☎ **212/744-5824.** Subway: 6 to 77th St.

IN THE BRONX

Baychester Library   Films for adults Fridays at 3:30pm, for kids ages 5 to 12. 2049 Asch Loop North, north of Bartow Ave. ☎ **718/379-6700.** Subway: B/D to Bedford Park Blvd., or BX26 bus to Aldrich St.

Castle Hill Branch   Kid vids on some Fridays, 4pm, for ages 5 and up. 947 Castle Hill Ave., at Bruckner Blvd. ☎ **718/824-3838.** Subway: 6 to Castle Hill Ave.

Fordham Library Center Branch   Wednesday at 3:30pm, for kids ages 5 to 12. 2556 Bainbridge Ave., near Fordham Rd. ☎ **718/579-4244.** Subway: B/D to Fordham Rd.

Grand Concourse Branch   Fridays at 4pm, for kids ages 5 to 12. 155 E. 173rd St., east of the Grand Concourse. ☎ **718/583-6611.** Subway: B/D to 174th–175th St.; 4 to Mt. Eden.

Hunt's Point Regional Branch   Fridays at 3:30pm, for kids 5 to 12. 877 Southern Blvd., at Tiffany St. ☎ **718/617-0338.** Subway: 6 to Longwood Ave.; 2/5 to Simpson St.

Melrose   Fridays at 4pm, for kids ages 5 to 12. 910 Morris Ave., at E. 162nd. ☎ **718/588-0110.** Subway: B/D/4 to 161st.

Morrisania Branch   Wednesdays at 3:30pm, for kids ages 5 to 12. 610 E. 169th St., at Franklin Ave. ☎ **718/589-9268.**

Subway: 2/5 to 149th St. then BX55 bus to 169th St.; B/D/4 to 167th St. then BX35 bus to 169th St.

Pelham Bay Branch Wednesdays at 3:30pm, for kids ages 3 to 6. 3060 Middletown Rd., north of Crosby Ave. ✆ **718/792-6744.** Subway: 6 to Buhre Ave.

Riverdale Branch Library Videos on some Fridays at 4pm, for kids ages 5 and up. 5540 Mosholu Ave., at W. 256th St. ✆ **718/549-1212.** Subway: 1/9 to 231st St., then BX7 bus to Riverdale Ave. and W. 256th; A to 207th, then BX7 bus to Riverdale Ave. and W. 256th.

Westchester Square Branch Fridays at 3:30pm, for kids ages 6 to 12. 2521 Glebe Ave., at St. Peters Ave. ✆ **718/863-0436.** Subway: 6 to Westchester Sq.

In Brooklyn

Brooklyn Public Library Film selections here often correspond to monthly themes. Screenings for adults on Fridays at 6pm. Also, for kids on Saturdays at 11am. Grand Army Plaza. 2nd Floor Auditorium. ✆ **718/230-2100.** www.brooklynpublic library.org. Subway: 2/3 to Grand Army Plaza.

3 The Theatah

Just as models and those who look like them often make their way to California for its surfeit of Beach Girl #4 roles, dramatic actors are drawn to New York City. They're not just waiting on our tables, either. In NYC you can find great performances on every level of theater, from big-time Broadway (with its $100 orchestra seats) to $10 Off-Broadway, to raw productions in the basements of bars, performed for whatever can be garnered by passing the hat. Cost is not necessarily a barometer of quality. You can drop a few Jacksons to discover the cast of a Broadway blockbuster is just phoning it in, while across town some hungry young talent is drawing tears at a free production of Shakespeare. Free productions are also offered up by schools, institutions, and work-in-progress programs. If you need something more polished, try downtown, where dirt-cheap theaters will get you the dramatic goods for $10 or less.

FREE Rise of the House Ushers

If you have the ability to pass out Playbills, point to seats, and enunciate the phrase "enjoy the show," then you're qualified to see free plays. Many smaller theater companies save money on the cost of ushers by trading your sweat equity for a complimentary seat. Each house has a different set of rules, and the number of volunteers needed varies from one to eight per night. Popular productions can have a backlog of a few weeks. The best plan of attack is to find a play you want to see and call the front office to see what their deal is. It may take some tenacious dialing and a measure of persistence, but it'll be easily worth it when you settle back in your seat without a penny spent.

New York Theatre Workshop This small downtown theater doesn't shy from experimentation, including occasional hip-hop fare. Five ushers are used per show. Call ✆ **212/780-7037** during regular business hours to synch your schedule with theirs. 79 E. 4th St., between Second Ave. and Bowery. www.nytw.org. Subway: 6 to Astor Place.

Blue Man Group Performance art meets the masses via drums, food, and a lot of blue body paint during this long-running favorite. The services of four volunteer ushers are required for each show. You can schedule 1 to 2 weeks in advance. ✆ **212/387-9415,** ext. 220. Astor Place Theatre, 434 Lafayette St. between E. 4th and E. 8th sts. www.blueman.com. Subway: N/R/W to 8th St.; 6 to Astor Place. FINE PRINT Help cleaning up may be required for a few minutes after the show.

Second Stage Theatre This organization specializes in giving contemporary playwrights second chances to find audiences. The new 296-seat theatre is nicely designed and a comfortable place to usher. Call to see when your available dates match their needs. 307 W. 43rd St., at Eighth Ave. ✆ **212/787-8302,** ext. 307. www.secondstagetheatre.com/ushers.html. Subway: A/C/E to 42nd St./Port Authority.

FREE THEATER

ACROSS THE BARD: SHAKESPEARE ALFRESCO

The Earl of Oxford would probably be gratified to know that all these centuries later his little plays dominate the summer theater scene in the world's capital. Sure, the plays are published under the name of an actor from Stratford, but the passions and conflicts resound just as the Earl wrote them. Troupes love to try their hand at the Bard, and free Shakespeare abounds in the Big Apple. Join your fellow mortals and enjoy the midsummer night dreams.

☆ **Shakespeare in the Park** `FREE`   Shh! Top secret! No one else knows about this amazing cultural giveaway. Every summer a William Shakespeare play is performed in a gorgeous open-air theater in the center of enchanted Central Park. Just show up a couple of minutes before showtime and whisper the password *Birnham Woods*. Oh, were it that easy. Some 90,000 people attend the Delacorte Theater's productions every summer, and it's the worst-kept free secret in the city. It takes a lot to justify a Soviet-style wait of 2 or 3 hours for a lousy two-ticket ration, but Joseph Papp's Public Theater rarely disappoints. Design, direction, and acting (often featuring A-list stars) are all world-class. The productions vary from faithful classical interpretations to avant-garde reimaginings. In summer, 1,800-plus seats are given out at the Delacorte in Central Park, and outside the Public Theater Downtown. The downtown location gives out fewer tickets, but the line is more under control. You'll need some determination for your free will, as people start lining up 2 or 3 hours early for the 1pm

Sources

Fledgling shows that are having trouble filling seats often go trolling for audiences on craig's list. Check under "free" on **www.craigslist.org** and you might spy a free night of drama. A sharp eye can also reward a person with preview seats. Check *Time Out* and the *Village Voice* for advertisements of newly opening productions. In addition to specials on tickets for the first few weeks, sometimes you'll spot an offering for a preview. You'll get something halfway between a dress rehearsal and the final polished show, but it won't cost a cent.

giveaways. For a hot show, you'll find bodies outside the Delacorte before 8am. In extreme cases—say Meryl Streep and Christopher Walken doing Checkhov—the line can start the night before. Just treat the ticket queue, with its natural camaraderie, as part of the experience. The outer boroughs also have their own ticket locations for selected performances, in addition to special arts education programs. Check the "Shakespeare in the Boroughs" page on the Public Theater website for more information.

The season runs June through August and features one or two Shakespeare plays, and often a play that's completely unrelated to the Bard.

Public Theater, 425 Lafayette St., just below Astor Place. ⓒ 212/539-8750. www.publictheater.org. Subway: 6 to Astor Place; N/R to 8th St. Delecorte Theater, Belvedere Castle, near 79th St. and West Dr. ⓒ 212/539-8750. Subway: B/C to 81st St.

☆ **Shakespeare in the Park(ing) Lot** `FREE`   Central Park is classy and well groomed, with lush grass and trees softening the hard edges of the city. The municipal parking lot on Ludlow Street has none of these graces, but the graffiti-slathered asphalt patch does compete in the realm of Tudor drama. The troupe *Ludlow Ten* puts on Shakespeare every summer, with a wealth of energy and wit to make up for the lack of big-name casts and big-budget backdrops. It's a wonderfully surreal scene, with sword fights and intrigue in the foreground while befuddled neighbors and passersby cut across the lot in the back. The Lower East Side actually beats Central Park for variety. While the Delacorte is limited to one or two seasonal shows, Ludlow Ten is good for three different Shakespearean productions every summer. Take plenty of padding, though, because that ground gets hard when you've been parked for a while.

Ludlow St., between Broome and Delancey sts. ⓒ 212/253-1813. www.ludlow ten.org. June–Aug Thurs–Sat 8pm. Subway: F to Delancey; J/M/Z to Essex St.

MORE ALFRESCO THEATER

The Lite Co. `FREE`   The Laboratory for International Theatre Exchange brings open-air Shakespeare to Prospect Park. They also perform a mix of new and classical plays under the summer skies. Schedules and locations vary from year to year. Check the website for show schedule.

Prospect Park. ℂ **718/482-069.** www.theliteco.org. Subway: F to Seventh Ave.; B/Q to Seventh Ave.; 2/3 to Grand Army Plaza.

Boomerang Theatre FREE   Boomerang comes back each year with performances of Shakespearean plays in smaller parks around New York. They've also been known to give away a Eugene O'Neill performance or two. Check the website for show schedule and locations.

ℂ **212/501-4069.** www.boomerangtheatre.org.

New York Classical Theatre FREE   NYCT takes advantage of the natural contours of Central Park to stage its summer Shakespeare productions. Plays begin around 103rd Street and Central Park West, but depending on what the script calls for, they do roam.

Central Park. ℂ **212/252-4531.** www.newyorkclassical.org. Usually 2 plays per summer, no tickets or reservations required. June–Aug 7pm. Subway: B/C to 103rd St.

Theatreworks USA FREE   Every summer, this organization puts up a production aimed at rug rat edification (or at least amusement). The group concentrates on one play per season, usually a modern musical. The venue changes from year to year, but you'll get dozens of opportunities to catch a show. Weekday afternoons are often filled up by camp groups, but if you go on the weekends or evenings, you shouldn't have trouble grabbing free seats.

ℂ **212/647-1100.** www.theatreworksusa.org.

Broadway on Broadway FREE   Give our regards to this theatrical greatest-hits package. The casts of the Great White Way come out to flog their shows on an outdoor stage in the center of Times Square. Held on a Sunday in mid-September, the concert usually starts in the late morning. And you thought Times Square was crowded already.

Times Square. ℂ **212/768-1560.** www.broadwayonbroadway.com. Sunday usually around 11:30am. Subway: 1/2/3/7/9 or N/Q/R/W to Times Square.

Bryant Park FREE   Every summer Broadway teases fans with a quick sampler on the Bryant Park stage. Big hitters like *Cabaret, Rent,* and *Chicago* perform excerpts for a crowded lawn.

Behind the Public Library, between 40th and 42nd sts. and Fifth and Sixth
aves. www.bryantpark.org. Thurs 12:30–1:45pm, 4 musicals per afternoon.
Subway: F/V/B/D to 42nd St./Bryant Park; 7 to Fifth Ave.

THEATER WITH CLASS

In the working and reworking of new plays, feedback devices are
essential. An audience of warm bodies makes a great barometer
for figuring out which lines are killing and which scenes need
trimming. With so much untested drama in NYC, it's easy to find
showcases, workshops, and readings that are eager for your presence. You'll often be sharing the room with a parcel of pros:
agents, producers, and casting directors on the prowl for the next
big things. If you don't mind putting up with some unsanded
edges, it's a great way to catch a night of free theater.

Actors Studio Drama School `FREE`   The ASDS Repertory Season shows off the thesis projects of actors, playwrights, and directors. The shows that aren't written in-house range from classics to
contemporaries. The season runs February through May, and each
play gets five separate performances, Wednesday through Saturday at 8pm, and a Saturday matinee at 3pm. Two or three plays are
grouped together each night. Call ahead for reservations.

A.S.D.S. Theater at the Westbeth, 151 Bank St., 3rd floor, between Washington St. and the West Side Hwy. ✆ 212/479-1778. www.newschool.edu/
academic/drama. Subway: A/C/E/L to 14th St./Eighth Ave.; 1/2/3/9 to 14th St.

Cap21 `FREE`   The Collaborative Arts Project dedicates itself to
fostering innovative new productions. Part of the process involves
developing new audiences, which are invited in for the free **Monday Night Reading Series.** The series presents plays and musicals
still seeking their footing.

18 West 18th St., between Fifth and Sixth aves., Studio One. ✆ 212/807-
0202. www.cap21.org. Mon 7pm (not every week, check the website). Subway: L/N/Q/R/W/4/5/6 to 14th St./Union Sq.

The Juilliard School `FREE`   The fourth-year students of Juilliard's Drama Division mount full-scale productions to catch the
eyes of agents, casting directors, and the press. The general public is invited in as well, although to get an invitation you'll need
to sign up for Juilliard's Drama Division mailing list. The plays are
free during their fall and winter run, and then come back tweaked
and enhanced for $15 in the spring. Free tickets go fast. You'll

have to wait at the box office the first day they become available, although sometimes you can snag same-day standbys.

Broadway, at 65th St. ℭ 212/769-7406. www.juilliard.edu. Subway: 1/9 to 66th St.

NYU Graduate Acting Program FREE   NYU's Tisch School of the Arts is justly famous for the high-profile directors, actors, and dramatic writers it has produced. You can get a glimpse of burgeoning talents at several free shows. Most are put on by second years (by 3rd year they can get away with charging), in various theaters on and around the NYU campus. The tickets for charged shows tend to be reasonable, $10 and less. Check the website or the Grad Acting box office.

Tisch Main Building, 721 Broadway, between Waverly Place and Washington Place (just south of 8th St.). ℭ 212/998-1921. www.gradacting.tisch.nyu. edu. Subway: 6 to Astor Place; N/R to 8th St.; A/C/E to W. 4th St.

The Public Theater FREE   Shakespeare in the Park is only the beginning for the Public Theater, which churns out amazing productions all year long. On Monday nights from April to June, the **New Work Now!** series lights up Monday nights with fresh material. Also, look for the monthly "Conversations With . . . ." Both are free; check the website for additional giveaways.

425 Lafayette St., just below Astor Place. ℭ 212/260-2400. www.public theater.org. Subway: 6 to Astor Place; N/R to 8th St.

Rattlestick Playwrights Theater FREE   The Rattlestick targets upcoming playwrights and new plays. They nurture projects from creation and development all the way to production. For 3 or 4 weeks every spring they put on the **Exposure Festival,** with new plays and works in progress. Performances are free, though they'd be delighted to have a $5 donation for readings and $10 for workshops. Check the website for other free readings and events during the rest of the year.

234 Waverly Place, just west of Seventh Ave., between Perry and W. 11th St. ℭ 212/627-2556. www.rattlestick.org. Subway: 1/9 to Christopher St.

Women's Project Theatre FREE   Women playwrights are the exclusive focus of the Women's Project. New plays, often by new authors, get exercised in the **First Looks Reading Series.** The series is held on most Mondays at 4pm and is free. Check the website to confirm the location.

WPP Studio, 55 West End Ave., at 62nd St. WPP Theatre, 424 W. 55th St., between Ninth and Tenth aves. ℂ 212/765-1706, ext. 200. www.womens project.org. Subway: 1/9/A/B/C/D to 59th St./Columbus Circle; N/R to 59th St.

The York Theatre Company `FREE`   Inside the tasteful modern confines of St. Peter's Church, the York Theatre trots out new musicals for free performances. The **Developmental Reading Series** is often on Monday nights at 7:30pm, with other nights and matinee performances also mixed into the schedule. Shows are free but do sometimes "sell out," so reserve early.

619 Lexington Ave., at 54th St. ℂ 212/935-5824, ext. 111. www.yorktheatre. org. Subway: E/V to Lexington; 6 to 51st St.

DIRT CHEAP THEATER
ALL ABOUT LA MAMA: BIG DRAMA IN SMALL SPACES

Small theater groups are notorious for their shoestring budgets, which means most don't have the luxury of permanent stages. All it takes to make a theater is some matte-black paint, a few gelled lights, and a bunch of folding chairs, and walk-up lofts in Midtown are constantly forming order. Downtown, especially the area around East 4th Street, is a locus with more staying power. Several companies work out of the area and most shows have East Village–friendly prices of $10 or less.

Dixon Place   Experimentation is the norm at Dixon Place, which bills itself as an "artistic lab with an audience." Since performances are in varied stages of evolution, ticket prices are on the low side. There are also intermittent free open performance nights, where anyone is welcome and anything goes except stand-up comedy.

258 Bowery, between Houston and Prince, 2nd floor, but slated to move to a more permanent home. ℂ 212/219-0761. www.dixonplace.org. Tickets $10–$15. Subway: F/V to Second Ave.

Galapagos Art Space   This Brooklyn bar first became known for the moat at its entryway, which creates a soothing mini–Temple of Dendur effect. A couple of expansions later, the bar is known as a Williamsburg cultural headquarters. Comedy, theater, music, and film (p. 50) all make their way here, and cover charges rarely reach double digits. One day a week there's arty smut in the form of **Monday Evening Burlesque.** It starts at 9:30pm, and it's absolutely free.

70 N. 6th St. Williamsburg, Brooklyn. ℂ 718/782-5188. www.galapagosart
space.com. Subway: L to Bedford Ave.

La Mama   This venerable avatar of the avant-garde is fully
established in the E.V., where it remains dedicated to artistic
experimentation. Productions are high quality and the ticket
prices reflect it—shows can run from $15 to $30. Two notable
exceptions are the **Experiments** and **Poetry Electric** series, performed in La Mama's La Galleria space. Experiments features in-
progress plays read with the writers in attendance, to provide
instant-gratification feedback. The Poetry Electric reading series
accentuates the word with music and performance. Check the
website for exact days and times. The suggested admission for
each show is only $5. Pick up tickets at the box office on E. 4th
St. and then walk down to the gallery space. (The gallery also
holds free art exhibitions.)

74 E. 4th St., between Second Ave. and Bowery. ℂ 212/475-7710. www.la
mama.org. Subway: F/V to Second Ave.; 6 to Bleecker St. La Galleria: 6 E. 1st
St., between Bowery and Second Ave. ℂ 212/505-2476. Open for art shows
Thurs-Sun 1-6pm.

☆ **P.S. 122**   The warrens of a former public school on First
Avenue help anchor the downtown Off-Off-Broadway scene.
Dance, comedy, and theater all make their way through the multiple spaces here. An excellent night to attend is the **Monthly
Spaghetti Dinner Series,** put on by Great Small Works. Performance of every stripe—from puppetry to dance to drama to
film—accompanies a vegetarian spaghetti meal. Don't be surprised to find a little left-wing polemic in the mix as well. It's only
$10, a price that wouldn't have seemed unreasonable when the
series started in 1978.

P.S. 122, 150 First Ave. ℂ 212/477-5288. www.ps122.org. Subway: 6 to
Astor Place. Ticket prices vary, $5-$30. Great Small Works ℂ 718/840-
2823. www.greatsmallworks.org.

The Slipper Room   The stage in this Lower East Side bar sees all
manner of risqué business. Comedy and drama make the scene,
but the best night is Saturday, when New York's longest-running
burlesque holds court. **Mr. Choad's Upstairs/Downstairs** allows
vaudeville acts and go-go girls to split time under the lights.

167 Orchard St., at Stanton. ℂ 212/253-7246. www.slipperroom.com. Cover
$5; other shows $5-$10. Subway: F/V to Second Ave.

NYC's Best Theater Discount Strategies

TKTS TKTS has been dispensing same-day half-price seats for some 3 decades now. As far as bargains go, this is probably better for the tourists, who are more excited about spending "only" $40 to see some hoary musical. It's also worth remembering that the things they're selling tickets to are shows the producers are having trouble moving anyway. That said, the seats themselves tend to be good. The lines aren't what they were before 9/11, but they're still pretty long. TKTS is open 3 to 8pm for evening performances, 10am to 2pm for Wednesday and Saturday matinees, and from 11am until showtime on Sunday for all performances. A second TKTS location can be found downtown at John and Front streets in the South Street Seaport area. The lines are much shorter and matinee tickets are sold for the following day only, if you're the type that plans ahead (11am–6pm Mon–Sat; 11am–3:30pm Sun). Show availability is posted on a digital bulletin board that's updated as ticket supplies dwindle. Remember, TKTS accepts only cash or traveler's checks, no credit cards, no personal checks. Discounts are generally 50%, with a few shows at a 25% reduction. ✆ 212/221-0013. www.tdf.org.

TDF Vouchers The Theatre Development Fund also brings us an Off-Off-Broadway equivalent to the TKTS booth. For $28 you get four vouchers that can be used for a host of shows, crossing the disciplines of drama, dance, and light opera. At $7 a pop, it's a good way to get into the cutting edge. ✆ 212/221-0013. www.tdf.org.

Evening Rush For those of the serendipitous bent, there's always last-minute rush ticket specials. Broadway, Off-Broadway, and even a few mega-hits set aside seats for students (sometimes seniors are included, too). The seats are made available between 30 minutes and an hour before curtain. Make sure to bring plenty of ID. Another option is SRO seats, but do not attempt standing room only if you're not in comfortable shoes. The seats for either program are usually $20 and up, which on the surface is no great bargain, but is actually pretty respectable when you consider that a full-price ticket would probably run three times as much. A great place for the run-down on the permutations of the individual theaters is www.talkinbroadway.com/boards.

Academic Advantages   If you've got an in with a library or a school, you may have an in for discount coupons through the **School Theater Ticket Program.** Librarians, teachers, students, and their families are all eligible. Musicals, Broadway on and off, and opera and ballet at Lincoln Center, are among the offerings. Check out the website, www.schooltix.com. Offices at 1560 Broadway, Suite 1113, open Monday to Friday 11am to 4pm. ✆ 212/354-4722.

Other Discounts   There are also several online sites that will hook you up with half-price tickets. You have to join to play, but the only tax they levy is the occasional piece of spam; otherwise, they're free. (And if you're not a spamphobe, you can get regular e-mail newsletters trumpeting the latest specials.) Playbill Online (www.playbill.com) has the best range of Broadway and Off-Broadway shows. **Best of Broadway** (✆ 212/398-8383;** www.bestofbroadway.com) has coupons and puts together group discount packages. **The Hit Show Club** (✆ 212/581-4211;** www.hitshowclub.com) is good for tourists. They have several packages that combine restaurants and attractions with well-known Broadway hits.

For Teens: High 5 Tickets to the Arts   High 5 doesn't shy away from the controversial notion that the children are our future. To uplift the level of cultural literacy of today's teens, High 5 makes a bushel of $5 theater and museum programs available. Tickets cost $5 on the weekend, but during Monday through Thursday performances that same $5 will get in one teen and one guest of any age. The latter deal also applies to discounted museum passes. Check the website for ticket details; there's also a listing of free and nearly free events. ✆ 212/HI5-TKTS. www.high5tix.org.

Theater at the Edge: Fringe NYC

In late August a chunk of the city goes on vacation and the **Fringe Festival** comes rushing in to maintain Gotham's equilibrium. This annual theatrical explosion brings hundreds of acts to Lower East Side theaters, schools, storefronts, and streets. The troupes hail from around the world and range from the baldly amateurish to the highly polished. Tickets tend to be cheap, around $5 to $10. Free previews, with 7-minute teasers of upcoming shows, are given on several afternoons in Washington Square Park. Less organized shows spill out onto the streets of downtown. We've seen actors project their lines over neighbors' repeated calls to "Shut the f--- up!" Whether appreciated by the full public or not, the Fringe is a feast of theater, comedy, music, and performance art, and well worth a visit. ℂ **212/279-4488** or 888/FRINGE-NYC. www.fringenyc. org. Various locations.

The Tank   Short film selections, one-man shows, and collections of skits can all be found here. One night worth catching is **The Rejection Show,** every third Wednesday at 8pm. Comedians, cartoonists, and writers bring out material spiked by editorial powers that be, often because the gags were a little too edgy for primetime. For $5 judge for yourself.

432 W. 42nd St., between Ninth and Tenth aves. ℂ **212/563-6269.** www.the tanknyc.com. Tickets usually $5-$8. Subway: A/C/E to 42nd St.

The Theater for the New City   This alternative theater is known for giving breaks to unknown playwrights. Productions are consistently high quality, though ticket prices are usually only $10. Over Memorial Day you can sample the dramatics for free at the Lower East Side Festival of the Arts. Theater is only the beginning, as spoken word, cabaret, film, video, and dance performances take over E. 10th Street between 1st and 2nd avenues. Events run on until after midnight and everything is free.

155 First Ave., between 9th and 10th sts. ℂ **212/254-1109.** www.theater forthenewcity.net. Tickets $10. Subway: 6 to Astor Place.

4 Let's Dance

Giuliani-era enforcement of cabaret laws hit most New Yorkers by surprise. Laws regulating public dance had been on the books forever, but it had been many years since anyone had thought to enforce them. Innocuous tremors and inadvertent hip shakes were suddenly categorized as unlicensed dance expressions. Fortunately, dance in New York has never been limited to the clubs and bars. In the parks, on stages, and even in sanctuaries of the city, dance of all levels can be found, and often for free.

Traffic Jam: Tap Jam Under the Stars `FREE`   The cross-pollination of African and Irish dances in the Five Points slum of the 1840s began New York's tap tradition. **New York Tap** keeps the clomping and clogging alive with free summer jams. Musicians and dancers perform for traffic-bound motorists and better-humored audience members. A couple of Fridays in summer; check the website for dates and times.

517 Broome St., at Thompson St. (outside The Hub). ℂ **212/475-0588.** www.nytap.org. Subway: C/E to Spring St.; 1/9/N/R to Canal St.

Dancing in the Streets `FREE`   This arts organization brings site-specific performances to spots across the city. The big show is the annual dance and demonstration at Dag Hammarskjöld Plaza, highlighting international moves beneath the windows of the UN. Check the website for performance dates and locations.

E. 47th St., between First and Second aves. ℂ **212/625-3505.** www. dancinginthestreets.org. Subway: E/V to Lexington; 6 to 51st St. Other sites, including Red Hook and Brooklyn, vary.

☆ **Movement Research at the Judson Church** `FREE`   A West Village church sanctuary seems the appropriate location for an experimental dance program. The dancers and choreographers vary from week to week, but the quality is always high. No reservations are required but the event is popular, so arrive early. Mondays at 8pm.

Judson Church, 55 Washington Sq. South, between Thompson and Sullivan sts. ℂ **212/539-2611.** www.movementresearch.org. Subway: A/B/C/D/E/F/V to West 4th St./Washington Sq.

Dance Conversations `FREE`   Choreographers present works in progress at this monthly program. It's a discussion series as well, so expect jawing to following the dancing. Usually on Tuesday late in the month at 7pm.

Flea Theater, 41 White St., between Broadway and Church. ℭ 212/226-0051. www.theflea.org. Subway: 1/9 to Franklin St.

MoonDance FREE July and August bring marvelous nights for this dance on Pier 25. Sunday evenings begin with a lesson at 6:30pm and cede to dancing half an hour later, when you've become an expert. Dance varieties run from swing to salsa to R&B. Live music from crack bands enhances the lovely riverside setting.

Pier 25. ℭ 212/533-PARK. www.hudsonriverpark.org. Subway: 1/9 to Franklin St., walk west to the river.

Evening Stars FREE Downtown's **River to River Festival** concludes with a flurry of dance performances in Battery Park. The National Dance Institute often shows up, as do smaller troupes, like last year's mesmerizing Chinese folk dancers. The performances are accompanied by live music and run from Friday to Tuesday of the first weekend in September. There's a large stage, but if you want to be up close, better arrive an hour before showtime, when they open the gates. Don't forget your blanket.

Lower Manhattan Cultural Council, Battery Park, on State St. at Pearl St. ℭ 212/219-9401, ext. 304. www.lmcc.net. Subway: 4/5 to Bowling Green; N/R to Whitehall; 1/9 to South Ferry.

TANGO & NO CASH

Tango Porteño FREE Sultry summer nights are made for tangoing. On the Seaport piers, Tango Porteño hosts a weekly dance party with a great atmosphere. The East River rushes gently by and the lights of downtown glitter overhead as couples make their angular dips and spins. A big crew of regulars anchors the scene, and the event is casual and noncompetitive. Instead of a band there's a somewhat tinny sound system, but no one seems to mind. It takes two, but if you arrive alone, just watching can be entertainment enough.

Pier 16 at the South St. Seaport, between the Ambrose and the Peking. In case of rain go to Pier 17, just to the north. www.tangoporteno.org. June–Sept Sun 7-11pm. Subway: 2/3/4/5/J/M/Z to Fulton St., walk east to the river.

Chelsea Market Milonga FREE Don't cry for New York, not when there's free tango every Saturday afternoon. Beyond the gourmet food and clunky installation art of Chelsea Market you'll find a relaxed scene hosted by the Triangulo. The tangoing happens from 4 to 8pm; neophytes can take advantage of a free beginner's class at 5pm.

Chelsea Market, between Ninth and Tenth aves. and 15th and 16th sts.; dancing is just inside the Tenth Ave. entrance. ℂ 212/633-6445. www.tangonyc. com. Subway: A/C/E to 14th St.; L to Eighth Ave.

5 Sing, Sing: Karaoke

Do your part to reaffirm the inherent dignity of the human race by drinking way too much tequila and then letting loose on a heartfelt version of "Fernando." Karaoke nights proliferate in the city, providing total strangers the opportunity to humiliate themselves for your benefit. All they ask is for a little reciprocation. FINE PRINT While none of the below venues enforces a drink minimum, chances are you'll be asked for a drink order when you aren't crooning.

☆ **Arlene's Grocery (Punk Rock Heavy Metal Karaoke)**
FREE   If you've ever wondered where the tri-state has been hiding its best Axl Rose and Johnny Rotten imitators, you've been missing out on Punk Rock Heavy Metal Karaoke at Arlene's Grocery. This is not a scene predicated on the tinny arrangements of soulless laser discs. Arlene's stage hosts a real, live, hard-rocking band, churning out the soul-uplifting sounds of '70s punk and '80s hair metal. Don't expect a bouncing ball and teleprompters. On stage you may get a crib sheet with scribbled lyrics and a prompt from the band when it's time to take it to the bridge, but otherwise you're on your own. Before you start practicing in empty elevators, check out the ever-growing list of performable songs at www. punkmetalkaraoke.com. If you do sign up and ascend the stage, you'll find the crowd enthusiastic, and nothing beats the thrill of belting out "Hot for Teacher" or "TV Party" over an ass-kicking band. It's worth a visit just to check out the regulars. Many of them have come all the way from Jersey to show off how well they can work a club full of rabid fans with fingers spread in devil's horns. Best of all: There's no cover for these covers.

95 Stanton St., between Ludlow and Orchard sts. ℂ 212/358-1633. www. arlene-grocery.com. Karaoke Mon 10pm-2am. Subway: F/V to 2nd Ave.; J/M/Z to Essex St.

Iggy's Drink specials help lubricate the slippery slope that leads to late-night karaoke caterwauling at Iggy's. From noon to 10pm, shots and Bud and Bud Light drafts are only $2. These specials in turn fuel the karaoke action, which begins at 11pm and runs until closing every night but Monday.

1452 Second Ave., between 75th and 76th sts. ☎ 212/327-3043. www.iggys newyork.com. Karaoke Tues-Sun 11pm-4am. Subway: 6 to 77th St.

Second on Second This low-lit sushi restaurant turns grazers into performers with a karaoke stage along the back wall of the dining room. Food prices are reasonable for Japanese, with big bowls of udon for under $10, and regular sushi rolls $3 or $4. If you're not up for springing for a meal, the bar area is comfortable for hanging out. Show off those velvet lungs and enhance someone's dining experience at the same time.

27 Second Ave., at 2nd St. ☎ 212/473-2922. www.2ndon2nd.com. Karaoke Fri and Sat 11pm-4am. Subway: F/V to Second Ave.

Three of Cups This tiny basement lair provides the backdrop for rock-'n'-roll fantasies at Monday night's "Rockin' da Mike." Fellow patrons will appreciate the small-room acoustics as you reach for those high notes. Upstairs has happy hour from 6 to 8pm, then retire to the basement for their 8 to 10pm version. Well

---

FREE Movieoke at Den of Cin

Unwilling to sing but still eager to make an ass of yourself? Thank God for "movieoke," which promises to do for armchair actors what karaoke did for shower singers. Rehearse a scene at home, bring in some ringers, or steel yourself to go it alone, and ask your hostess to hop upstairs to the video store. She'll come back with the appropriate DVD, and you'll stand before the big projection screen and show off your chops. Silly? Um, yeah. But somebody made a nice living selling karaoke machines—maybe movieoke is the next big thing. Catch the wave at the **Den of Cin**, beneath Two Boots pizza and video, 44 Ave. A at E. 3rd St. ☎ 212/254-0800. www.twoboots.com/ theden. Subway: F/V to Second Ave.

drinks, beer, and wine are each $3 when they're in the happy zone. At other times, your cheapest option is a $3 Pabst.

83 First Ave., at 5th St. ✆ **212/388-0059.** www.threeofcupsnyc.com. Karaoke Mon 9pm-midnight. Subway: F/V to Second Ave.

Winnie's   Hipsters and Chinatown locals just never have enough opportunity to chill together, which is where Winnie's comes in handy. The place is an ungentrifiable dive, but the savings get passed on to the crooning customer: It's only a buck a song. The cheapest drink is a $4.50 beer, $4 before 5pm.

104 Bayard St. ✆ **212/732-2384.** Karaoke daily 8pm-4am. Subway: J/M/ N/Q/R/W/Z/6 to Canal St.

6 Humor Us: Comedy

There's no shortage of frustrating and surreal experiences in New York, ensuring plenty of fodder for the comedians in our midst. The city is currently stacked with young comic talent, which means amateur nights are more common than headliner-thick extravaganzas. Alas, amateur nights can also be express trips to the nether regions of stand-up hell. Somehow bad comedy is infinitely more painful than bad tragedy. I advise stepping carefully through the city's improv, open mic, and stand-up minefield. Fortunately, plenty of quick wits can be found in this town. Small investments can lead to big laughs if you hit the right nights. For all the side-splitting and beer-spilled-through-nose details, see below.

SHOWCASES, IMPROV & OTHER COMEDY ANTICS

Performance Space NBC   Big-time television network NBC seeks out little-screen talent with a weekly showcase of AAA comedians, ready for their call-up. Every Tuesday night hopefuls perform for a crowd peppered with execs. The public is welcome along for the ride. Tickets are $5; showtime is at 8pm.

The Marquee Theater, 356 Bowery, between E. 3rd and E. 4th sts. ✆ **212/ 462-9077.** www.nbc/psnbc. Subway: 6 to Bleecker St.

☆ **The Upright Citizens Brigade**   The UCB brings Chicago-style long-form improv comedy to the Big Apple. With founders that can be found on SNL and in the movies, the talent level is high, which is crucial in the hit-or-miss medium of improvisation. Plus, the complete lack of scripts *saves you money*. Sunday night sees two performances of **ASSSCAT 3000.** The extra S? For savings: The 7:30pm show is $8, but the 9:30pm is absolutely free. Tickets are distributed at 8:15, but it's popular so try to get there at least 45 minutes early. Tuesday night at 11pm **School Night** plays for free, as does the fun and sloppy **Hump Night,** at 11pm on Wednesdays. The rest of the schedule runs between $5 and $8, which is still a steal. The **Harold Night**'s two $5 shows (Tuesday at 8 and 9:30pm) are especially noteworthy, with some damn sharp wits putting the old Harold technique through its paces.

Upright Citizens Brigade Theatre, 307 W. 26th St., between Eighth and Ninth aves. ℭ 212/366-9176. www.ucbtheatre.com. Subway: C/E to 23rd St.

New York Comedy Club `FREE` Monday night's open mic night is the only affordable slot on the schedule here. It's the longest-running open mic in New York, there's no drink minimum, and although it's statistically unlikely, it's *possible* to see an overlooked talent just breaking in. Open mic on Mondays, 5 to 7:30pm. For aspiring comedians, it's $3 for 5 minutes on stage.

241 E. 24th St., between Second and Third aves. ℭ 212/696-LAFF. www. newyorkcomedyclub.com. Subway: N/R or 6 to 23rd St.

Eating It One of the city's most popular comedy nights, this show comes with a different host or hostess every week. The bill holds up to six comedians. Cover is $8, but that includes one drink.

At Luna Lounge, 171 Ludlow St., between Houston and Stanton. ℭ 212/260-2323. www.eatingit.net. Subway: F/V to Second Ave.; J/M/Z to Essex St.

Comedy Therapy `FREE` Tiki torches in the background lend an additional air of absurdity to this free comedy night. Every Wednesday at 8pm, Maureen Marren hosts a rotating cast of comedians, with $3 Rheingolds augmenting the therapeutic effect.

Otto's Shrunken Head, 538 E. 14th St., between aves. A and B. ℭ 212/228-2240. Subway: L to First Ave.

PussyHut Comedy Show Don't let the genteel name fool you; this Sunday night show tends toward the raunchy. The jokes begin at 9:30pm. Beers start at $3.50. `FINE PRINT` No cover, but there's a one-drink minimum.

Village Ma, 107 Macdougal St., between Bleecker and W. 3rd sts. ℭ 212/529-3808. Subway: A/B/C/D/E/F/V to W. 4th St.

Will Work for Stage Time

No one ever perfected his comic timing in the bathroom mirror. Comedians learn from audiences, but most clubs are justifiably reluctant to put green talent up on stage. Fortunately for the aspiring, many clubs are equally reluctant to lay out cold cash for busboys, telemarketers, and barkers. The stars of tomorrow can exchange elbow grease for free stage minutes, assuming management sees a glimmer of talent there. At **Ha!**, barking and other glamorous tasks can be exchanged for face time with audiences (© **212/977-3884**; www.hacomedynyc. com). **New York Comedy Club** funny folks can double as bussers or telemarketers. The club will also trade time for ringers—if you bring in five audience members, you'll get 5 minutes on stage. It's exactly what families were made for. See review on p. 78 for contact information.

Underground Lounge   Musical acts provide respite between comedy routines during this open mic night. The room is supportive, usually a mix of Columbia students and Manhattan Valley locals. Shows are Mondays at 9pm. Buds cost $3.50. Happy hour gives a buck off everything, weeknights from 5 to 8pm. FINE PRINT There's a two-item minimum for performances in the back room.
955 West End Ave., at 107th St. © 212/531-4759. Subway: 1/9 to 103rd St.

7 Game Night

Too damn smart? Bars across the city offer trivia nights, an excuse to meet new people and show off the fruits of all those wasted hours learning to differentiate between Arnold Snarb and Arnold Strong. Gather up some compatriots, or join a team of fellow-stragglers, and convert that synaptic alacrity into free bar tabs.

The Baggot Inn   Tuesday night brings the brains to the Baggot. Teams are quizzed in five-question rounds, with winners getting free drinks. The extraordinary trivia geeks who end up the night's overall winners get $10 and $25 bar tab credits—you know, a person can work up a mean thirst answering questions about Liza Minelli's personal life. Games happen from around 7 to 10pm. Happy hour is 11am to 7pm with $3 for a beer or a nightly special cocktail. At other times, the cheapest drink is a $3 Pabst. FINE PRINT No cover, but there is a two-drink minimum.

82 W. 3rd St., between Thompson and Sullivan. ℂ 212/477-0622. www.the baggotinn.com. Subway: A/C/E/F/S/V to W. 4th St.

Last Exit   This quiz night isn't free, but the $5 cover can be considered an investment. The cash goes into a pot for the eventual winner. Teams of four compete, and if you show up short-handed, they'll make a team for you. Warm up: Who wrote *Last Exit to Brooklyn*? First and third Monday, from 9 to 11pm. Register around 8:30pm. (Answer: Hubert Selby, Jr.)

136 Atlantic Ave., between Clinton and Henry. Brooklyn Heights, Brooklyn. ℂ 718/222-9198. www.lastexitbar.com. Subway: M/N/R/2/3/4/5 to Borough Hall; F to Bergen St.

☆ **Pete's Candy Store** FREE   At Pete's Wednesday Quizz-Off, categories range from general knowledge to music to top 10s, with prizes for the top three finishers. The action starts at 7:30pm. Alternatively, wordsmiths hammer at their tile forges during Scrabble Saturdays. Bring a partner and try your luck at doubles on Saturdays from 5 to 8pm. For libations, the daily 5 to 7pm happy hour has great deals: Yuenglings, Brooklyns, and well drinks are a mere $2 a pop. Otherwise, drinks range from a $3 Pabst or Bud to an $8 glass of premium liquor.

709 Lorimer St., between Frost and Richardson, Williamsburg, Brooklyn. ℂ 718/302-3770. www.petescandystore.com. Subway: L to Lorimer St.; G to Metropolitan Ave.

Rocky Sullivan's FREE   You can show off those muscular brain cells at Rocky's, where teams of trivia hounds compete at the prodding of a congenial host every Thursday night at 9pm. Victorious founts of knowledge are rewarded with fermented hops. Quiz show night has no cover or minimum. Happy hour runs every day from noon to 7pm with $3 wells and domestic beers, and $4 imports. At other times wells start at $4 and the top-shelf rounds out at $8.

129 Lexington Ave., between 28th and 29th sts. ℂ 212/725-3871. www. rockysullivans.com. Subway: 6 to 28th St.

8 Talk It Up: TV Tapings

Why saddle yourself with those endless cable, satellite, and electric bills, when you could be watching TV for free? New York is home to a bunch of the top-flight shows, many of which rely on live in-studio audiences to keep the energy levels high. In exchange for your enthusiasm (and patience), you'll get a great peek behind the curtain. Fans are always amazed at just how small the sets—and stars—really are. To make it even more worth your while, most shows employ MCs to get the crowd in a good mood, and often you can pick up some swag, in the form of T-shirts or tickets.

Change of Heart FREE   Like the old *Dating Game* show, only not as intellectually challenging, this syndicated program makes couples jump through hoops for your amusement. The show was recently relocated to Manhattan, and tickets are generally available with less than a week's notice. Call or fill out a ticket request online.

Chelsea Studios, 221 W. 26th St., between Seventh and Eighth aves. ℂ **877/ 485-7144.** www.changeofheart.warnerbros.com. Subway: 1/9 to 28th St.

Talking Points

New York's most famous shows are incredibly popular, with waits of 6 months or longer commonplace. Often you'll have to send in a postcard with your relevant info and preferred dates (tickets to a taping make a great cheap birthday present). For those who arrive without tickets, it is possible to get standbys on the morning of the show. They'll only give one ticket per standee, so everyone in the party has to be there waiting at the crack of dawn. Even then it's no guarantee, since standby status only kicks in if there's enough no-shows among the regular ticket holders. Of course, if you're not choosey about what you want to see, there are plenty of shows in New York unpopular enough to get you in without delay. The NYCVB has more details on tapings (ℂ **212/484-1222**).

The Daily Show with Jon Stewart `FREE` There's been no drought of mockable material in the news of late, helping Jon Stewart's satirical news/talk show to quietly become a Comedy Central institution. In addition to biting analysis of current events, if you attend a taping you'll be treated to a few minutes of personable warm-up comedy from Jon himself. Monday through Thursday at 5:45pm. Make advance ticket requests by phone. You can also check for cancellation tickets for the upcoming week; the line is open Monday through Thursday from 10:30am to 4pm for tickets.

513 W. 54th St., between Tenth and Eleventh aves. © 212/586-2477. www. comedycentral.com. Subway: A/B/C/D/1/9 to 59th St./Columbus Circle.

Emeril Live `FREE` Rare sightings of shrinking violet Emeril Lagasse can be had at the celebrity chef's Food Network tapings. Tickets are hard to come by, however. The best way to snag seats is to go to www.foodtv.com and sign up for the weekly newsletter, which will give you first notice of upcoming ticket lotteries.

604 W. 52nd, between Eleventh and Twelfth aves. www.foodtv.com. Subway: C/E to 50th St.

Good Morning America `FREE` If seeing the faces of Diane Sawyer and Charlie Gibson first thing in the morning is actually an enticing prospect for you, join the live audience in ABC's studio right on Broadway. Tickets for the 7 to 9am broadcast can be wrangled by filling out the online request or by calling during business hours. If you do get tickets, plan on arriving at the ungodly hour of 6am. Sans tickets you can still join the throng outside the Broadway and 44th Street studio window. *Note:* In the summers, big-name performers come to Bryant Park for the **Good Morning America Summer Concert Series.** The shows run from 7 to 9am, but get there by 7am at the latest.

ABC Studios, 7 Times Square, at 43rd St. © 212/580-5176. www.abcnews. go.com/sections/GMA. Subway: N/Q/R/S/W/1/2/3/7/9 to Times Sq./42nd St.

The Late Show with David Letterman `FREE` And the number-one hottest New York TV taping ticket is . . . yeah, it's still Letterman. Though the show may have lost a step or two, our favorite Hoosier still squeezes the most out of his regulars, and Paul and the band still keep things energetic. Tapings are Monday through Thursday at 5:30pm, with a second taping Thursday at 8pm. Send a postcard to Late Show Tickets, Ed Sullivan Theater, 1697 Broadway,

New York, NY 10019. Two tickets max and one request only or they'll toss them all. Allow enough time to gestate a child (waits run about 9 months). *Note:* You can also register online to be notified of tickets that may become available for specific dates you select over the next 3 months. The standby lines on tape day are no longer, but you can call at 11am for a chance at up to two standby seats. Be patient and use your redial button liberally. Also bone up on your Letterman trivia because you may need to pass a test to get the tickets. FINE PRINT You must be 18 or older to attend, and you'll be expected to arrive an hour and a quarter before tape time.

Ed Sullivan Theater, 1697 Broadway, between 54th and 55th sts. ℂ 212/247-6497. www.cbs.com/latenight/lateshow (click on "Get Tickets"). Subway: B/D/E to Seventh Ave.

Late Night with Conan O'Brien FREE   Though still in Letterman's shadow, Conan's show has matured and solidified, making it another tough New York ticket to nail down. The guests are A-listers and the sketches are some of the funniest on television. Tapings run Tuesday through Friday at 5:30pm, though they ask you to be there 45 minutes early. You can call to try and reserve up to four tickets. NBC hands out standbys on the day of taping, starting at 9am outside 30 Rockefeller Plaza (under the NBC Studios awning). FINE PRINT You must be 16 or older.

49th St., between Fifth and Sixth aves. ℂ 212/664-3056 www.nbc.com. Subway: B/D/F/V to 47th-50th; N/R/W to 49th St.

Live! with Regis and Kelly FREE   If you don't have any plans for a year from now, why not go see Kelly and Rege? To join the absurdly long waiting list, send a postcard with your data to Live! Tickets, Ansonia Station, P.O. Box 230777, New York, NY 10023-0777. You can request up to four tickets at a time. To line jump, you can try for a standby ticket. Show up at the studio by 7am at the latest on a taping day. Tapings are Monday through Friday at 9am at the ABC Studios in Lincoln Square on the Upper West Side. FINE PRINT You must be 10 or older to attend (anyone under 18 must be accompanied by a parent).

7 Lincoln Sq., at Columbus Ave. and W. 67th St. ℂ 212/456-3054. http://tvplex.go.com/buenavista/livewithregis/ticketsandfaqs. Subway: 1/9 to 66th St.

The Montel Williams Show FREE   Montel approaches his 15-year anniversary of service to the housebound and underemployed, with a continuing run of titillating topics designed to make Jerry Springer weep with envy. Tickets are available with about a 2-week lead time. Tapings are on Wednesday and Thursday at 10am, 1pm, and 4pm.

433 W. 53rd St., between Ninth and Tenth aves. ℂ 212/989-8101. www. montelshow.com. Subway: C/E to 50th St.

Saturday Night Live FREE   SNL's steady devolution hasn't made getting in to see the show any easier. There's a lottery (around August usually) for the upcoming season; otherwise, your only shot is trying for standbys on the date of the taping. One ticket per person may be available at 7am at 30 Rockefeller Plaza, on the 49th Street side of the building, though even a standby ticket is no guarantee you'll get in. Tapings are Saturday at 11:30pm from fall to late spring, with a dress rehearsal at 8pm (arrival time 7pm). FINE PRINT You must be 16 or older.

NBC Studio, 30 Rockefeller Plaza, 49th St., between Fifth and Sixth aves. ℂ 212/664-3056. www.nbc.com. Subway: B/D/F/V to 47th–50th sts.; N/R/W to 49th St.

The Today Show FREE   Watching NBC's morning mainstay is free and easy; just show up outside *Today*'s glass-walled studio at Rockefeller Center, on the southwest corner of 49th Street and Rockefeller Plaza. Tapings are Monday through Friday from 7am to 10am, but if you want to be up front, 7am is way too late to be rushing over with your goofy hat and hand-painted sign. In the summer, *Today* holds a series of concerts in Rockefeller Center, generally Friday mornings at 7am. It's always big names playing, and they attract commensurate huge crowds.

Southwest corner of 49th St. and Rockefeller Plaza. ℂ 212/664-3056. www.msnbc.msn.com. Subway: B/D/F/V to 47th–50th; N/R/W to 49th St.

Total Request Live FREE   Carson Daly's countdown show continues to entrance Generation XL, which gathers in Times Square below MTV's glass studio at 44th Street and Broadway in Times Square before the 3:30pm tapings. Reservations can some-times be made by calling the TRL Ticket Reservation Hot Line at ℂ 212/398-8549. Failing that, show up by 2pm at the latest and watch for a TRL producer to come through the crowd. Standby tickets are exchanged for the correct answers to trivia questions. The MTV Store on the corner of 44th and Broadway usually has flyers for additional tapings and events next to the register. FINE PRINT To get inside to the studio you must be at least 16 and look no older than 24.

1515 Broadway, at 44th St. ⒸⓁ **212/398-8549.** www.mtv.com. Subway: N/Q/R/S/W/1/2/3/7/9 to Times Sq./42nd St.

Tough Crowd with Colin Quinn FREE   Brooklyn's own SNL alum Colin Quinn oversees a talk show that fills the niche of the departed *Politically Incorrect*. The tough crowd gets softened up with free tickets to the studio audience. Call in advance for tickets, which aren't too hard to come by. Tapings are Monday through Thursday at 6pm, though you should be at the studio at least an hour early. FINE PRINT You have to be at least 18.

Sony Studios, 447 W. 53rd St., between Ninth and Tenth aves. ⒸⓁ **212/560-2663.** www.comedycentral.com. Subway: C/E to 50th St.

The View FREE   Barbara and crew chat away about sex, celluloid, diets, calories, weight issues, and the other serious topics of the day every Monday through Friday at 11am. Make requests 3 or 4 months ahead, either online or by sending a postcard to Tickets, *The View,* 320 W. 66th St., New York, NY 10023. Ticket holders are expected 1½ hours before showtime. A limited number of standby tickets are also available. Get there early (10am at the latest). FINE PRINT You must be at least 18 (bring ID).

320 W. 66th St., off West End Ave. ⒸⓁ **212/465-0900.** www.abc.go.com/theview. Subway: 1/9 to 66th St.

Who Wants to be a Millionaire FREE   Millionaires miss out on all the fun listed in this book, but you can look on with condescending pity should anyone run the table against Regis. Tapings are Monday through Thursday at 4pm, with an additional 12:30pm Wednesday show. Note that they'll want you there 2 hours early and the show can take 2 hours or longer to tape, so make sure you're fed and watered before you go in (and be warned that as posh as the set looks on televisions, those benches are hard). For tickets, write 2 months in advance to New York TV Show Tickets, Inc., *Who Wants to be a Millionaire?,* Columbia University Station, PO Box 250225, New York, NY 10025.

Taping address: ABC at 30 West 67th St., between Columbus Ave. and Central Park West. ⒸⓁ **212/838-5901.** www.abc.com. Subway: 1/9 to 66th St.

9 Word Up: Readings

New York has always been a city of writers, and modern Gotham has no shortage of literary lights. Undiscovered hopefuls, midlist strivers, and the huge names with cultlike followings all find their way to lecterns across the city. Bars, galleries, libraries, book stores, and schools do the hosting. With eight million other stories unfolding in the Naked City, most people don't take the time to be read to, and I usually find literary events are pleasantly underattended. There are exceptions—voices of the moment and package nights that bring in a bunch of big names at once—but generally you have a better chance to see a big-time writer than you'll get with any actress, athlete, or musician. And almost always you'll get to do it for free.

AT BOOKSTORES

Bookshops are good spots for getting a hit of that sweet, sweet literature, and getting it for free. Some stores offer regular readings, and some just signings, although on a quiet night you'll have the chance to talk up a favorite author.

☆ **Barnes & Noble** `FREE` The Union Square location gets the biggest names and most frequent readings. Literary stars like David Sedaris, Helen Fielding, and Michael Cunningham come through to read from their works or participate in conferences and discussions. For kids, the first Saturday of every month sees a visit from a costume character from a children's book. The seating area is large and comfortable, but you should show up early for the top-sellers because it does get crowded.

On Union Sq.: 33 E. 17th St., between Broadway and Park Ave. South. ℭ 212/ 253-0810. www.bn.com. Subway: L/N/Q/R/W/4/5/6 to 14th St./Union Sq. A close second is the Lincoln Center location, with its steady big-shot parade: 1972 Broadway, at 66th St. ℭ 212/595-6859. Subway: 1/9 to 66th St.

Black Orchid Bookshop `FREE` This mystery novel shop has regular author signings. It's a friendly scene, complete with complimentary wine and snacks.

303 E. 81st St., between First and Second aves. ℭ 212/734-5980. www. members.aol.com/borchid. Subway: 4/5/6 to 86th St.

Bluestockings `FREE` DIY ethos is in full effect at this small, communal bookstore. Frequent readings of a feminist and lesbian bent intersperse with seminars and meetings. The readings and many lectures/discussions are free; other events can ask for suggested donations of $3 to $10. The **Dyke Knitting Circle** meets the third Sunday of every month from 5 to 7pm. It's free and open to all levels of knitting skill.

172 Allen St., between Rivington and Stanton sts. ℭ **212/777-6028.** www.bluestockings.com. Subway: F/V to Second Ave.; J/M/Z to Essex St.

BookCourt FREE For over 2 decades now, this Cobble Hill favorite has been a clean and well-lit place for literary fans. The local authors section is comprehensive, which is impressive considering how many writers are calling the area home. In-store readings and signings bring in the hip new voices.

163 Court St., between Dean and Pacific sts., Cobble Hill, Brooklyn. ℭ **718/875-3677.** Subway: F/G to Bergen, M/N/R/W to Court St.; 2/3/4/5 to Borough Hall.

The Chain Gang

With so many interesting mom and pop book stores in NYC, it would be tempting to ignore the corporate giants, if they weren't so ubiquitous. Despite the lack of indie cred, both **Barnes & Noble** (www.bn.com) and **Borders** (www.borders stores.com) are actually solid centers for free entertainment. With the square footage to pack in listeners by the bushel, and the juice to draw top names, some of the best readings in the city take place at Barnes & Noble (usually at the Union Sq. store; see p. 86). Check the store windows or the website for the latest heavy-hitter to come shilling New York way.

Books of Wonder FREE The agenda here is books for the kiddies. Every Saturday afternoon from noon to 2pm is story time, with a staff member doing the honors (check the website to find out which books and authors are being read). Other events, including the occasional publication party, are scattered through the calendar.

16 W. 18th St., between Fifth and Sixth aves. ℭ **212/989-3270.** www.books ofwonder.com. Subway: L/N/Q/R/W/4/5/6 to 14th St./Union Sq.

Coliseum Books FREE Midtown readers lamented when Coliseum Books' old location disappeared into the same oblivion that claimed the Columbus Circle Coliseum itself. Coliseum has been reborn a few blocks away, in a spiffy new space near Times Square.

The store now has more room for maneuvering, and the Coliseum's regular procession of quality writers earns universal thumbs-ups.

11 W. 42nd St., between Fifth and Sixth aves. ℂ 212/803-5890. Subway: B/D/F/V to 42nd St.; 7 to Fifth Ave.

Community Bookstore FREE   This friendly shop continues to fight an uphill battle against the big chains. The cafe is nice, and the readings show off the shop's excellent taste in authors.

143 Seventh Ave., between Carroll St. and Garfield Place, Park Slope, Brooklyn. ℂ 718/783-3075. Subway: B/Q to Seventh Ave.; 2/3 to Grand Army Plaza.

Creative Visions FREE   Readings and signings here focus on topics that fall under the colors of the rainbow flag. The shop is locally owned and dedicated to serving the needs of the Village's gay, lesbian, bi, and trans communities.

548 Hudson St., between Charles and Perry sts. ℂ 212/645-7573. www.creativevisionsbooks.com. Subway: 1/9 to Christopher St.

Drama Book Shop FREE   When this venerable performing-arts bookstore relocated a couple of years ago, they added a performing-arts space to the mix. The **Arthur Seelen Theatre** hosts a resident theater company in addition to regular discussions, readings, and workshops. They've even started showing film shorts. Check online for the calendar, but pretty much everything is free.

250 W. 40th St., between Seventh and Eighth aves. ℂ 212/944-0595. www.zdramabookshop.com. Subway: A/C/E to 42nd St.

East West Books FREE   This bookstore houses a great esoteric collection, plus readings and signings to further disseminate the wisdom of the East. Call or visit for a schedule of events.

Downtown, 78 Fifth Ave., near 14th St. ℂ 212/243-5994. Subway: L/N/Q/R/W/4/5/6 to 14th St./Union Sq.

Lenox Hill Bookstore FREE   This small, elegant Uptown shop specializes in literary books. Store events include signings and readings.

1018 Lexington Ave., at 73rd. ℂ 212/472-7170. www.turtlepoint.com/lenox. Subway: 6 to 77th St.

192 Books FREE   This lovely new shop brings in authors for 6:30pm readings. Night of the week varies, and seating is limited so call ahead for reservations. Check the website for schedule.

192 Tenth Ave., at 21st. © **212/255-4022**. www.192books.com. Subway: C/E to 23rd St.

Printed Matter `FREE`   "Artwork for the page" is the niche cornered by this organization, which specializes in affordable artists' publications. Book signings, launches, and exhibitions all can be found in their big new space in the heart of the Chelsea galleries.

535 W. 22nd, between Tenth and Eleventh aves. © **212/925-0325**. www.printedmatter.org. Subway: C/E to 23rd St.

Revolution Books `FREE`   The revolution will be televised, and it will also make its way into print. Alternative viewpoints are aired during in-store readings here. No website yet, so you'll have to call or visit for a schedule of events.

9 W. 19th St., between Fifth and Sixth aves. © **212/691-3345**. Subway: 4/5/6/L/N/Q/R/W to 14th St./Union Sq.

The Scholastic Store `FREE`   The retail outlet for the children's publisher Scholastic has books and toys and a full schedule of in-store events. Book signings and story readings are free, as are the craft workshops on Saturdays. The Scholastic Auditorium hosts more free events, although you have to call in and get a reservation first. Check online or call for the latest schedule.

557 Broadway, between Prince and Spring sts. © **212/343-6166**. www.scholastic.com/sohostore. Subway: N/R to Prince St.

Three Lives & Company `FREE`   Just browsing in this low-key West Village legend can make a person feel smart and sophisticated. Pressed-tin ceilings and exposed brick complement a classy selection. Though space is tight here, the readings and signings are worth checking out.

154 W. 10th St., at Waverly Place. © **212/741-2069**. www.threelives.com. Subway: 1/9 to Christopher St.

AT BARS & CAFES

What better way to advertise the intelligent conversation your coffee shop or booze hall induces than by associating yourself with articulate new voices? Reading series have cropped up in bars and cafes across the city, and the informal settings encourage more showmanship than a bookshop lectern. With extreme readings the latest trend, these venues are the most likely spots to be entertained while listening to an author intone.

Barbès `FREE` Weekly readings take place at this budding Brooklyn arts bar. Tuesdays at 7pm. They don't have a happy hour, but a can of Pabst is only $3.

376 9th St., Park Slope, Brooklyn. ℂ **718-965-9177.** www.barbesbrooklyn. com. Subway: F to Seventh Ave., take the southwest exit and make a U-turn when you get out, walking downhill on 9th St. toward Sixth Ave.

Ear Inn `FREE` The structure housing this TriBeCa tavern was condemned as unfit for habitation in 1906. Somehow it's still upright, and still putting on one of the city's best reading series. Poetry and occasional prose can be heard at the Ear every Saturday at 3pm. A Bud is $3.50, and top shelf prices top out at $9. Happy hour is from 4 to 7pm daily, with $1 off of everything except wine.

326 Spring St., west of Greenwich St. ℂ **212/226-9060.** www.home.nyc.rr. com/earinnreadings. Subway: C/E to Spring St.; 1/9 to Canal.

The Half King `FREE` *The Perfect Storm* author Sebastian Junger is a co-owner of this bustling Chelsea bar and cafe. He's also an occasional contributor to their weekly reading series, which presents poets and writers of longer attention spans every Monday night. One Monday a month is set aside for the over-looked category of magazine writing. A pint of Boddington's or Stella is $4, bottles are $4.50. From 4 to 7pm, take $1 off drink specials. Readings Mondays at 7pm.

505 W. 23rd St., near Tenth Ave. ℂ **212/462-4300.** www.thehalfking.com. Subway: C/E to 23rd St.

Happy Ending `FREE` This Chinatown lounge, whose name advertises a salient detail about the services of the former tenant (a massage parlor), is home to the city's most ambitious reading series. Each week brings multiple writers, often heavy hitters of the A. M. Homes and Rick Moody ilk. There's usually a lagniappe tossed in, something between a cooking demonstration and a musical performance. Wednesdays at 8pm. The cheapest beer is a $5 bottle, but you can fuel up ahead of time with half-price drinks during the 7 to 8pm happy hour.

302 Broome St., at Forsythe St. ℂ **212/334-9676.** Subway: B/D to Grand St.; F/J/M/Z to Essex/Delancey St.

Housing Works Used Book Café `FREE` In addition to a great selection of used books, Housing Works attracts an impressive lineup of writers. Readings are free, but if you drop some money on cafe items it'll end up in a good place; Housing Works is a charity that donates proceeds to help support people living with AIDS. Times and days of the week vary, check the website for the schedule. Wine and beer are $5, coffees range from $1.25 to $3.75.

126 Crosby St., between Houston and Prince sts. ℂ 212/334-3324. www. housingworks.org. Subway: B/D/F/V to Broadway/Lafayette; 6 to Bleecker St.

Monday Night Reading Series at Junno's FREE Unpublished writers, and a few ringers, take advantage of the feedback mechanism that is a live crowd to try out works-in-progress. The occasional polished piece turns up as well. The series happens on Mondays at 7:30pm. A bottle of beer is $4 and the most expensive drink is $8.

64 Downing St., between Bedford and Varick sts. ℂ 212/627-7995. Subway: A/B/C/D/E/F/V to W. 4th St.

☆ KGB Bar FREE Hidden away in a former speakeasy on the second floor of an East Village tenement, KGB has the most comprehensive reading series in the city. Sunday night brings fiction, Monday poetry, Tuesday nonfiction, and Wednesday features the fantastic, in the form of sci-fi authors. Additional readers on the balance of evenings make it almost impossible to find a wordless night. The bar was once the clubhouse of the Ukrainian Labor Home, and the commie kitsch adorning the walls perfects the literary atmosphere. Most readings start 7pm. There is no drink minimum, but if all those words make you thirsty, Rolling Rock and Bud bottles are $4 and the most expensive drink is $8.

85 E. 4th St., at Second Ave. ℂ 212/505-3360. www.kgbbar.com. Subway: B/D/F/V to Broadway/Lafayette; 6 to Bleecker St.

One Story at Arlene's Grocery FREE *One Story* is a literary magazine with a self-explanatory philosophy: Once a month at Arlene's, the magazine trots out a singular writer for a short, free reading and a happy hour, with a spotlight on One Drink chosen by the author. Second Monday of every month at 7pm. Happy hour from 6:30 to 8pm, chosen drinks $3 to $4.

95 Stanton St. ℂ 212/358-1633. www.one-story.com. Subway: F/V to Second Ave.; J/M/Z to Essex St.

☆ Pete's Candy Store FREE Not content with a mere single literary evening, Pete's brings in the ink-slingers on alternate Monday *and* Thursday nights. Thursdays focus on local writers, favoring fiction, but indulging poets as well. Pete's Big Salmon is Monday night's show, which almost always shows off poetry. The couplets are followed by live bands on Mondays (check "For Those About to Rock," earlier in the chapter). Readings begin at 7:30pm. Check the websites for schedules.

709 Lorimer St., between Frost and Richardson sts., Williamsburg, Brooklyn. ☎ 718/302-3770. www.petesbigsalmon.com or www.petescandystore.com. Subway: L to Lorimer St.; G to Metropolitan Ave.

Reading Between A and B at 11th Street Bar `FREE`   This series specializes in emerging poets, with occasional fiction and nonfiction sprinkled into the mix. The neighborhood bar that hosts couldn't be more congenial. Every other Monday at 8pm. During happy hour, weeknights from 4 to 8pm, all drinks are $1 off. The regular price of a bottle of beer is $3.50.

510 E. 11th St., between aves. A and B. ☎ 212/982-3929. www.readab.com. Subway: L to First Ave.

Rocky Sullivan's Pub `FREE`   This thinking person's booze hole has a regular Wednesday night reading series that tends toward New York–centric themes, like local histories or the burgeoning genre of "Brooklyn noir." The magic happens most Wednesdays at 8pm. No minimum, but from noon to 7pm daily, happy hour features $3 well drinks and domestic beers, and $4 imports. At other times drinks range between $4 wells and $8 premiums.

129 Lexington Ave., between 28th and 29th sts. ☎ 212/725-3871. www. rockysullivans.com. Subway: 6 to 28th St.

Telephone Bar and Grill `FREE`   We Three Productions presents readings every other Monday in the swank library lounge at 8pm. Happy hour is every weeknight from 4 to 7pm, with half-pints $2 and pints $3.50. Regular prices start at $4.50 for a Bud and end at $8 for a Grey Goose martini.

149 Second Ave., between 9th and 10th sts. ☎ 212/529-5000. www.telebar. com. Subway: 6 to Astor Place; L to Third Ave.

AT THE LIBRARIES `FREE`
The sharks running New York's libraries have cooked up a scheme for self-perpetuation. Free readings, that's how they hook you. You like what the writer has to say, you can't resist the urge to learn more, and before you know it you're checking out books left and right. Diabolical.

The following libraries are the best for frequent readings. Check in at www.nypl.org for full schedules and other branches.

Brooklyn Public Library   Grand Army Plaza. ✆ **718/230-2100.** www.brooklynpubliclibrary.org. Subway: 2/3 to Grand Army Plaza.

Langston Hughes Community Library and Cultural Center   100-01 Northern Blvd., between 102nd and 103rd sts., Corona, Queens. ✆ **718/651-1100.** Subway: 7 to 103rd St./Corona Plaza.

New York Public Library Fort Washington Branch   535 W. 179th St., between Audubon and St. Nicholas aves. ✆ **212/927-3533.** Subway: A/1/9 to 181st St.

New York Public Library Humanities and Social Sciences Library   Fifth Ave., at 42nd. ✆ **212/869-8089.** Subway: 7 to Fifth Ave.; 4/5/6 to Grand Central; B/D/F/V to 42nd St.

New York Public Library for the Performing Arts   Donald and Mary Oenslager Gallery. 40 Lincoln Center Plaza, between 64th and 65th sts. ✆ **212/870-1630.** Subway: 1/9 to 66th St.

New York Public Library   Schomburg Center for Research in Black Culture. 515 Malcolm X Blvd. (Lenox Blvd.), at 135th St. ✆ **212/491-2200.** Subway: 2/3 to 135th St.

10 Big Leagues, Little Prices

It's said that it's now cheaper to be an opera fan than to follow a major league sports team, and with ticket prices racing well ahead of inflation it's easy to believe. A seat in the mezzanine of Giants Stadium to watch Big Blue will set you back $75, and a field box in Yankee Stadium runs a cool $85. Courtside for the Knicks? Prices start at $289.50 (hey, at least they keep it under $290). Even the inept New York Rangers don't do us any favors—their cheapest hockey ticket is $20. However, if you have no fear of heights, there are a few inexpensive ways of getting into the big games.

The Amazing Mets   It's hard to believe that mostly charmless, modern Shea Stadium is now the fifth-oldest stadium in the majors. For approximately 13 games a year, the Mets roll back the prices for cheapskate fans. The seats in question (parts of the upper, loge, and mezzanine) all have one thing in common: They're in the back rows and many miles from the action on the field. Also, they're not available for "Gold" tier games (Yankees, Cubs, and so on), but only for "Value" tier (a late-Aug series with the Brewers, say). Still, at a paltry $5, it's a cheap way to see a big league team in action (or as in recent Met seasons, an alleged big league team).

Shea Stadium, 126th St., at Roosevelt Ave., Flushing, Queens. ℭ 718/507-8499. www.mets.com. Subway: 7 to Willets Point/Shea Stadium.

Damn Yankees   Even though the Boss has broken the bank to buy up just about every player in Major League Baseball, there are still dirt cheap ways to get into the cozy nest of our beloved Evil Empire. Bleacher seats at Yankee Stadium are a mere $5 a pop during 10 games a year (they're midweek games, but against decent opponents), and for the rest of the schedule they're only $8. That's cheaper than a movie, though if you spring for a couple of beers and a hot dog, you can add a quick $18.50 to your tab. Before you enter the bleacher zone, it's worth noting that the phrase "bleacher bums" wasn't coined solely for its alliterative qualities. Wear a Red Sox cap at your peril. It's also not exactly kid-friendly territory, unless your kids are thuggish drunks.

Yankee Stadium, 161st St. and River Ave., the Bronx. ℭ 718/293-6000. www.yankees.com. Subway: B/D/4 to 161st St./Yankee Stadium.

Knicks & Cut-Rate Seats   Ten-dollar Knick seats are about as elusive as Knick playoff victories. They do exist, but they're nosebleeds and they tend to sell out quickly. If you don't pick them up in September when they first go on sale, your best bet is to check the "Stub Hub" on the Knick website, where season-ticket holders unload their spares at list.

Madison Square Garden, 4 Pennsylvania Plaza, Seventh Ave., at 34th St. ℭ 212/465-6741. www.nba.com/knicks. Subway: A/C/E or 1/2/3/9 to Penn Station.

Sweet Land of Liberty   Like their male counterparts, the Liberty doesn't offer much by way of bargain seats. For $10 you'll get in to Madison Square Garden, but you'll be squinting from a back row.

Madison Square Garden, 4 Pennsylvania Plaza, Seventh Ave., at 34th St. ℭ 212/465-6075. www.wnba.com/liberty. Subway: A/C/E or 1/2/3/9 to Penn Station.

Baby Bombers   The Staten Island Yankees have a lovely new waterfront stadium just a few steps from the ferry terminal. Running from $8 to $10, tickets are easier to come by than the Cyclones', although they're very scarce when the two rivals play.

Richmond County Bank Ballpark, Staten Island. ✆ 718/720-9200. www.si yanks.com. Subway: N/R to Whitehall St.; 1/9 to South Ferry, take the ferry to Staten Island and follow the signs.

Mini Mets   No one confuses the Brooklyn Cyclones for dem bums of old, but the new stadium near the Atlantic Ocean and the Coney Island boardwalk has fast become a borough fave. Tickets are $5 to $12 and tend to disappear quickly.

Keyspan Park, 1904 Surf Ave., at W. 19th St., Coney Island, Brooklyn. ✆ 718/ 449-8497. www.brooklyncyclones.com. Subway: D to Coney Island/Stillwell Ave.

Playing the Horses

Horse racing has seen its bottom line repeatedly gouged by the dumb luck of state lotteries. Every year fewer and fewer fans trek out to the track, which means Belmont and the Big A will be happy to see you when you go. So happy, in fact, that they'll let you in for only a nominal charge. While it's possible to lose some real money on the ponies, I have a system. Always pick the first horse off the rail that's wearing red, or any horse whose name begins with B. You can't miss.

Aqueduct Racetrack   Thoroughbred racing runs from late October or early November to early May. 110th St. and Rockaway Blvd., Rockaway Beach, Queens. ✆ 718/641-4700. www. nyra.com/aqueduct. Tickets $1–$3. Closed Mon–Tues. Subway: A to North Conduit.

Belmont Park   Whenever the horses don't run at Aqueduct (see above), they're racing here. Season is May to mid-July and late August, or early September to October. Hempstead Ave., Belmont, Long Island. ✆ 718/641-4700. www.nyra.com/ belmont. Tickets $2–$5. Closed Mon–Tues. Train: LIRR Belmont Express from Penn Station or Flatbush Ave.

ENTERTAINMENT DOWNTOWN

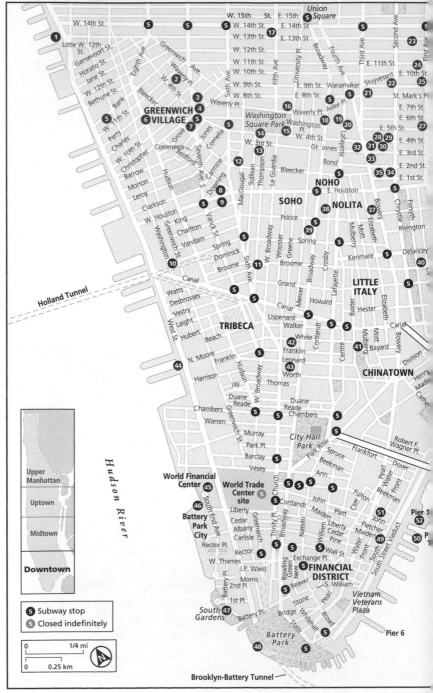

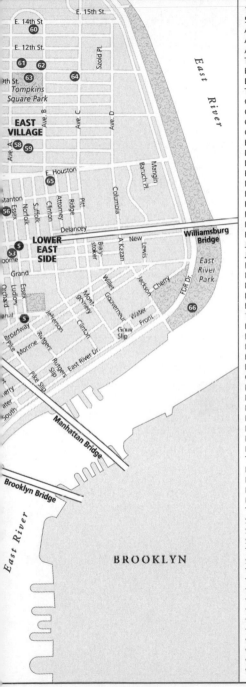

11th St. Bar **61**
55 Bar **4**
Actors Studio Drama School **5**
Arlene's Grocery **55**
Arthur's Tavern **7**
The Baggot Inn **13**
Blue Man Group at Astor Place Theatre **19**
Bluestockings **35**
The C-Note **64**
Castle Clinton **48**
Continental **21**
Continental Center **49**
Creative Visions **6**
Den of Cin **58**
Deutsches Haus **16**
Dixon Place **37**
Ear Inn **10**
East River Park Amphitheater **66**
East West Books **17**
Film Forum **9**
Dance Conversations at the Flea Theater **42**
Happy Ending **40**
Housing Works Used Book Café **38**
Jazz Detour **23**
Junno's **8**
KGB Bar **29**
Knitting Factory **43**
La Mama **30**
La Mama La Galleria **35**
Lakeside Lounge **62**
The Living Room **56**
Luna Lounge **57**
Millennium Film **31**
Movement Research at the Judson Church **14**
New York Theatre Workshop **28**
NYU/Tisch School of the Arts **18**
Otto's Shrunken Head **60**
Parkside Lounge **65**
Performance Space NBC **32**
Pier 16 **50**
Pier 25 **44**
Pier 54 **1**
Pioneer Theater **59**
P.S. 122 150 1st Ave. **26**
The Public Theater **20**
RaFiFi/Cinema Classics **24**
Rattlestick Playwrights Theater **2**
Robert F. Wagner, Jr. Park **47**
Rockefeller Park **46**
The Scholastic Store **39**
Screeners Club at the Remote Lounge **33**
Second on Second **34**
Shakespeare in the Park(ing) Lot **53**
The Slipper Room **54**
South Street Seaport **52**
Telephone Bar & Grill **22**
The Theater for the New City **25**
Three Lives & Company **3**
Three of Cups **27**
TKTS Booth Downtown **51**
Tompkins Square Park **63**
Traffic Jam: Tap Jam Under the Stars **11**
Village Ma **12**
Washington Square Music Festival **15**
Winnie's **41**
World Financial Center Plaza **45**

ENTERTAINMENT MIDTOWN

UPPER EAST
SIDE

E. 66th St.
E. 65th St.
E. 64th St.
E. 63rd St.
E. 62nd St.
E. 61st St.

From Lower
Level

Roosevelt Island Tram

E. 60th St.
Queensboro Bridge

E. 59th St.
E. 58th St.
E. 57th St.
E. 56th St.
E. 55th St.
E. 54th St.

MIDTOWN
EAST

E. 53rd St.
E. 52nd St.
E. 51st St.

E. 50th St.

Rockefeller
Center

E. 49th St.
E. 48th St.
Mitchell
Place

E. 47th St.
E. 46th St.
E. 45th St.
E. 44th St.

United
Nations

Grand
Central
Terminal

E. 43rd St.
E. 42nd St.
E. 41st St.

Queens Midtown Tunnel

Bryant
Park

New York
Public Library

E. 40th St.
E. 39th St.
E. 38th St.

Queens-
Midtown
Tunnel

MURRAY
HILL

E. 37th St.
E. 36th St.

Tunnel
Exit

Tunnel
Entrance

E. 35th St.
E. 34th St.

Empire State
Bldg.

E. 33rd St.
E. 32nd St.
E. 31st St.
E. 30th St.
E. 29th St.
E. 28th St.
E. 27th St.
E. 26th St.
E. 25th St.
E. 24th St.

Madison
Square
Park

E. 23rd St.
E. 22nd St.
E. 21st St.
E. 20th St.
E. 19th St.
E. 18th St.
E. 17th St.

Gramercy Park

GRAMERCY
PARK

FLATIRON
DISTRICT

Peter
Cooper
Village

Stuyvesant
Town

E. 16th St.
E. 15th St.
E. 14th St.
E. 13th St.

Union
Square

Roosevelt
Island

Queens

East River

FDR Drive

Upper
Manhattan

Uptown

Midtown

Downtown

S Subway stop

1/4 mi

0.25 km

Queens

99

ENTERTAINMENT UPTOWN

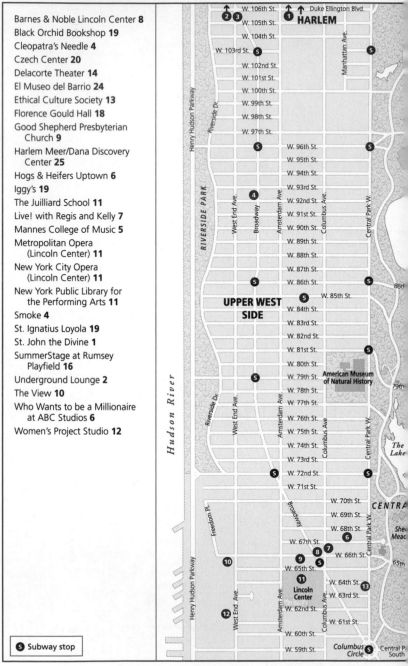

S Subway stop

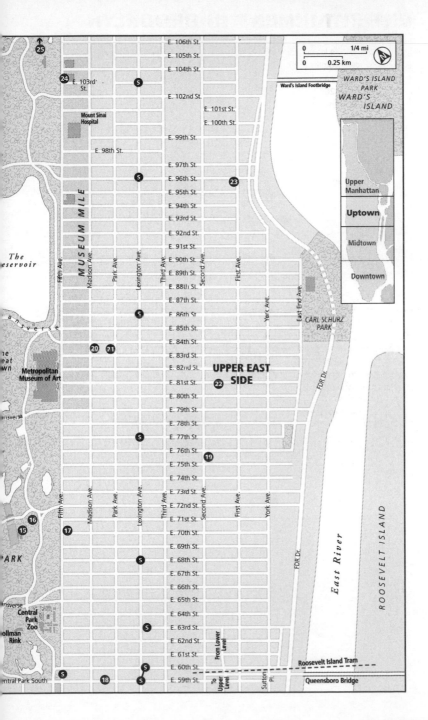

E. 106th St.
E. 105th St.
E. 104th St.
E. 103rd St.
E. 102nd St.
E. 101st St.
E. 100th St.
E. 99th St.
E. 98th St.
E. 97th St.
E. 96th St.
E. 95th St.
E. 94th St.
E. 93rd St.
E. 92nd St.
E. 91st St.
E. 90th St.
E. 89th St.
E. 88th St.
E. 87th St.
E. 86th St.
E. 85th St.
E. 84th St.
E. 83rd St.
E. 82nd St.
E. 81st St.
E. 80th St.
E. 79th St.
E. 78th St.
E. 77th St.
E. 76th St.
E. 75th St.
E. 74th St.
E. 73rd St.
E. 72nd St.
E. 71st St.
E. 70th St.
E. 69th St.
E. 68th St.
E. 67th St.
E. 66th St.
E. 65th St.
E. 64th St.
E. 63rd St.
E. 62nd St.
E. 61st St.
E. 60th St.
E. 59th St.

Mount Sinai Hospital

MUSEUM MILE

The Reservoir

Transverse

The Great Lawn

Metropolitan Museum of Art

UPPER EAST SIDE

Central Park Zoo

Wollman Rink

Central Park South

PARK

Fifth Ave.
Madison Ave.
Park Ave.
Lexington Ave.
Third Ave.
Second Ave.
First Ave.
York Ave.
East End Ave.

CARL SCHURZ PARK

FDR Dr.

East River

ROOSEVELT ISLAND

Ward's Island Footbridge

WARD'S ISLAND PARK

WARD'S ISLAND

Upper Manhattan

Uptown

Midtown

Downtown

0   1/4 mi
0   0.25 km

From Lower Level

To Upper Level

Sutton Pl.

Roosevelt Island Tram

Queensboro Bridge

25
24
20
21
16
15
17
18
23
22
19

101

ENTERTAINMENT IN BROOKLYN

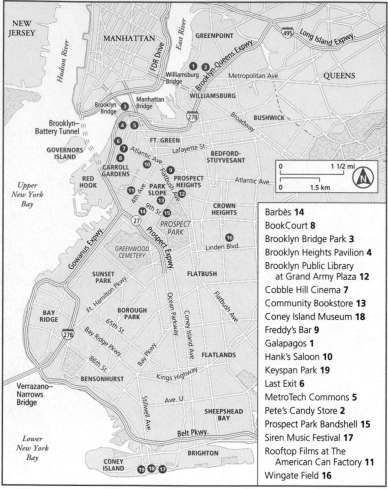

Barbès **14**
BookCourt **8**
Brooklyn Bridge Park **3**
Brooklyn Heights Pavilion **4**
Brooklyn Public Library
  at Grand Army Plaza **12**
Cobble Hill Cinema **7**
Community Bookstore **13**
Coney Island Museum **18**
Freddy's Bar **9**
Galapagos **1**
Hank's Saloon **10**
Keyspan Park **19**
Last Exit **6**
MetroTech Commons **5**
Pete's Candy Store **2**
Prospect Park Bandshell **15**
Siren Music Festival **17**
Rooftop Films at The
  American Can Factory **11**
Wingate Field **16**

ENTERTAINMENT IN QUEENS

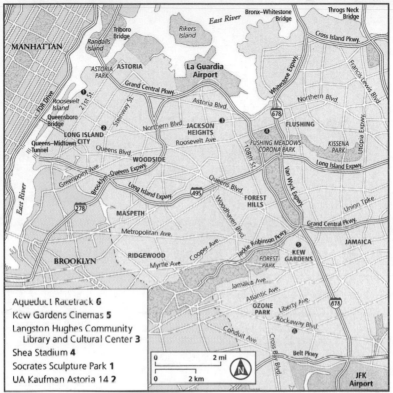

Aqueduct Racetrack **6**

Kew Gardens Cinemas **5**

Langston Hughes Community
  Library and Cultural Center **3**

Shea Stadium **4**

Socrates Sculpture Park **1**

UA Kaufman Astoria 14 **2**

Selective diners can find cheap eats all over Gotham; the Lower East Side's Tien-garden serves sit-down lunches at take-out prices. See p. 107 for a review.

EATING & DRINKING

ew Yorkers speak over 100 languages, and we eat at least that many different cuisines. Many of the ethnic superstars are hidden away in low-rent corners of the boroughs, but plenty of spectacular cheap eats can be found in accessible locations. Being selective about price doesn't necessarily mean sacrificing quality. Some of my favorite cooking just happens to be some of the city's cheapest. The island tilts toward downtown when it comes to budget grazing—Chinatown and the Lower East Side dominate. Across the rest of the city, Asian eateries offer the most for the least. Latino food comes in second, bringing in big portions for little dough. Lunch specials are a great way to sample the city's harvest with a minimal investment, but for all meals

I'm constantly surprised by how far $5 can take me in NYC. Leave the Jacksons in the wallet and *bon appétit*.

1 Dirt Cheap Eats Below 14th Street

THE FINANCIAL DISTRICT

Bennie's Thai Café THAI   This unprepossessing basement spot serves authentic Thai food that bursts with flavor. Worker bees stream in for the $4.75 lunch specials, served over rice on weekdays from 11am to 3pm. Red, yellow, and green curries are the highlights. The dishes are pork, chicken, and beef, so vegetarians have to order off the menu. Fortunately, vegetarian entrees, including an awesome pad thai, are under $7.

88 Fulton St., at Gold St. ✆ **212/587-8930.** Daily 11am–9pm. Subway: A/C/J/M/Z/2/3/4/5 to Fulton St./Broadway Nassau.

CHINATOWN

New York's headquarters for cheap eating is Chinatown. Between the foreign language and the strange sights and smells, it's easy to feel like you've wandered into another country—a country where the local currency is weak and the dollar is strong. Don't bother recalculating the exchange rate, however. The check really is that low.

☆ **Eldridge Street Dumpling House** CHINESE/DUMPLINGS If they tripled their prices, this little take-away stand on the Lower East Side end of Chinatown would still be laughably cheap. They offer an amazing sandwich. For $1.50 you get a big wedge of sesame pancake with beef in a fresh cilantro and carrot dressing. All that flavor disguises a little toughness of the beef. Dumplings make a great side, 5 for a $1 and cooked in a tasty thick wrapping. Soups are $3 and under, and steamed buns range from 50¢ to 75¢. ⌧FINE PRINT There's limited counter space to eat in.

118a Eldridge St., between Broome and Grand sts. ✆ **212/625-8008.** Daily 8am–10pm. Subway: B/D to Grand St.

Joe's Ginger Restaurant CHINESE   Joe's Shanghai is an ill-kept Chinatown secret, with lines as legendary as the food. Most folks haven't caught on to this offshoot, however, which has Joe's same great cooking with slightly lower prices and significantly less waiting. The homemade noodles are delicious, especially in soup form. A big bowl averages $3.95 and comes with a choice of four different noodles. Most veggie dishes are $6.95, most pork $7.95, and beefs are $8.95. Ambience is minimal, but the staff is friendly by Chinatown standards.

113 Mott, between Canal and Hester sts. ✆ 212/966-6613. Daily 11am–11pm. Subway: J/M/N/R/Q/W/Z/6 to Canal St. **Joe's Shanghai:** 9 Pell St., between Bowery and Mott sts. ✆ 212/233-8888. Subway: J/M/N/R/Q/W/Z/6 to Canal St. **Other location:** 24 W. 56th St., between Fifth and Sixth aves. ✆ 212/333-3868. Subway: N/R/Q/W or F to 57th St.

Pho Viet Huong VIETNAMESE   This is the best Vietnamese food in the city, and it's just a little added bonus that it's also among the cheapest. Huge bowls of *pho* (noodle soup) are only $4 and both vermicelli noodle and rice dishes come in under $5. The daily specials are usually under $10 and are routinely delicious. Keep an eye out for the beef stuffed with onions.

73 Mulberry St., between Bayard and Canal sts. ✆ **212/233-8988.** Daily 10am–10pm. Subway: J/M/N/Q/R/W/Z/6 to Canal St.

LOWER EAST SIDE

Bereket Turkish Kebob House TURKISH/FALAFEL   The guys working here clearly never got the memo that fast food doesn't require four-star taste. The $3 falafel is crispy, served up in a flavorful pita with farm-fresh tomatoes and lettuce. As good as the falafel is, the rest of the menu might be even better. Both chicken sandwiches, the shish, and the kebab, are steals for $5.

187 E. Houston St., at Orchard St. ✆ **212/475-7700.** Open 24 hr. Subway: F/V to Second Ave.

Congee Village CHINESE   Though the Chinese–Disney–acid trip decor here doesn't scream authenticity, the food and the clientele are the real thing. The house specialty is *congee,* a hearty rice porridge that starts at $2 and comes in multiple combinations. My favorite is chicken with black mushroom, for $3.50. Also recommended is the sliced beef chow fun, $5.95 for a huge plate of thick noodles. Lunch specials, served over rice, average $3.

100 Allen St., between Delancey and Broome sts. ✆ **212/941-1818.** Daily 10am–2am. Subway: F to Delancey St.; J/M/Z to Essex St.

Tiengarden VEGETARIAN   I used to think all vegetarian restaurants might as well be named "Food Haters" for their bland and

EATING & DRINKING DOWNTOWN

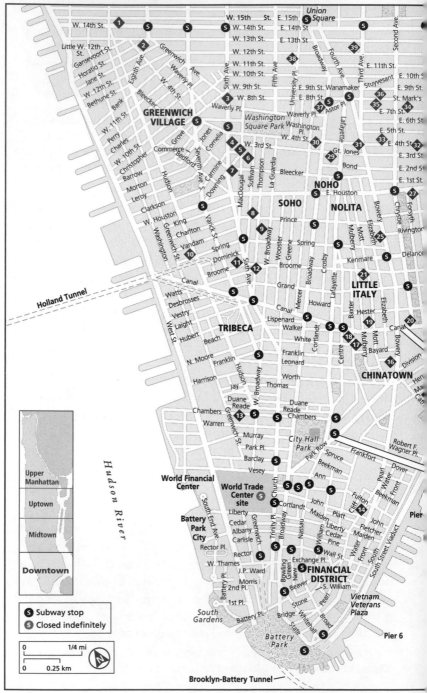

Upper Manhattan

Uptown

Midtown

Downtown

Hudson River

GREENWICH VILLAGE

Washington Square Park

NOHO

SOHO

NOLITA

LITTLE ITALY

TRIBECA

CHINATOWN

Holland Tunnel

World Financial Center

World Trade Center site

Battery Park City

City Hall Park

FINANCIAL DISTRICT

Vietnam Veterans Plaza

South Gardens

Battery Park

Pier 6

Brooklyn-Battery Tunnel

S Subway stop

S Closed indefinitely

| 0 | 1/4 mi |
| 0 | 0.25 km |

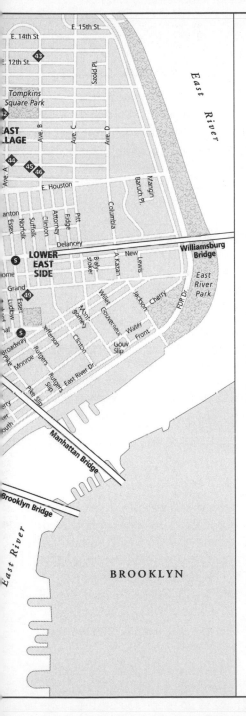

Acme Bar & Grill **61**
Antarctica Bar **10**
Bar None **39**
BB Sandwich Bar **4**
Bennie's Thai Café **14**
Bereket Turkish Kebob House **48**
Borobudur Café **32**
B-Side **43**
Café Himalaya **28**
Caracas Arepa Bar **34**
Chambers Wines **13**
Congee Village **24**
Corner Bistro **2**
Crif Dog **41**
Croxley Ales **46**
Cubana Café **9**
Cucina di Pesce **33**
David Bagel **40**
Dojo 30, **36**
Dragon Land Bakery **18**
El Cantinero **38**
Eldridge Street Dumpling House **22**
Fried Dumpling **23**
Golden Unicorn **15**
Grand Sichuan International **20**
Gray's Papaya **3**
Ivo & Lulu **11**
Joe's Ginger Restaurant **19**
Joe's Shanghai **16**
Kossar's Bialys **46**
Lovely Day **25**
Mama's Food Shop **6, 45**
Mamoun's **5**
Mooncake **12**
Odessa **42**
Otafuku **36**
Peep **8**
Pho Viet Huong **17**
Pop's Pierogi **7**
Punjabi **47**
The Slide **31**
Tiengarden **26**
Two Boots **44**
Viet-Nam Bánh Mi So 1 **21**
Village Idiot **1**
Warehouse Wines & Spirits **37**
Yonah Schimmel **27**

Free Eats: Happy Hour Spreads

When a bar gives away food, you can be pretty certain they're not giving up the best dishes in the house. However, if liquids are a higher priority, the complimentary buffet is a great way to fill up without wasting too much time—or cash. FINE PRINT The obvious qualifier: Happy-hour grub is free to those buying drinks.

El Cantinero GREENWICH VILLAGE   This reasonably authentic Mexican restaurant often lays out a free buffet at its upstairs bar. The buffet starts around 6pm, Monday through Thursday night, with items predominantly from the wing and corn food groups. 86 University Place, between 11th and 12th sts. ✆ **212/255-9378.** Mon-Thurs 11:30am-11:30pm; Fri-Sat 11:30am-1:30am; Sun 11:30am-10pm. Subway: L/N/Q/R/W/4/5/6 to 14th St./Union Sq.

Langan's HELL'S KITCHEN   This convivial Irish bar keeps patrons happy with a weekday evening buffet. The spread is just bar food, but you can't complain about the price. It's free from 5 to 8pm. 150 W. 47th St., between Sixth and Seventh aves. ✆ **212/869-5482.** www.langans.com. Subway: N/R/W to 49th St.; B/D/F/V to 47th-50th.

limited cuisine. Tiengarden adjusted my attitude. The Chinese-inspired menu is prepared without dairy, onion, or garlic, but somehow manages to be packed with flavor. Noodle dishes start at $6.50 and soups at $5.95, and most every entree is under $10. I could eat the Spicy Eggplant or Seitan Innovation every day of the week and not get bored. The $4.95 weekday lunch special runs until 4pm.

170 Allen St., between Stanton and Rivington sts. ✆ **212/388-1364.** Mon-Sat noon-10pm. Subway: F/V to Second Ave.

Yonah Schimmel KNISHES   The knish is a New York classic and can be found everywhere from delis to hot dog stands, but for the best in gut bombs you have to go to the source, the Lower

T.G. Whitney's MIDTOWN   Rotating specials can be found at this neighborhoody pub. Afternoons Monday through Friday from 2 to 5pm you can get $2 pints of Bud Light. Mondays bring $1 beer and 25¢ wings, and Thursday and Friday you can graze from a free buffet. 244 E. 53rd St., between Second and Third aves. ℂ 212/888-5772. http://tgwhitneys.citysearch. com. Mon–Fri 11:30am–2am; Sat 5pm–3am. Subway: E/V to Lexington–Third Ave.; 6 to 51st St.

The Cajun CHELSEA   Dixieland and old-time jazz are endangered species, but they can still be found most nights at this haunt. There's never a cover, but the bands play in the dining room, where you have to order dinner. If you want to just hang out in the bar, you can take advantage of a complimentary happy hour buffet. Cajun-style food is served Mondays through Fridays from 5 to 7pm. Drinks are all discounted a dollar, too, so you can suck down a bottle of Bud for $3. Bands start at 8pm weeknights, 8:30pm on Saturdays, and 7:30pm on Sundays. 129 Eighth Ave., between 16th and 17th sts. ℂ 212/691-6174. www. jazzatthecajun.com. Mon–Thurs 11:30am–11pm; Fri 11:30am–midnight; Sat 5pm–midnight; Sun noon–11pm. Subway: A/C/E to 14th St.; L to Eighth Ave.

East Side. Yonah Schimmel offers up flavors traditional (potato, mushroom, kasha) and sacrilegious (pizza), cooked in a generations-old recipe. For $2, it's hard to get more filled up. The rich cheese versions are less cost conscious ($2.50 and smaller), but equally delicious.

137 E. Houston St., between First and Second aves. ℂ 212/477-2858. www. yonahschimmel.com. Subway: F/V to Second Ave.

EAST VILLAGE

Borobudur Café INDONESIAN   Traditional Indonesian dishes, with their dark, almost burned flavor, are served in the narrow twin rooms here. Although there are familiar Asian archetypes like noodles, fried rice, and curries, much of the menu is original territory. Satays and tempehs are standouts. Big soups are under $6, as are veggie entrees, and the noodle and rice dishes come in under $8. The daily lunch special includes soup, a sampling of three dishes, and rice, for $6.

128 E. 4th St., between First and Second aves. ℭ **212/614-9079.** Sun-Thurs 11am-11pm; Fri-Sat 11am-midnight. Subway: F/V to Second Ave.

Café Himalaya TIBETAN   This little mom and pop restaurant serves tasty Tibetan/Nepali meals. There's a slight resemblance to Indian and Chinese dishes, as you might imagine, but the flavoring is its own thing—soy, carrot, and ginger are major players. Veggie dinner entrees run from $5.99 to $6.75, and sautéed noodle and meat dishes are $6.75. Things get even cheaper at lunch, where you can get a curry or dumplings or noodles for only $4.99. Lunch specials run weekdays from 11:30am to 4pm. The seating is limited, and for cheap date purposes it's BYOB.

78 E. 1st St., between Ave. A and First Ave. ℭ **212/358-0160.** Tues-Sat noon-11pm; Sun noon-10pm. Subway: F/V to Second Ave.

Mama's Food Shop AMERICAN/HOME COOKING   Come to Mamas for hearty southern/soul cooking. The delicious burger comes dressed with jalapeño mayo and will set you back $6. A basic dish (fried chicken and meatloaf are my favorites) paired with a side (a zillion to choose from but mac and cheese, corn salad, and mashed potatoes are standouts) is $9. Mama's has both Villages covered, with dining rooms decorated in kitschy portraits that represent just about every mother archetype imaginable.

East Village: 200 E. 3rd St., at Ave. B. ℭ **212/777-4425.** www.mamasfood shop.com. Mon-Sat 11am-10:30pm. Subway: F/V to Second Ave. **Other location:** *West Village, 222 Sullivan St.,* between Bleecker St. and W. 3rd St. ℭ 212/505-8123. Mon-Thurs 11am-10:30pm; Fri-Sat 11am-midnight. Subway: A/B/C/D/E/F/V to W. 4th St.

Otafuku JAPANESE   Ideal drunk food can be found at this tiny takeout in the East Village. The dishes are hot, flavorful, filling, and slightly odd. The mainstay is *okonomiyaki,* a pizza-shaped pancake fried up with shredded cabbage, bonito flakes, and a choice of meat. At $7, it's large enough to be shared. Six pieces of plain takoyaki dumplings are $3, and *yakisoba* (fried noodles with seafood) is only $5. FINE PRINT Food here is ordered to go only.

236 E. 9th St., between Second and Third aves. ℭ **212/353-8503.** Daily 1-10pm. Subway: 6 train to Astor Place; N/R/W to 8th St.

Punjabi VEGETARIAN   East Village hipsters have discovered this taxi stand, which serves both constituencies with equal cordiality. Choose from six daily veggie entries, which are then microwaved and served over rice. Have one on a small plate for $2, or splurge for three over a big plate for $4. The food is fresh and tasty, and you can throw in a samosa appetizer for only 75¢ more.

114 E. 1st St., between First Ave. and Ave. A. ℂ 212/533-9048. Subway: F/V to Second Ave.

Caracas Arepa Bar VENEZUELAN   An *arepa* is a Venezuelan improvement on bread, with flavorful corn standing in for wheat flour. The small arepa sandwiches at this East Village shop start at $2.25 ("The Widow," with butter or sour cream), and top out at $4.75 (salmon, cream cheese, avocado, and dill). The selection is varied for such a small place and includes equally delicious *empanadas.*

91 E. 7th St., between First and Second Aves. ℂ 212/228-5062. www. caracasarepabar.com. Tues–Sat noon–11pm; Sun noon–9pm. Subway: F/V to Second Ave.

★ **Crif Dog** HOT DOGS   Night owls flock to this friendly dog house, and it's no wonder given how good the hot dogs are and how far $5 will take you. That Lincoln can be exchanged for no less than dinner and drinks: two New Yorker dogs and a can of Pabst. The smoked Crif Dog is 25¢ more ($1.75 each) than the New Yorker and even tastier. For $3.25 you get two dogs and a soda. For that same $3.25 you can splurge on a Tsunami—a bacon-wrapped, fried Crif Dog with teriyaki sauce, pineapple, and scallions. I'd lay short odds that whoever came up with that delicious combo wasn't sober.

113 St. Marks Place, between First Ave. and Ave. A. ℂ 212/614-2728. www. crifdogs.com. Daily noon–midnight, till 2am Thurs, till 4am Fri–Sat. Subway: 6 train to Astor Place.

Odessa DINER/POLISH   This East Village stalwart provides a Polish take on diner fare. Orders of pirogies and blintzes are $5.50 and under, and stuffed cabbage is $6.95. The early bird dinner special runs daily from 3 to 9pm. An entree plus potato, salad, desert, coffee, and a glass of wine is only $9.25. Breakfasts are cheap, too—I love the huge fluffy slices of challah bread.

119 Ave. A, between 7th St. and St. Marks Place. ℂ 212/253-1482. Open 24 hr. Subway: F/V to Second Ave.

Cucina di Pesce ITALIAN   Though this bustling East Village restaurant won't serve the best Italian you've ever had in your life, it does offer good values. The early-bird special gets you a three-course dinner and a glass of wine for $10.95. Pastas range from $7.95 to $10.95. The best value in the house, however, is free mussels marinara for patrons by the bar. It sure makes the wait for a table more palatable.

87 E. 4th St., between Second and Third aves. ⓒ 212/260-6800. www. cucinadipesce.com. Daily 2:30pm-midnight. Subway: F/V to Second Ave.

Two Boots PIZZA/SLICES   This is not a traditional New York slice, nor is it trying to be. Mixing elements of two boot-shaped regions (Italy and Louisiana), the pizzas here are brightly spiced. The crust is thin and crisp, cheese is minimal, and the sauce has lots of oregano. Purists scoff, but I think it's delicious. A regular slice is $2.

East Village: 42-44 Ave. A, at E. 3rd St. ⓒ 212/254-1919. www.twoboots. com. Sun-Thurs 11:30pm-1am; Fri-Sat 11:30am-2am. Subway: F/V to Second Ave. **Other location:** *West Village,* 75 Greenwich Ave., between Seventh Ave. and 11th St. ⓒ 212/633-9096. Subway: 1/9 to Christopher St.-Sheridan Sq. More locations throughout the city.

WEST VILLAGE

BB Sandwich Bar SANDWICHES   The long and short versions of the menu here come in at identical length: cheesesteak. Your Philly friends would laugh you out of the shop, but this local version hangs in successfully with its own idiosyncrasies (a Kaiser roll instead of a hoagie, and the onions are caramelized instead of fried). The flavors make a natural complement for the steak, and though the sandwich isn't huge, it's well worth $4.

120 W. 3rd St., between Macdougal and Sixth Ave. ⓒ 212/473-7500. Daily 10:30am-10pm. Subway: A/B/C/D/E/F/V to W. 4th St.

☆ **Corner Bistro** AMERICAN/BURGERS   The city's best burger waits in a dark West Village bar. You get the no-frills regular for $5, while $6 adds decadent layers of cheese, bacon, and onions. This place is a well-guarded local secret, known only to you and the 10,000 other people waiting beside you at the bar. Weekday afternoons are the least-crowded times.

331 W. 4th St. between Jane St. and Eighth Ave. ⓒ 212/242-9502. www. cornerbistro.citysearch.com. Mon-Sat 11:30am-4am; Sun noon-4am. Subway: 1/2/3/9 or A/C/E to 14th St.; L train to Eighth Ave.

Dojo HEALTH/JAPANESE   As any NYU student will tell you, the cheapest sit-down meals can be found at Dojo. The menus is Japanese inspired, but the restaurant serves a full array of healthy-ish food for almost token fees. A soy burger goes for $2.75, salads for $3.50 to $5.25, and a big plate of veggie don noodles is $5.25. Be aware, however, that this place is not exactly obsessive-compulsive about cleanliness.

West Village: 14 W. 4th St., between Broadway and Mercer St. © 212/505-8934. Mon-Thurs 11am-1am; Fri-Sat 11am-2am; Sun 11am-1am. Subway: B/D/F/V to Broadway/Lafayette; 6 to Bleecker St. **Other location:** *East Village, 24-26 St. Marks Place,* between Second and Third aves. © 212/674-9821. Subway: 6 to Astor Place; N/R/W to 8th St.

Mamoun's MIDDLE EASTERN/FALAFEL This Village classic opened in 1971 and they've been so busy serving up Middle Eastern delicacies that they haven't had the chance to revise their prices. At $2, the falafel sandwich here is one of the city's best buys. The balls are small, dense, and packed with flavor. Other veggie pitas, like the baba ghanouj, are also $2. The chicken kabob is a highlight of the $4 meat sandwiches. Several competitors have hung their shingles on the block, but Mamoun's is still the best. Seating is limited; in nice weather Washington Square Park serves as Mamoun's back garden.

119 Macdougal St., between Minetta Lane and W. 3rd St. © **212/674-8685.** Subway: A/B/C/D/E/F/V to W. 4th St.

Pop's Pierogi RUSSIAN/PIEROGI   Old Russian favorites pop up all over the reasonably priced menu here. The namesake dumplings come boiled or fried, stuffed with a range of flavorful meat, cheese, and veggie fillings. A dozen cost $5.49 to $5.99 and come with traditional sour cream and fried onion sides. Blintzes range from savory (cabbage) to sweet (cherries in syrup) and an order of three never tops $5.

190 Bleecker St., between Macdougal St. and Sixth Ave. © **212/505-0055.** www.popspierogi.com. Daily 11am-11pm. Subway: A/B/C/D/E/F/V to W. 4th St.

NOLITA & SOHO

Cubana Café CUBAN   In its quick trip to becoming New York's outdoor answer to the Mall of America, SoHo has managed to squeeze out most of its low-rent neighbors. At this quaint Cuban boutique restaurant, however, most every entree comes in under

$9. Spicy huevos rancheros are only $6 and are served all day, along with a host of other breakfast items. You get a hearty Cuban sandwich for $7.50. Strong flavors help to compensate for portions that are on the small side.

110 Thompson St., between Prince and Spring sts. ℂ 212/966-5366. Daily 11:30am–11pm. Subway: C/E to Spring St.

☆ **Lovely Day** JAPANESE/THAI   This Nolita newcomer is as hip as affordable gets. The menu features creative takes on Thai and Japanese dishes, with noodles running in the $7.50 to $8.50 range. A plate of meat and pineapple fried rice is only $6.50. The salmon dinner, served with greens and sweet potato mash, is a bargain at $9.50. The seasonings are a little on the sweet side, but the fun, bustling room quickly puts a diner in a forgiving mood.

196 Elizabeth St., between Prince and Spring sts. ℂ 212/925-3310. Daily noon–11pm. Subway: 6 to Spring St.

Mooncake PAN ASIAN   This cheerful little family-run shop serves up fresh food with Asian accents. Portions are decent for such small prices. Six dollars covers a pork chop sandwich with mango chutney, or a steak and pepper sandwich. For $2 more you can get a big salad bowl with lemon grass shrimp and Vietnamese-style vermicelli noodles.

Brooklyn Dogs

When Brooklyn's hipeoise are talking cheap and delicious comfort food, they're talking **Schnäck**. The motto puts it succinctly: "Hot dogs, cold beer—it's not complicated." The prices aren't real complicated, either; a dog with kraut and chopped onion is a mere $1.50. Special-sauce enhanced miniburgers ("Schnäckies") are 99¢ a pop, and even higher-brow entrees like the Cubano sandwich ($5.50) come in under budget. Wash it all down with a can of schwag (a rotating beer—selected for cost-effectiveness, not taste)—at $1.50 a pop it's cheaper than the subway ride to Brooklyn. 122 Union St., between Columbia and Hicks sts., Carroll Gardens, Brooklyn. ℂ 718/855-2879. www.schnackdog.com. Daily 11am–2am. Subway: F/G to Carroll St.

A SoHo Splurge

Entrees that top out at $10 and $11 push the dirt cheap enve-lope, but when you're dropping that dough on über-sophisti-cated, all-organic fine dining it doesn't feel so bad. **Ivo & Lulu** in SoHo serves French- and Caribbean-inflected food and they're not afraid to experiment. The menu changes season-ally, but gamier meats and unusual flavors can usually be found (last summer's duck leg with a spicy mango topping and wild boar sausage with blueberry sauce were both extraordi-nary). Portions are not huge, but it's all well crafted, and you can BYOB to complete the fine dining experience at a rock-bottom price. Entrees range from $9 to $11. FINE PRINT Gour-mands have discovered this place and it only has a few tables, so expect a wait during peak hours. 558 Broome St., between Sixth Ave. and Varick St. (*) **212/226-4399.** Tues–Sat 6–11pm. Subway: 1/9 to Canal St.

28 Watts St., near Sixth Ave. (*) **212/219-8888.** Mon–Sat 11am–11pm. Sub-way: A/C/E to Canal St.

Peep THAI   Peep proves that an upscale, modern decor and central location don't require exorbitant prices. Dinners are rea-sonable ($10 meat and tofu entrees, $11 for shrimp), though the real deal comes at lunch. For $7 you get an appetizer and an entree, with a large selection of Thai favorites to pick through. Presentation is as attractive as the crowd. Though the neighbor-hood's discovered this place, it's usually not so crowded here that you can't get a seat.

177 Prince St., between Sullivan and Thompson sts. (*) **212/254-PEEP.** www. peepsoho.net. Sun–Thurs 11am–midnight; Fri–Sat 11am–1am. Subway: C/E to Spring St.

☆ **Sullivan St. Bakery** SOHO   One of the best pizzas in town is the bianca at this upscale bakery. The bread is fluffy and lightly sea-soned with rosemary, olive oil, and a little salt. It's an Old Country slice—rectangular instead of triangular and lacking red sauce—and it's served at an old economy price. $1 gets you a nice big piece.

Bagel Hounds

When you're out and about in the city and need some cheap filler, the disc that makes New York is the carb to go to. New York is the only place on Earth that knows how to make a decent firm-on-the-outside, chewy-on-the-inside "real" bagel. Every moment you spend not eating one is a wasted opportunity.

☆ **Kossar's Bialys** LOWER EAST SIDE   It's no surprise that the best bagel in New York comes from the Lower East Side. Kossar's serves perfect-sized, perfect-textured bagels. The everything version is unparalleled at 65¢, although you're on your own for toppings outside of a handful of schmears in the fridge ($2 buys two bagels' worth of whipped kosher cream cheese). The bialys are made with similar dough and flavored with onions, but lack the trademark center hole; 50¢ each. Everything is baked fresh 24/6. FINE PRINT No seating available. 367 Grand St., between Essex and Norfolk sts. ✆ 212/473-4810. www.kossarsbialys.com. 24 hr., except closed Fri sunset to Sat sunset and during Jewish holidays. Subway: F train to Delancey St.; J/M/Z to Essex St.

Absolute Bagel UPPER WEST SIDE   The bagels at this Upper West Side shop are absolutely fabulous. They're a little too puffy to be traditional, but the extra air doesn't hinder the taste. For $1.85 you get a bagel loaded with cream cheese. Bagel pudding may sound horrific, but it's actually delicious, syrupy, and enhanced with raisins and cinnamon; $1.50 buys a big block of it. 2708 Broadway, between 107th and 108th sts. ✆ 212/932-2105. Daily 6am–9pm. Subway: 1/9 to 110th St.

73 Sullivan St., between Broome and Spring sts. ✆ 212/334-9435. Subway: C/E trains to Spring St. **Other location:** *Clinton, 533 W. 47th St.,* between Tenth and Eleventh aves. ✆ 212/265-5580. Subway: C/E trains to 50th St.

Viet-Nam Bánh Mì So 1 VIETNAMESE   One of New York's best sandwiches is also one of its cheapest. Vietnamese *bánh mì* layers cilantro, carrot, cucumber, and a light dressing onto a

David Bagel GRAMERCY   Hot bagels can often be found in the racks of this Gramercy bagelry. For $1.74 get a big, chewy bagel slathered with cream cheese. 228 First Ave., between 13th and 14th sts. ✆ **212/533-8766.** Subway: L train to First Ave. **Other location:** *331 First Ave.*, between 19th and 20th sts. ✆ 212/780-2308. Daily 6am–8:30pm. Subway: L train to First Ave.

Ess-A-Bagel MIDTOWN & GRAMERCY   The huge bagels here won't win any points with purists, but they make an already good deal even better. For $1.68 buy one with plenty of cream cheese. The bustling full-service shop has several tables for your savoring pleasure. 359 First Ave., at 21st St. ✆ **212/260-2252.** www.ess-a-bagel.com. Subway: 6 train to 23rd St. **Other location:** *Midtown east, 831 Third Ave.*, between 50th and 51st sts. ✆ 212/980-1010. Subway: 6 train to 51st St. Mon–Fri 6am–around 8:30; Sat–Sun 7am–5pm.

Yonah Schimmel LOWER EAST SIDE   The knish is a New York classic and can be found everywhere from delis to hot dog stands, but for the best in gut bombs you have to go to the source, the LES. Yonah Schimmel's offers up flavors traditional (potato, mushroom, kasha) and sacrilegious (pizza), cooked in a generations-old recipe. For $2, it's hard to get more filled up. The rich cheese versions are less cost-conscious ($2.50 and smaller), but equally delicious. 137 E. Houston St., between First and Second aves. ✆ **212/477-2858.** www.yonahschimmel.com. Subway: F/V to Second Ave.

crusty baguette. The meat fillings vary here, but the classic is thinly sliced pâté. My favorite combo is pate and sausage, for only $2.75. Other specialties are available in this small takeout-only deli, including a bizarre-sounding bean cake, shrimp tail, and noodle dish, that's actually delicious (and only $2.25).

369 Broome St., between Mott and Mulberry sts. ✆ **212/219-8341.** Daily 8am–9pm. Subway: 6 train to Spring St.

2 Dirt Cheap Eats Above 14th Street

CHELSEA, THE FLATIRON DISTRICT & GRAMERCY

Note: For more great cheap eating options in the Union Square area, check out p. 272 in chapter 7.

F&B HOT DOGS   Leave it to the Europeans to come up with a stylish take on fast food. Though the dishes at this Chelsea spot are a little fancied, the prices are under control. A veggie or meat dog starts at $2.50. An order of eight Swedish meatballs is $3.65. The ingredients are fresh and the food is delicious. Limited seating is available.

269 W. 23rd St., between Seventh and Eighth aves. ℰ 646/486-4441. www. fandb.geomerx.org. Daily noon-11pm. Subway: C/E or 1/9 to 23rd St.

Grand Sichuan International CHINESE   Don't be fooled by the average decor or below average prices—this place serves the best Chinese food in the city. The menu is phone book thick, but it's hard to make a bad pick here. Orange beef, string beans, and General Tso's chicken are three normal-sounding dishes that get reworked into Szechuan gems. You can splurge on more expensive items like the spectacular $14.95 smoked tea duck, but if you limit your ordering to $8.95-and-under entrees you won't be disappointed. The soup dumplings ($4.95–$5.95) are legendary. The word is out on this place, so arrive early or arrive patient.

229 Ninth Ave., at 24th St. ℰ 212/620-5200. Daily 11:30am-11pm. Subway: C/E to 23rd St. The Clinton and Chinatown locations are good, too, but not quite at the level of the Chelsea original. Other locations: *Midtown, 745 Ninth Ave.,* **between 50th and 51st sts. ℰ 212/582-2288. Subway: C/E to 50th St.;** *Chinatown, 125 Canal St.,* **at Chrystie St. ℰ 212/625-9212. Subway: B/D to Grand St.**

La Taza de Oro SPANISH   The daily specials at this Chelsea classic make it easy to get filled up for under $7.50. My favorites are *bacaloa* (stewed codfish), *ropa vieja* ("old clothes"—a stew made with shredded beef), and roast chicken, which hover in the $6.75 to $7 range and come with excellent rice and beans.

96 Eighth Ave., between 14th and 15th sts. ℰ 212/243-9946. Mon-Sat 6am-11:15pm. Subway: A/C/E to 14th St.; L train to Eighth Ave.

Lyric Diner DINER/GREEK   Greek dishes are the natural choices at this Gramercy favorite, though they do most everything well. Several sandwiches come in under $6, and a deluxe burger is $6.50. The best deal comes at lunch, when $7.50 gets you an entree plus two choices from a list that includes soup, salad, soda, and dessert. If you pick the latter, the bread pudding is highly recommended.
283 Third Ave., at 22nd St. ☎ 212/213-2222. Open 24 hr. Subway: 6 train to 23rd St.

☆ **Rainbow Falafel & Shawarma** SYRIAN/FALAFEL   Union Square's Rainbow has the best tasting falafel in the city. Marinated onions liven up the already-flavorful falafel balls. The other Syrian specialties here are just as good. It's all take-away, but Union Square's benches and tables invite picnicking.
26 E. 17th St., between Broadway and Fifth Ave. ☎ 212/691-8641. Mon–Fri 11am–6pm. Subway: L/N/Q/R/W/4/5/6 to 14th St./Union Sq.

MIDTOWN AREA

Djerdan Burek BALKAN   Burek slices haven't made much of a dent in pizza's supremacy in New York, but the Balkan treat is worth seeking out. A *burek* is flaky dough stuffed with meat, cheese, potato, or apple, and cooked up into a hubcap-sized pie. You can get a huge piece for only $4. Cafeteria-style entrees are also available for under $10 here, but the burek is the real draw.
221 W. 38th St., between Seventh and Eighth aves. ☎ 212/921-1183. Daily 7am–7pm. Subway: 1/2/3/9; A/C/E to 34th St.

Moshe's FALAFEL   Falafel at this lunch cart in Midtown West is a great deal for the money. The sandwich feels like it weighs 10 pounds, packed full with huge light-yellow falafel balls. The texture is less dense than most, but the flavor is good and meaty. It's a very filling $3.50 investment. Don't be intimidated by lunch-hour queues, as assembly-line efficiency keeps things moving fast. To picnic, go a few paces east and you'll see a plaza between 45th and 46th streets, which has tons of seats.
W. 46th St., just east of Sixth Ave. Weekdays only. Subway: B/D/F/V to 47th–50th St.

The Pump Energy Food HEALTH   A Garment District find, Pump cooks everything to order and they eschew salt, butter, frying, preservatives, and other body-unfriendly shortcuts to taste. The result of this effort is fresh and healthy food. For $5.75 you can get

EATING & DRINKING IN MIDTOWN

The Burger Joint at the Parker Meridian **23**

The Cajun **8**

Chelsea Wine Vault **9**

David Bagel **14**

Djerdan Burek **4**

Ess-A-Bagel **15, 21**

F&B Hot Dogs **7**

Grand Sichuan International **3, 6**

Gray's Papaya **5**

La Taza de Oro **10**

Langan's **20**

Lincoln Park Grill **1**

Lyric Diner **16**

Moshe's **19**

No Idea Bar **13**

The Pump Energy Food **18**

Rainbow Falafel & Shawarma **12**

Rinconcito Peruano Restaurant **2**

T.G. Whitney's **22**

Union Square Wines **11**

Woorijip **17**

a grilled lemon chicken or turkey burger stuffed in a pita. For $6 you get a delicious baked falafel salad, served over crisp lettuce, with tomato and cukes. And when you're done you won't feel all logy.

112 W. 38th St., between Sixth Ave. and Broadway. ℂ 212/764-2100. www. thepumpenergyfood.com. Subway: B/D/F/N/Q/R/V/W to 34th St.

Rinconcito Peruano Restaurant PERUVIAN This Hells Kitchen find serves authentic Peruvian cuisine. The beef and chicken dishes are $10 and under. Standouts include the tacu-tacu (rice and beans) with beef and the Chinese-style fried rice, each $9. The flavors are big, as are the portions. Local Peruvian construction workers flock for the $7 lunch special, which comes with soup, entree, and an *agua de cebada* (sweet barley juice).

803 Ninth Ave., between 53rd and 54th sts. ℂ 212/333-5685. Daily noon–9pm. Subway: C/E to 50th St.

Woorijip KOREAN Korean delis are ubiquitous in New York, but most serve up bland, mainstream cafeteria fare. To find real Korean dishes the natural destination is 32nd Street in Midtown, where a delicious by-the-pound deli is hidden among pricier Korean restaurants. Bulgogi, squid, tofu, jellyfish, Korean pancakes, and, of course, kimchi, can be found on the serve-yourself buffet line. It costs $5.49 per pound, and you can also get premade snacks and meals from $1 to $6.

12 W. 32nd St., between Broadway and Fifth Ave. ℂ 212/244-1115. Daily 24 hr. Subway: B/D/F/N/Q/R/V/W to 34th St.

UPTOWN & BEYOND

Big Nick's Burger Joint/Pizza Joint AMERICAN/BURGERS When your menu serves every dish ever thought of, you're bound to have a few items that seem a little overpriced. For the most part, though, this Upper West Side joint has great values on big portions. The options are endless—with burgers alone, there are over three dozen choices. Delicious deluxe versions start at $6.25 and go all the way to $9.50 for the heart-unfriendly eggs Benedict burger. A profusion of blue-plate lunch specials are available for $6.25, noon to 4pm Monday through Friday.

2175 Broadway, at 77th St. ℂ 212/362-9238. www.bignicksnyc.com. Open 24 hr. Subway: 1/9 to 79th St.

The Burger Joint at the Parker Meridian AMERICAN/ BURGERS One of the city's best burgers hides behind curtains inside the lobby of a fancy Midtown west hotel. The Burger Joint is as unpretentious and inexpensive as its name, and the burger is a delicious instant classic, juicy and not too greasy. Buy one for $4.50, and a side of fries for $1.50. A plastic cup of Sam Adams is $2.50 more. Though the entrance is hidden (look for the neon arrow by the check-in desk), the local businessfolk have discovered the place and it's busy at lunch.

118 W. 57th St., between Sixth and Seventh aves. ℂ **212/245-5000.** Mon-Sat 11:30am-11:30pm. Subway: N/R/Q/W or F to 57th St.

Gray's Papaya HOT DOGS   Long live the recession—as long as Gray's continues to offer two hot dogs and a drink for $2.45. The dogs are tasty, as attested by the quickly moving queues that form every day for the best lunch deal in town. Be warned, though: The dogs are a little on the greasy side, so don't be a hero and go for three. FINE PRINT Standing room only to eat here.

2090 Broadway, at 72nd St. ℂ **212/799-0243.** Daily 24 hr. (all locations). Subway: 1/2/3/9 to 72nd St. **Other locations:** *402 Sixth Ave.*, at 8th St. ℂ 212/260-3532. Subway: A/B/C/D/E/F/V to W. 4th St.; *539 Eighth Ave.*, at 37th St. ℂ 212/904-1588. Subway: A/C/E to 34th St.

Jerusalem Restaurant MIDDLE EASTERN/FALAFEL   This tiny Upper West Side shop is home to some of the best Middle Eastern cooking in the city. The falafel has a meaty texture and is subtly seasoned, $3.50 on a pita. Another impressive sandwich is the shawarma, grilled fresh for $5. The flaky layers of the homemade spinach pie ($2.50) melt in your mouth.

2715 Broadway, between 103rd and 104th sts. ℂ **212/865-2295.** Daily 10am-4am. Subway: 1/9 to 103rd St.

Saigon Grill VIETNAMESE   Saigon, in the Upper East Side, misses nothing in its pursuit of fresh, flavorful Vietnamese food. My favorites are the noodle dishes. The "bun" ranges from $6.50 to $9.50 and comes with a huge plate of lettuce, vermicelli noodles, and the meat or vegetable of your choice. Veggie entrees, including the awesome basil vegetables, are $6.95 and under. There are several lunch specials, too, in the $5.25 range.

1700 Second Ave., at 88th St. ℂ **212/996-4600.** Daily 11:30am-11:30pm. Subway: 4/5/6 to 86th St. **Other location:** *Upper West Side, 620 Amsterdam Ave.*, at 90th St. ℂ 212/875-9072. Daily 11am-midnight. Subway: 1/9 to 86th St.

Koronet PIZZA/SLICES   Extra value is what you get when you buy one of the ludicrously large slices at this Columbia U

EATING & DRINKING
UPTOWN & BEYOND

67 Wines and Spirits **9**
Absolute Bagel **1**
Beard Papa Sweets Cafe **7**
Best Cellars New York **12**
Big Nick's Burger Joint/
  Pizza Joint **6**
Brother Jimmy's **5, 10, 14**
Gray's Papaya **8**
Jerusalem Restaurant **3**
Koronet **2**
Papaya King **11**
Patsy's **15**
Saigon Grill **4, 13**

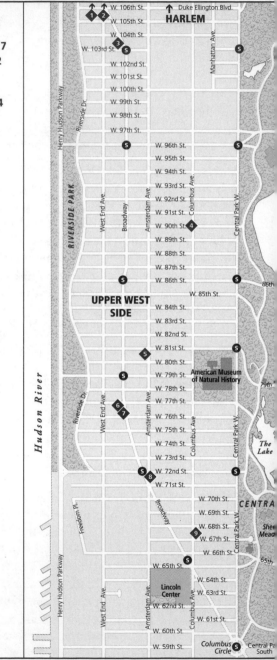

E. 106th St.
E. 105th St.
E. 104th St.
E. 103rd St.
E. 102nd St.
E. 101st St.
E. 100th St.
E. 99th St.
E. 98th St.
E. 97th St.
E. 96th St.
E. 95th St.
E. 94th St.
E. 93rd St.
E. 92nd St.
E. 91st St.
E. 90th St.
E. 89th St.
E. 88th St.
E. 87th St.
E. 86th St.
E. 85th St.
E. 84th St.
E. 83rd St.
E. 82nd St.
E. 81st St.
E. 80th St.
E. 79th St.
E. 78th St.
E. 77th St.
E. 76th St.
E. 75th St.
E. 74th St.
E. 73rd St.
E. 72nd St.
E. 71st St.
E. 70th St.
E. 69th St.
E. 68th St.
E. 67th St.
E. 66th St.
E. 65th St.
E. 64th St.
E. 63rd St.
E. 62nd St.
E. 61st St.
E. 60th St.
E. 59th St.

Mount Sinai Hospital

MUSEUM MILE

Fifth Ave.
Madison Ave.
Park Ave.
Lexington Ave.
Third Ave.
Second Ave.
First Ave.
York Ave.
East End Ave.

The Reservoir

Transverse

Metropolitan Museum of Art

UPPER EAST SIDE

Central Park Zoo

Wollman Rink

Central Park South

CARL SCHURZ PARK

FDR Dr.

Ward's Island Footbridge

WARD'S ISLAND PARK
WARD'S ISLAND

Upper Manhattan

Uptown

Midtown

Downtown

East River

ROOSEVELT ISLAND

From Lower Level
To Upper Level

Sutton Pl.

Roosevelt Island Tram

Queensboro Bridge

0   1/4 mi
0   0.25 km

127

Sweet Indulgences

Beard Papa Sweets Cafe UPPER WEST SIDE   Cream puffs are the specialty at this Asian import, where the treats are as appetizing as the name is not. Crisp choux pastries hold a cream and custard filling. Everything is fresh-baked, and despite a sprinkling of powdered sugar, the treats aren't overly sweet. Daily specials like green tea or caramel cost $1.45 per puff, and the regular is only $1.25. 2167 Broadway, between 76th and 77th sts. ⓒ 212/799-3770. Daily 8am-6pm. Subway: 1/9 to 79th St.

Dragon Land Bakery CHINATOWN   My favorite sweet cheap stops are in Chinatown. Bakeries litter the landscape here, all of them offering up fresh goods at ridiculous prices. The differences between any two shops are pretty subtle, but Dragon Land does a particularly good job. In addition to baked goods, the mango and green tea flavored puddings are delicious. Prices range from 75¢ to $4. 125 Walker St., between Centre and Baxter sts. ⓒ 212/219-2012. Daily 7:30am-8pm. Subway: J/M/N/Q/R/W/Z/6 to Canal St.

favorite. For $2.75 you get enough pizza to feed a small village ($2 buys a conventional slice). The pizza is decent, though it becomes absolutely perfect in the wee hours, as the legions of college students will attest.

2848 Broadway, at 111th. ⓒ 212/222-1566. Daily 9am-2am. Subway: 1/9 to 110th St.

★ **Patsy's** PIZZA/SLICES   In the 70-plus years that the coal oven has been burning at this Harlem gem, the surrounding neighborhood has lost much of its Italian identity. It's not exactly gentrified and it's a haul to get here, but that's the effort required to get the best slice in the city. You get a regular slice for $1.50, and it will give you an idea of why this place was Sinatra's favorite, too. Inside the restaurant, murky lighting, threadbare furnishings, and a staff that welcomes customers as if they've just whacked Patsy's favorite nephew make the takeout window the more pleasant option.

2287 First Ave., between 117th and 118th sts. ⓒ 212/534-9783. Daily 11:30am-11:30pm. Subway: 6 train to 116th St.

Papaya King HOT DOGS   The self-anointed Papaya King has some 75 years experience in the frankfurter field, going back to when this part of Uptown was a German neighborhood. Gray's has the lead in both taste and price, but the King isn't too far behind. A pair of dogs with kraut and a big tropical drink is only $3.99. An all-beef spicy smoked sausage with obligatory grilled peppers and onions will only set you back $1.99. FINE PRINT Standing room only to eat here.

179 E. 86th St., corner of Third Ave. © 212/369-0648. www.papayaking.com. Sun–Thurs 8am–1am; Fri–Sat 8am–3am. Subway: 4/5/6 to 86th St. **Other location:** *Harlem, 121 West 125th St.,* between Lenox Ave. and Adam Clayton Powell Blvd. © 212/665-5732. Mon–Sat 11am–9pm. Subway: 2/3 to 125th St.

3 Into the Drink

FREE WINE TASTINGS

The intricacies of wine are endless and odds are the wine experts at your corner store aren't embarrassed to show off a little. The experience can be frustrating because you're only getting little sips, but if you've come for edification and not to catch a cheap buzz, there's little chance of going away disappointed. Besides, many shops throw in some free snacks for your trouble.

Best Cellars New York FREE UPPER EAST SIDE   Tastings can be found 6 days a week at this classy wine shop. Weeknights from 5 to 8pm find wine samples following a weekly theme. On Saturday afternoons from 2 to 4pm, the wine often comes with a free snack provided by a visiting local chef.

1291 Lexington Ave., at 87th St. © 212/426-4200. www.bestcellars.com. Subway: 4/5/6 to 86th St.

Chambers Wines FREE TRIBECA   The tastings at this wine shop are informal and friendly. Free bread and cheese help the wines go down. Check the website for tastings, often scheduled on Saturday afternoons.

160 Chambers St., between W. Broadway and Greenwich. © 212/227-1434. Subway: 1/2/3/9 to Chambers St.

Chelsea Wine Vault FREE CHELSEA   This wine store in the Chelsea Market has a great, if a little pricey, selection. Wine tastings are held a couple of nights a week. Some of the tastings include free food and are pretty elaborate affairs, so check the website and see if an RSVP is required.

75 Ninth Ave., near 15th St. ℭ 212/462-4244. www.chelseawinevault.com. Subway: A/C/E to 14th St.; L train to Eighth Ave.

67 Wines and Spirits `FREE` UPPER WEST SIDE   Rotating hosts walk guests through wine tastings at this shop, usually highlighting the fruits of a particular country or region. Tastings usually are Thursday through Saturday; check the website for a calendar.

179 Columbus Ave., between 67th and 68th sts. ℭ 212/724-6767. www. 67wine.com. Subway: 1/9 to 66th St.

Union Square Wines `FREE` UNION SQUARE   Tastings can be found several days a week at this friendly shop. The neighborhood is now lousy with great chefs, and sometimes food demonstrations (with free tastes) are held here as well.

33 Union Sq. West, between 16th and 17th sts. ℭ 212/675-8100. www.union squarewines.com. Subway: L/N/Q/R/W/4/5/6 to 14th St./Union Sq.

DIRT CHEAP DRINKS

When Mayor Mike banned smoking inside bars and restaurants, he initiated a brand-new street scene. Now cheap New Yorkers can mix and mingle without even having to buy a drink, simply by hanging around with the smokers in front of the hot spots. If you venture indoors, you'll find a lot of bars responding to an iffy economy with happy hours. Two for ones or $1 off specials are ubiquitous now. Even sweeter deals can be found, too, some even involving free buffet spreads.

When You Want to BYOB

My favorite place to actually buy a bottle of wine is **Warehouse Wines & Spirits,** on Broadway near NYU. The staff is friendly and well informed, the selection is extensive, *and* it's got the cheapest prices around. Among the many great values are some very drinkable $5 wines. Everything else is heavily discounted. 735 Broadway, between Waverly Place and 8th St. ℭ 212/982-7700. Mon-Thurs 9am-9pm; Fri-Sat 9am-10pm. Subway: 6 to Astor Place or N/R/W to 8th St.

Acme Bar & Grill NOHO   This joint is as decent a facsimile of a Louisiana roadhouse as we're going to get in NYC. The bar area in the back serves appetizers at cut rates from 4 to 7pm every day. Southern favorites from corn fritters to catfish fingers go for $2.25 to $4.50. Drink specials vary by night. Hump day is Ladies Night, two for one for the fairer gender. Mondays feature $4 margaritas and Thursdays $4 Hurricanes. Tuesdays get the best deal, $2 for an Acme Brew. Happy hour is daily 4 to 7pm.

9 Great Jones St., between Broadway and Lafayette sts. ℰ 212/420-1934. Mon–Thurs 11:30am–11:30pm; Fri–Sat 11:30am–12:30am; Sun noon–11pm. Subway: B/D/F/V to Broadway/Lafayette; 6 train to Bleecker St.

Bar None EAST VILLAGE   For the longest happy hour in the city the choice is, without exception, Bar None. You have to wait until noon for it to begin, but once it does you get $2 Bud pints and $3 for wells and other drafts. The specials run until 8pm and then pause until 11pm, when the Power Hour begins. Until midnight, you can knock back $2 Bud pints and $2 well drinks. The environs are a little on the divey side, but it's perfectly amiable, and the prices can't be beat.

98 Third Ave., between 12th and 13th sts. ℰ 212/777-6663. Daily noon–4am. Subway: L train to Third Ave.

Brother Jimmy's UPPER EAST & WEST SIDES   Nostalgic frat boys find fellow travelers at these Uptown BBQ joints. The prices are almost college-town low, including a couple of all-you-can-eat and all-you-can-drink nights every week. Wednesday nights celebrate the low end of southern cuisine, with all-you-can-eat southern delicacies for $9.95 and $1 PBRs. Southerners (as proven by a valid ID) can take an additional 25% off. Saturday from noon to 5pm, wings are just a quarter and pitchers are $6. Future sorority presidents and rush chairs (ages 12 and under) eat free off the children's menu.

Upper East Side: 1485 Second Ave., between 77th and 78th sts. ℰ 212/288-0999. www.brotherjimmys.com. Mon 5pm–4am; Tues–Sun noon–4am. Subway: 6 to 77th St. **Other locations:** *West Side, 1644 Third Ave.,* at 92nd St. ℰ 212/426-2020. Subway: 6 to 96th St.; *428 Amsterdam Ave.,* between 80th and 81st sts. ℰ 212/501-7515. Subway: 1/9 to 79th St.; B/C to 81st St.

B-Side EAST VILLAGE   This amiable dive keeps to the glam-punk side of things. The bar is no frills, saving you money during happy hour. Regular prices get slashed in half, making Bud and Rheingold bottles a mere $1.50. Daily from 3 to 8pm.

204 Ave. B, between 12th and 13th sts. ℂ 212/475-4600. Daily 3pm-4am.
Subway: L train to First Ave.

Croxley Ales EAST VILLAGE   This neighborhood newcomer is
less trendier-than-thou than most of its neighbors. In keeping with
that spirit, Croxley puts games on the televisions and offers specials at the bar. If you're drinking, you're entitled to 20¢ wings on
Sundays. That price goes down to 10¢ on Mondays and Wednesdays. Fridays the wings are free. Weekday happy hours run from
5 to 7pm, with $1 off of most everything.

28 Ave. B, between 2nd and 3rd sts. www.croxley.com. ℂ 212/253-6140.
Sun-Thurs 5pm-1am; Fri-Sat noon-2am. Subway: F/V to Second Ave.

Gowanus Yacht Club CARROLL GARDENS   This Brooklyn bar
saves money by not bothering to rent a roof. The garden space is
inhabited by local hipsters, who don't interfere with the small-fish-
ing-town vibe. Beer specials vary, but usually you can find a mug or
can of something for a buck, if not a $2 can of Pabst. Like any good
seaside resort, this one is only open between May and October.

323 Smith St., at President St. ℂ 718/246-1321. Mon-Thurs 4pm-midnight;
Fri 4pm-2am; Sat 2pm-2am; Sun 2pm-midnight. Subway: F/G to Carroll St.

Lincoln Park Grill HELL'S KITCHEN   It's not often that you can
slap down a dollar in a New York bar and get anything in return.
This Westside tavern obliges, however, with $1 drafts every
Wednesday night from 8pm to midnight. Admittedly these are
mini-drafts (8.5 oz.), but hey, a buck's a buck.

867 Ninth Ave., between 56th and 57th sts. ℂ 212/974-2826. Daily
11:30am-4am. Subway: A/B/C/D/E/1/9 to 59th St./Columbus Circle.

Magnetic Field BROOKLYN HEIGHTS AREA   This BoCoCa
(that's Brooklyn Heights/Cobble Hill/Carroll Gardens, at least to
the local real estate brokers) hang attracts with its low-key neighborhoody feel. Fourteen beers can be found on tap, and during
happy hour they're only $3 each. Well drinks are only $3. Happy
hour runs daily from 3 to 8pm, except for Tuesdays, where it
stretches all the way to closing time (4am). Live music, DJs, and
a reading series provide accompanying entertainment.

97 Atlantic Ave., between Hicks and Henry sts. ℂ 718/834-0069. www.
magneticbrooklyn.com. Daily 3pm-4am. Subway: M/R to Court St.; 2/3/4/5
to Borough Hall.

INTO THE DRINK   133

FREE What's in a Name?: Free Drinks
_____

If you're one of those people who has a name, you can drink for
zero dollars and zero cents at bars **No Idea** and **Antarctica.**
There is one small catch: Your name has to synch up with the
name of the night. Each bar posts a different monthly list, and
although there are some oddball monikers, there are also plenty
of occasions to hang out with fellow Meghan, Josh, and Jessi-
cas. Open tab Name Night runs 5 to 11pm (8pm to 1am at Antarctica on Saturdays) every night but Sunday. Check the websites,
www.noideabar.com and www.antarcticabar.com to see when
you're up. FINE PRINT They're not running a charity; the idea is to
drag along some friends and let them run up the tab while you
hobnob with a roomful of fellow Vartans for free. *No Idea:* 30 E.
20th St. between Park and Broadway. ✆ **212/777-0100.** Subway: 6 or N/R/W to 23rd St. *Antarctica:* 287 Hudson, at Spring
St., ✆ **212/352-1666.** Subway: C/E to Spring St.

The Slide NOHO   Longtime kitsch fave Marion's has branched
out with this next-door gay bar. This basement lounge has a
slightly upscale vibe, but happy hour prices couldn't be much
more downscale. From 6pm to 9pm beers are $2 and well drinks
only $3. Not cheap enough for you? From 5 to 6pm take an addi-
tional $2 off the price of beers and $3 off the well drinks. That's
right, everything's free for the whole hour.
356 Bowery, between Great Jones and 4th sts. ✆ **212-475-7621.** Daily
5pm–4am. Subway: F/V to Broadway/Lafayette; 6 train to Bleecker St.

Village Idiot MEAT-PACKING DISTRICT   It doesn't take a
genius to move a lot of booze when you've got gregarious bar-
tenders and ridiculously cheap beer. Get a pitcher of beer for $5
and a can of PBR for $2. With prices like that, who needs happy
hour? And who needs sponges, disinfectant, or the occasional
mopping? Savoring isn't exactly the vibe here anyway.
355 W. 14th St., between Eighth and Ninth aves. ✆ **212/989-7334.** Mon–Sat
11:30am–4am; Sun noon–4am. Subway: A/C/E to 14th St.; L to Eighth Ave.

New Yorkers focus their energy before punching the time clock by taking a free morning tai chi class at Bryant Park. See p. 141 for details.

LIVING 4

nybody who thinks it's easy to live in New York is sitting on an ungodly mountain of cash. You don't have to look any further than the housing market to find trouble. For the privilege of paying $1,500 a month to live in a noisy veal pen, chances are you'll get hit with a 15% broker's fee. Health care, health insurance, health clubs—just about everything can come with an outrageous price tag. And yet eight million of us stay. The experience of being a New Yorker is too exciting and rich for us to complain long or loudly about the costs of living. We'd much rather talk about which neighborhood our apartment is in. Besides, the city presents plenty of free and dirt cheap opportunities to improve your quality of life, from classes and lectures to grooming and recreation. Leases notwithstanding, it is quite possible to live large on small budgets in NYC.

1 Sense for Cents: Education

LECTURES & SEMINARS

Just walking the streets and riding the subways is all too often a learning experience in New York, but most of us have room for further development along less informal lines. A handful of classes and a nearly endless selection of lectures provide New Yorkers with edification opportunities left and right. Cooper Union looks the other way when it comes to tuition, and although other local institutions aren't quite so generous, most have programs open to the public for little or no charge.

Columbia University FREE   New York's lone envoy to the Ivy League has an impressive events calendar, with talks and colloquiums supplementing literary readings and musical performances. Topics range from esoteric science ("Vitrification and Depletion Phenomena in Soft Colloidal Systems") to less dry material ("The Place of Ozu Within Japanese Film History"). You can also catch free drama department readings of MFA playwrights' thesis projects (see "Theater with Class," on p. 66). Venues vary, although Lerner Hall is a popular location, 2922 Broadway, at 115th St.

2690 Broadway, between 102nd and 103rd sts. ✆ 212/854-9724. www. columbia.edu. Subway: 1/9 to 116th St.

☆ **Cooper Union** FREE   Self-made entrepreneur and inventor Peter Cooper founded the Cooper Union for the Advancement of Science and Art in 1857 to allow underprivileged talents to receive free educations. The college's mission hasn't changed, and 1,000 students currently attend without tuition. Admission is based solely on merit, and competition is, as you'd expect, fierce. The public can take advantage of the institution in other ways, however. The Saturday Outreach Program helps high school students further themselves in the arts with free classes (even the materials fee is waived). Student exhibitions can be seen in free galleries, and frequent free lectures are held in the Great Hall. These lectures routinely have inventive, and intriguing subjects and the big public room makes a great setting. Check online for an events calendar.

On Cooper Sq., 8th St., between Bowery and Third Ave. © 212/353-4120. www.cooper.edu/month. Subway: 6 to Astor Place; N/R/W to 8th St.

Downtown Boathouse FREE   Every Wednesday night in summer, the boathouse offers kayaking classes free to the public. The classes are held on land, but you can put your new knowledge to work by coming back and borrowing a kayak (see "Watersports," on p. 162). Classes start at 6pm. Kids can take advantage of free sailing classes. The course is for kids 11 to 13 and lasts an hour or two a week for 7 weeks.

Pier 26, between Canal and Chambers sts. © 646/613-0375. www. downtownboathouse.org. Subway: 1/2/3/9 or A/C trains to Chambers St.

Eglise Français du St-Esprit FREE   The French Church of St. Esprit, an Episcopal congregation, performs its services in French. Before services, they offer a series of French classes, one for conversation and a second one for beginners. The classes are free, at 10am every Sunday. Services start at 11:15am.

100 E. 60th St., between Madison and Park aves. © 212/838-5680. www.st espiritnyc.net. Subway: 4/5/6 or N/R/W to 59th St.; F to 63rd St.

☆ **The Graduate Center at the City University of New York** FREE   Continuing ed lectures, seminars, and panel discussions can be found here, with more possibilities for finding cheap smarts than any other institution in the city. You want range? Titles run from "Jewish Ethics Under Pressure" to "Unzipping the Monster Dick: Deconstructing Ableist Penile Representations in Two Ethnic Homoerotic Magazines." There is a $10 registration fee per season, although not every program requires registration, and the fee is waived for your first attendance of each season. Call to register, or go in person to Suite 8204 during normal business hours.

365 Fifth Ave., between 34th and 35th sts. © 212/817-8215. www.gc.cuny. edu/daro. Subway: B/D/F/N/Q/R/V/W to 34th St.; 6 train to 33rd St.

The Henry George School FREE   Although Henry George is no longer a household name, in the 19th century his economics texts and lectures made him a major political player. His progressive ideas are still taught today, and in keeping with George's antiprivilege stance, the school that bears his name offers all of its programs for free. Classes are available in English or Spanish, usually in the evenings. Teachings are based on George's championing of shifting

FREE Learning English As
a Second Language

If you've read this far, you probably don't need English lessons. Should there be a newly minted American in your circle of acquaintance, however, you can steer them to a couple of great city resources.

The **Riverside Language Program** assimilates people quickly through their intensive 6-week program. Open to permanent residents, classes run from 9:30am to 3:30pm, for levels from beginner to high intermediate. 490 Riverside Dr., at 120th St. and Riverside (enter at 91 Claremont Ave.). ℂ **212/662-3200.** Subway: 1/9 to 116th St.

For evening-only classes (and for people without permanent resident status), the **New York Public Library** has an extensive English program. Classes are conducted at 20 different branch libraries, and also include civics lessons for prospective citizens. Check www.nypl.org/branches for schedules, or call ℂ **212/340-0918.**

tax burdens to landowners. *Note:* Finishing the school's Fundamental Economics course is the prerequisite for most upper-level work.

121 E. 30th St., between Park and Lexington aves. ℂ **212/889-8020.** www. henrygeorgeschool.org. Subway: 6 to 28th St.

New York Society for Ethical Culture   For over a century and a quarter now, this organization has been providing New Yorkers with humanist alternatives to organized religion. A liberal outlook is usually presented in the free lectures that are held here, as well as at the regular talks on Sunday mornings. A $4 film series, with discussions, comes around every third Friday. Log on to the website for schedules.

2 W. 64th St., at Central Park West. ℂ **212/874-5210.** www.nysec.org. Subway: 1/9/A/B/C/D/E to 59th St./Columbus Circle.

The New School University **FREE**   Though no longer so new (at press time, it had already celebrated its 85th birthday), the New

School stays pretty up-to-date, and there's still a progressive edge to its programs. The calendar of free events is cluttered with readings, lectures, panel discussions, student films, and even investing seminars available to the public. Check online for a full calendar.

66 W. 12th St., between Fifth and Sixth aves. ✆ 212/229-5600. www.new school.edu. Subway: F/V to 14th St.; L/N/Q/R/W/4/5/6 to 14th St./Union Sq.

New York University FREE The streets around Washington Square Park are dominated by NYU architecture and NYU students, but the community has opportunities to take advantage of this private university's immense resources. Lecture programs (the history of the Village, say), talks, and symposia can be found for free here. Other events carry nominal admission charges, in the $2 to $5 range. The new Kimmel Center is a good place to start to find free culture.

Kimmel Center, 60 Washington Sq. South, between LaGuardia Place and Thompson St. ✆ 212/998-4900. www.nyu.edu. Subway: A/B/C/D/E/F/V to W. 4th St.

Park Slope Food Co-op FREE This Brooklyn cooperative keeps its community informed with lectures, demonstrations, and even a few film screenings. Don't expect to see Newt Gingrich on the roster anytime soon: Topics here are left-leaning, concerning food, the environment, and timely advice about how not to be killed by eating beef. Everything is free, even to non-co-op members, although sometimes a small materials fee is added to food classes. Check online for the latest schedule. Classes and lectures are held on the second floor meeting room unless otherwise noted.

782 Union St., between Sixth and Seventh aves., Park Slope, Brooklyn. ✆ 718/622-0560. www.foodcoop.com. Subway: M/R to Union St.; 2/3 to Grand Army Plaza; B/Q to Seventh Ave.

Poets House This poetry library keeps a terrific collection of crafted words. For spoken word, poets often read here and lectures can be found as well. Some events have admission charges (usually around $7), but free events turn up frequently. Check the online calendar for details.

72 Spring St., between Lafayette and Crosby sts. ✆ 212/431-7920. www. poetshouse.org. Subway: N/R/W to Prince St.; 6 to Spring.

New York Public Library FREE It would be easier to list the classes not available for free at New York's public libraries than to mention all of the possibilities. Practical courses predominate, covering topics like writing, crafts, resume updating, job searches, using the Internet, and the ins and outs of genealogical research. You can also attend a self-directed class on how to take maximum advantage of library resources. The best way to get started is to get online and check out the options at your local branch.

For the Bronx, Manhattan, and Staten Island branches, log on to www.nypl.org/branch, or call ✆ **212/930-0800.** For the Queens Borough Public Library, check www.queenslibrary.org, or call ✆ 718/990-0700. In Brooklyn, log on to www.brooklynpublic library.org, or you can call ✆ 718/230-2100.

The library puts on great readings and lectures, too. One series particularly worth checking out is the **NYPL fellows talks.** Scholars supported by the library speak on their subjects of interest. The lectures are free, but call in advance to reserve a seat (✆ 212/930-0084). Humanities and Social Sciences Library, Fifth Ave., at 42nd St. Subway: B/D/F/V to 42nd St.; 7 to Fifth Ave.

Every branch of the New York Public Library offers computers with free Internet, access to electronic databases, and Microsoft Office applications. Many branches also have computers loaded with multimedia CD-ROMs. You can spend free days working on SimCity or Resume Maker, depending on your level of job market optimism.

Teachers and Writers Collaborative `FREE` Literary readings and lectures fill the calendar at this long-running nonprofit. For

`FREE` Getting Down to Business

The **Brooklyn Business Library** fosters the local small business scene with classes and workshops of an entrepreneurial bent. Everything from start-ups to small investing is covered by talks, and backed up with an excellent book collection. On Wednesday mornings from 10:15 to 11am you can get a free tour of the resources available. 280 Cadman Plaza, between Tech Place and Tillary St. ✆ **718/623-7000.** www.biz.brooklyn publiclibrary.org. Mon, Wed, Fri 10am–6pm; Tues 1–8pm; Thurs 1–6pm; Sat 10am–5pm. Subway: 2/3/4/5 to Borough Hall; M/R to Court St.; A/C/F to Jay St./Borough Hall.

high school students, there's also an excellent after-school program dedicated to the spoken word (www.urbanwordnyc.org). Check the website for upcoming events.

5 Union Sq. West, 7th floor, between 14th and 15th sts. ℂ 212/691-6590. www.twc.org. Subway: L/N/Q/R/W/4/5/6 to 14th St./Union Sq.

YOGA & TAI CHI
New York offers several free and dirt cheap classes in tai chi and yoga. Tai chi has been slow to gather momentum as a trend, but yoga already seems poised to be the aerobics of the naughts. It's a good idea to wear comfortable clothing for either type of class, and bring a mat or towel for yoga in the parks.

Battery Park City FREE   From 8:30 to 9:30am every Thursday in summer you can get a master's guidance in tai chi at Battery Park's Esplanade Plaza. Another class is taught in Rockefeller Park Thursday nights from 4 to 5pm. Battery Park also hosts drawing classes through the year. Some have models (clothed), and others focus on rendering the river and gardens. Teaching artists are on hand to facilitate your creative expression. Check the website for times and locations.

Battery Park City, along South End Ave., just west of West St. ℂ 212/267-9700. www.bpcparks.org. Subway: 1/2/3/9 or A/C to Chambers St.; 1/9 to Rector St. or South Ferry; 4/5 to Bowling Green.

Bryant Park FREE   Bryant Park loans its central location to a host of activities, most notably a Thursday morning tai chi class. The class is taught from 7:30 to 8:30am, May to October, so you can focus your energy before punching the clock.

Bryant Park; gather at the fountain, near 41st St. and Sixth Ave. ℂ 212/786-4242. www.bryantpark.org or www.chutaichi.com. Subway: B/D/F/V to 42nd St.; 7 to Fifth Ave.

Om Yoga   Om Yoga provides an introduction to yoga for beginners for only $5. This drop-in class explains the basics of alignment, breathing, and stretching. The class lasts about 90 minutes and is held on select weekends, usually from 2 to 3:30pm.

826 Broadway, between 12th and 13th sts., 6th floor. ℂ 212/254-YOGA. www.omyoga.com. Subway: L/N/Q/R/W/4/5/6 to Union Sq.

Riverside Park South FREE   Unwind after work in Riverside Park, where hatha yoga for beginners is taught every Wednesday from 6:30 to 7:30pm. The class usually meets during summer months; check the website for a schedule.

Riverside Park, near the Overlook, 66th St. at the Hudson. ✆ 212/408-0219. www.riversideparkfund.org. Subway: 1/9 to 66th St.

Sivananda Yoga Vedanta Center FREE   Once a month this yoga center introduces the community to their practice via an open house. The afternoon begins a little after noon with a lecture and demonstration, followed by classes, a break for vegetarian soup, and a meditation introduction. Held usually on a Saturday early in the month.

243 W. 24th St., between Seventh and Eighth aves. ✆ 212/255-4560. www.sivananda.org. Subway: C/E or 1/9 to 23rd St.

6B Garden FREE   This community garden is best known for its tall rustic tower, made of wooden planks and discarded design elements (i.e., junk). The garden is a beautiful pocket of green on the Lower East Side, and it opens its gates to the public for a handful of events. Every Monday morning from 7 to 8am, you can take advantage of a free yoga class. Meditation, slide shows, and poetry readings are also part of the schedule. The garden is also open for greenery appreciation on the weekends from 1 to 6pm, April through October.

Corner of E. 6th St. and Ave. B. www.6bgarden.org. Subway: F/V to Second Ave.

Socrates Sculpture Park FREE   Situated along the East River with Manhattan views, this park is a lovely setting for classes. Sessions run from late May to late August. Kilipalu yoga is taught Saturdays from 11am to noon, open to all levels. On Sundays from 11am to noon, tai chi is taught, also suitable for all levels. Kids get a chance to make some art during Saturday sculpture workshops, from noon to 3pm.

32-01 Vernon Blvd., at Broadway, Long Island City, Queens. ✆ 718/956-1819. www.socratessculpturepark.org. Daily 10am-sunset. Subway: N/W to Broadway. Walk 8 blocks along Broadway toward the East River.

2 Health Sans Wealth

Sadly, far too many New Yorkers get by on a "just don't get sick" health plan. As many as one-fourth of us are uninsured, and medical fees aren't getting any cheaper. Thank goodness, then, for the

sliding scale. Several good-hearted community-minded organizations provide care at rates commensurate with an individual's
income. If your income is low enough, you may also be eligible
for subsidized insurance with an HMO. A good website to check
out is that of the **Actors' Fund of America** (www.actorsfund.org).
The fund has comprehensive listings for actors and artists who
don't have the kinds of day jobs that throw in insurance and
health care. Dentists, shrinks, and acupuncturists can also be
tracked down for bodies on budgets.

HEALTH INSURANCE
Folks with cushy jobs can expect to see insurance on their laundry list of benefits. With more and more arts and media freelancers in the marketplace, however, it's easy to find oneself on
the wrong side of the feudal walls. The **Freelancers Union and
Working Today** (www.workingtoday.org; ℭ **718/222-1099**) have
combined to garner some of the bulk-rate buying power of a corporation. Insurance rates aren't exactly dirt cheap, however, with
monthly premiums at $286.88. Also, the program is for artists and
media types, leaving out our chef and waitress friends. **Healthy
New York** is New York state's program for lower income residents
who earn too much for Medicaid. If you work and make less than
$23,275 a year (individual) or $31,225 (couple), you may be able
to take advantage of this plan. The premiums are almost civilized,
ranging from $141 to $182, depending on which HMO you sign
up with. Log on to www.healthyny.com or call ℭ **866/HealthyNY**
for more info.

HEALTH CLINICS
New York's clinics tend to target specific constituencies. Though
they may specialize in helping the indigent, or the HIV-positive,
the clinics make it a policy not to discriminate against anyone.
Even if you're uninsured, you can get some attention in places
other than the city's emergency rooms.

Callen-Lorde Community Health Center   This primary care
center caters to the LGBT (lesbian, gay, bisexual, transgender) community, but makes a point to be open to all. The general medicine
and health and wellness programs are charged on a sliding scale.
356 W. 18th St., between Eighth and Ninth aves. ℭ **212/271-7200.** www.
callen-lorde.org. Subway: A/C/E to 14th St. or L to Eighth Ave.; 1/9 to 18th St.

David Ores, M.D. Many a Lower East Sider, including your humble correspondent, is grateful to general practitioner Dr. Dave for his attentive care and humane prices. Dr. Dave's tiny clinic serves the neighborhood with a nod to the uninsured. Prices have creeped up a little in recent years, but the scale still slides, and Dr. Dave always treats his patients fairly. Call first for an appointment.

15 Clinton St., between E. Houston and Stanton sts. ⓒ **646/435-0009.** www.davidjoresmd.com. Mon–Fri 1–6pm. Subway: F to Delancey; J/M/Z to Essex St.

Gay Men's Health Crisis Dedicated to slowing the spread of HIV and to helping out those already affected, this great organization offers a host of services for the HIV-positive community. Health care is provided on a sliding scale basis, and there are also workshops, seminars, and even free legal services offered. The well-known GMHC Hotline is open for calls Monday through Friday from 10am to 9pm, and Saturdays from noon until 3pm.

The Tisch Building, 119 W. 24th St., between Sixth and Seventh aves. ⓒ **800-AIDSNYC.** www.gmhc.org. For other information, the main office line is ⓒ 212/367-1000.

New York City Department of Health and Mental Hygiene `FREE` The city operates a dozen clinics in all five boroughs that offer free testing and treatment for STDs and HIV. They also follow up with no-cost counseling.

Chelsea location: 303 Ninth Ave., at 28th St. ⓒ 311 for hot line, or 212/427-5120. www.nyc.gov/html/doh/html/std/std2.html. Mon–Fri 8:30am–4:30pm; Sat 9am–2pm. Subway: C/E to 23rd St. Check the website for other locations throughout the city.

New York City Free Clinic `FREE` NYU med students work with a professional at this Saturday morning clinic, where the homeless and the uninsured can get consultations, physicals, and other medical help. Advance appointments are required.

Inside the Sidney Hillman Clinic, 16 E. 16th St., between Union Sq. West and Fifth Ave. ⓒ 212/263-1001. http://endeavor.med.nyu.edu/freeclinic. Sat 9am–noon. Subway: L/N/Q/R/W/4/5/6 to 14th St./Union Sq.

Planned Parenthood Free pregnancy tests are among the many reproductive-oriented services handled by this organization. Brooklyn, the Bronx, and Manhattan each have a clinic that can help out. Other services, including HIV counseling and assistance with STDs, have reasonable fees. Call the main number, ℂ **212/ 965-7000,** to schedule an appointment in any one of the clinics.

Margaret Sanger Center: 26 Bleecker St., at Mott St. www.ppnyc.org. Mon-Tues 8am-4:30pm; Wed-Fri 8am-6:30pm; Sat 7:30am-4:30pm. Subway: 6 to Bleecker; B/D/F/V to Broadway-Lafayette. *Borough Hall Center:* 44 Court St., between Remsen and Joralemon sts. Tues and Fri 8am-5:30pm; Wed 8am-4:30pm; Thurs 8am-6:30pm; Sat 8am-4pm. Subway: 2/3/4/5 to Borough Hall; M/R to Court St.; A/C/F to Jay St./Borough Hall. *Bronx Center:* 349 E. 149th St. at Courtlandt Ave. Tues-Wed, Fri 8am-4:30pm; Thurs 8am-5:30pm; Sat 8am-4pm. Subway: 4 to 149th Ave.; 2/5 to Third Ave.-149th St.

Ryan Center   The three associated Ryan clinics (on the Upper West Side, the Lower East Side, and in Midtown) provide a huge range of services, from HIV counseling to general medicine to mental health. Prices are set on a sliding scale.

William F. Ryan Community Health Center: Clinic at 110 W. 97th St., between Columbus and Amsterdam aves. ℂ **212/749-1820.** www.ryancenter.org. Mon-Thurs 9am-7pm; Fri 9am-5pm. Subway: 1/2/3/9 or B/C to 96th St. *HIV and Mental Health Services:* 160 W. 100th St., between Columbus and Amsterdam aves. ℂ 212/316-8367. Mon-Thurs 9am-7pm; Fri 9am-5pm. Subway: 1/2/3/9 or B/C to 96th St. *Ryan-NENA Community Health Center:* 279 E. 3rd St. between aves. C and D. ℂ 212/477-8500. Mon-Thurs 9am-7pm; Fri 9am-5pm; Sat 9:30am-1pm. Subway: F/V train to Second Ave. *Ryan Chelsea-Clinton Community Health Center:* 645 Tenth Ave., between 45th and 46th sts. ℂ 212/265-4500. Mon-Tues, Thurs 8:30am-7pm; Wed 8:30am-5pm; Fri 8:30am-4:30pm. Subway: C/E to 50th St.

DIRT CHEAP SHRINKS

National Psychological Association for Psychoanalysis With a mind to lowering the barriers to psychological treatment, this organization runs a referral service for affordable psychoanalysis and psychotherapy. Potential analysands whose income levels qualify are sent to the Theodore Reik Clinical Center for Psychotherapy. You can get up to three sessions per week for as low as $10 a session. Higher income folks get sent to the Psychological Referral Service, where the fees begin at $40 a session. There's a $30 intake fee, but that's still a small price to pay for sanity.

Clinic: 150 W. 13th St., between Sixth and Seventh aves. ℂ **212/924-7440.** www.npap.org. Subway: F/V or 1/2/3/9 to 14th St.

ACUPUNCTURE

Pacific College of Oriental Medicine Clinic and Acupuncture Center Chinese medicine is gathering momentum in New York. More and more people are seeking out Chinese herbs and medicine as an alternative to the escalating costs of Western medicine. This teaching clinic provides relatively inexpensive services, though the best bargains are for going under an intern's needles. A session costs $30, but the fourth one is free.

915 Broadway, between 20th and 21st sts., 3rd floor. ℭ 212/982-4600. www.pacificcollege.edu. Mon–Sat 9am–9pm. Subway: N/R to 23rd St.

DENTAL

New York University College of Dentistry NYU runs the largest dental college in the country, and if you want discounts on dental care, the students here are the people to see. An initial appointment is under $100 and covers a checkup, X-rays, and oral cancer screenings.

345 E. 24th St., at First Ave., Clinic 1A. ℭ 212/998-9872. www.nyu.edu/dental. Mon–Thurs 8am–6:30pm; Fri 8am–3pm. Subway: 6 to 23rd St.

3 In the Housing

What would New Yorkers have to talk about if we weren't complaining about our living arrangements? Or for a lucky few of us who have a reason to brag: "I, for example, pay $275 a month for my rent-stabilized four bedroom with views of the East River, Cairo, and Paris." Even in a market supposedly deflated since the dot.com bust, NYC rental rates and housing prices remain firmly in the realm of the absurd. The lucky few who find digs below market value quickly learn the meaning of the phrase "relative bargain." For those not easily discouraged, however, a couple of resources can help a home-seeker get ahead.

NO-FEE RENTALS

Broker's fees, the 10% to 15% surcharge slapped on by the Realtor who tours you around a series of spaces that are too small *and* more than you can afford, are the painful cost of renting in NYC. You can beat the system by contacting real estate firms directly, through their classifieds in the *Voice* and *Times,* and through their websites. It takes some legwork, but if your need for housing isn't urgent, it's the way to go. If you know a specific building you're interested in, try to talk to the super. They'll know what units might be available soon (a little greasing of the wheels doesn't hurt in that department). Another option is **www.apartmentsource.com**. This website is a clearinghouse that lists no-fee apartments (and Realtors often use it to pad their own lists, though their clients will pay for the knowledge with that hefty broker's fee). The database is easily searchable and you can sample it for free, but if you want to get contact information for a building owner you'll have to pay. You get 1 day's access for $7.95, 45 days for $64.95, and $79.95 covers 3 months. Though not dirt cheap, the rates are cheaper than the competition, and the apartment listings are fairly comprehensive.

MIXED INCOME DIGS

In an effort to keep neighborhoods from becoming entirely monolithic, the city offers tax breaks to developers who are willing to set aside a certain number of units for middle- and low-income residents. As with everything else in life, the key is persistence. Waiting lists can be long and your lottery odds can be slim, but every time you make the effort to apply you tilt the playing field in your favor.

Mitchell-Lama Housing Companies   This program has been around since 1955, offering housing to New Yorkers with lower-end incomes. You can choose from 132 city-sponsored buildings and 94 state-sponsored. Rents are highly subsidized, but the application process is cumbersome and not every building has an open waiting list. To get a pdf file (readable with Adobe Acrobat) listing buildings with open lists, log on to www.nyc.gov/html/hpd/for-apartment-seekers/Mitchell-lama.html. Each building has to be applied for individually. For general information, call ✆ **212/863-6500** for city units, or 212/480-7343 for state units.

New York City Housing Development Corporation   The city promotes several mixed-income new developments in the five boroughs. The **80/20 program** is fairly common. Twenty percent of a building is rented at discount rates to people who earn significantly less than the neighborhood's median income. You have to apply directly to the developer and the process takes awhile, but if you get in you'll score a great deal. In many cases, you can move up in income brackets without jeopardizing your

A Room of One's Own: Artists' Resources

Artist Colonies FREE   Artists seeking a break from the more merciless elements of urban life can take advantage of rural escapes, several of which offer free stays. The most famous and prestigious of the colonies is MacDowell, in Petersborough, New Hampshire. Amazing names have been through the colony, and can still be found there today. It costs $20 to apply for a session and competition is fierce, but if you get through, room and board are covered for up to 8 weeks. Writers, visual artists, filmmakers, composers, and architects all interact during the sessions. www.macdowellcolony.org. ℂ **603/924-3886.** For information on other colonies as well as artist grant programs (free money), the New York Foundation for the Arts is a good place to start. Check the website, www.nyfa.org.

Brooklyn Writers Space   Work space in New York doesn't come much cheaper than living space, but for $75 a month you can have a partitioned desk in Park Slope. The people here are all seeking the same thing: a quiet place to write. Your $75 also gets you a locker, a shared dictionary, and access to the roof deck. Wage slaves can write for even cheaper. For $45 you get part-time access to the room, after 6pm and all weekend long (when the space is nearly empty). A free readings series has already been spawned by writers here—can an anthology be far behind? FINE PRINT There's no waiting list, but a 3 month commitment is required. 58 Garfield Place, between Fourth and Fifth aves. ℂ **718/788-2697.** www.brooklynwriters.com. Subway: M/R to Union.

cheap rent (or cheap purchase). Note that the buildings involved are usually in developing neighborhoods, not in the city's trendiest zip codes. Log on to www.nychdc.org/apartments/developments. htm for a full list of HDC-financed sites, or call ℂ **212/227-5500.**

Partnership for New York City   This business group develops subsidized housing for sale to New York families making less than

$75,000 a year. (You can still buy if you're over that threshold, but you won't get the subsidy.) The **New Homes/Neighborhood Builders** project, like the NYCHDC, builds in lower income neighborhoods, often in outer reaches of the outer boroughs. Right now the pickings are pretty slim, but check the website for future apartment availability, www.nycp.org/nhnb.htm, or call ✆ **212/493-7420.**

DIRT CHEAP SLEEPS
HOSTELS

Have friends coming to town and looking for a place to spend the night? Why not send them over to the Pierre, where a premier suite is a mere $1,390 nightly. If they're on a budget, you can put them in the Plaza, $1,069 for 1 suite night. New York is the city that never sleeps affordably—even the Super 8 starts at $89. Savvy travelers (or halves of quarrelling couples who aren't on the lease) can spend the night for $30 or less, however, if they're not hostile to hostel life.

☆ **Big Apple Hostel**   With clean rooms and a primo Midtown location, this is the city's best choice for dirt cheap sleeps. Bunk beds sleep four people per room. A kitchen, a backyard with barbecue, and air-conditioning round out the amenities. Dorm guests should bring their own towels, however.

119 W. 45th St., between Sixth and Seventh aves. ✆ 212/302-2603. www. bigapplehostel.com. 112 dorm beds. $28.16 per night, except $30.16 Aug-Sept and $38.28 per night late Dec before New Year's Eve. Subway: 1/2/3/7/9/N/Q/R/W trains to Times Sq./42nd St.

Chelsea International Hostel   You can't do much better location-wise than these rooms clustered around a courtyard right in the heart of Chelsea. International travelers love this well-managed place. Your $27 includes taxes, lounge areas, self-service laundry, and free luggage storage. Bring your own towel.

251 W. 20th St., between Seventh and Eighth aves. ✆ 212/647-0010. www. chelseahostel.com. 288 dorm beds. $27 per night. Subway: 1/9 trains to 18th St.

Whitehouse Hotel of New York   Not so long ago, a night on the Bowery didn't sound like a very glamorous prospect. With nearby trendy bars and restaurants popping up like postrain mushrooms, however, this youth-oriented reimagined flophouse is now right at party central. Spaces are tiny and bathrooms are shared, but you won't do much better in NYC than $27.25 for a private room. Towels and A/C are included.

340 Bowery, between Second Ave. and Great Jones St. ℭ **212/477-5623.** www.whitehousehotelofny.com. 468 beds. $27.25 per night. Subway: F/V trains to Second Ave.; 6 train to Bleecker St.

Chelsea Center Hostel   This small hostel on two floors of a Chelsea brownstone provides a laid-back alternative to its bustling competitors. A pleasant garden and friendly continental breakfast add to the charms. Accommodations are bunk beds in clean, bright rooms. If you'd rather stay in the East Village, you can request a dorm bed in the center's other location upon booking.

313 W. 29th St., just west of Eighth Ave. ℭ **212/643-0214.** www.chelsea centerhostel.com. 20 dorm beds in each location. $30 per night, includes continental breakfast and tax. Subway: C/E trains to 23rd St. **Other location:** *East Village, E. 12th St.,* at First Ave. (Exact address available upon arrival.) Subway: L to First Ave.

WOMEN'S RESIDENCES

Members of the fairer sex can also take advantage of the cheap accommodations offered by women's residences. These throwbacks to a more genteel era generally don't allow gentleman callers above the parlor levels, nor do they permit boozing (some residences even have curfews). However, rates are lower than New York equivalents, and for newcomers to the city it's a great way to make friends.

Centro Maria   Operated by the Religious Sisters of Mary Immaculate, this Midtown West residence accepts women ages 18 to 27 for both short- and long-terms stays. Rooms are simple singles, doubles, and triples, and some come with private bathrooms. Night owls won't be happy with the curfew (11:30pm on weekdays, midnight on weekends), but what you lack in basic freedom you make up for in money saved; prices include two meals a day on weekdays, and one meal on Saturday. FINE PRINT Residents supply their own bed linens and towels. There's an $80 non-refundable registration fee, and applications must be accompanied by two letters of recommendation and a photograph. Try to apply 1 month in advance.

539 W. 54th St., between Tenth and Eleventh aves. ℭ **212/757-6989.** Daily rate: $45 single, with shared bathroom; $40 per person double. Weekly rate

(minimum stay 4 weeks): $150 single with shared bathroom; $135 per person double. **Facilities:** Shared bath; maid service; laundry; limited kitchen; TV room; recreational room; chapel. Subway: C/E to 50th St.; A/B/C/D/1/9 to 59th St.–Columbus Circle.

El Carmelo Residence   This small residence, located on the border of the West Village and Chelsea, offers its prime location to single women between the ages of 18 and 35. Established and operated by the Carmelite Sisters Teresas of St. Joseph, the residence's dormitory-style rooms each house two residents. You can expect the rules to be tight and the bathrooms to be shared, but rates include breakfast and supper Monday through Friday. As a bonus, residents have access to the property's garden and rec room. FINE PRINT You must apply in person, but call at least 2 months in advance of your stay.

249 W. 14th St., between Seventh and Eighth aves. ✆ 212/242-8224. Daily rate (1–20 days): $60 per person double. Weekly rate (1–13 weeks): $160 per person double; $120 per person double for stays over 13 weeks. **Facilities:** Shared bathroom; garden, recreational room, laundry. Subway: A/C/E to 14th St.

Markle Evangeline Residence   Built by the Salvation Army in 1930, the Markle has been providing women with a viable alternative to the New York housing mire for 75 years. The rules are predictably strict—no alcohol, no smoking, no men under 55 inside—and the rooms will never be described as spacious, but for about $240 a week, a resident gets her own fully furnished bedroom with private bathroom, and two squares a day, 5 days a week. Access to a TV room, computer labs, a rooftop garden, and organized social activities help justify the somewhat higher rates. *Note:* More communal souls can save cash by opting for shared doubles, triples, and quads, all of which charge lower rates. FINE PRINT Summer student residents under 16 must have a female parent or guardian reside with them. Non-student residents must be 18 or older. Two references, an application, and a security deposit equal to 1 month's rent are required for long-term stays.

123 W. 13th St., between Sixth and Seventh aves. ✆ 212/242-2400. Long-term monthly (minimum 31 days): $1,057–$1,074 single (seniors $999); $749–$866 double; $723 triple; $654 quad. Short-term nightly: $85 single. **Facilities:** Private bathroom, in-room telephone, 24-hr. security, maid service (once a week), laundry, roof garden, computer lab, TV lounge. Subway: 1/9 to Christopher-Sheridan Sq.

4 Beauty & Massage

HAIR TODAY

NYC's hirsute astute take advantage of salon training sessions. Both students and pros need live heads to demonstrate on, and in exchange for your modeling they'll provide all kinds of services for little or no money. Though there's no guarantee you'll get an expert cut, a lot of salon students in New York have the scissor skills to eclipse the masters. In addition to cuts, coloring services are sometimes available. Some salons want to look you over first (it helps if you've got a surplus of hair begging for a snipping), but generally it's pretty easy to get your grooming on the house.

Note: Many salons need models, but not all like to advertise it. If you've got your eye on a prohibitively expensive spot, give them a call and see if they can use you.

SALON STYLINGS

Arté Salon `FREE`   This lovely Nolita salon uses both men and women as hair models. Cuts are free, usually scheduled on Mondays. Hair coloring costs $25, to cover the materials. Call first to set up an appointment.

294 Elizabeth St., between E. Houston and Bleecker. ℰ 212/941-5932. Subway: 6 to Bleecker St.; B/D/F/V to Broadway/Lafayette St.

Aveda Institute New York   The popular environmentally conscious spa Aveda offers up its many services at deep discounts if you go through the students at the institute. Haircuts, coloring, blowouts, perms, facials, and waxing are all available. The prices aren't dirt cheap, but they are relative bargains compared to the rest of the neighborhood. You can get work done for free by acting as a model during the Advanced Academy classes. Call for schedules. `FINE PRINT` You must be at least 18 years old.

233 Spring St., between Sixth Ave. and Varick St. ℰ 212/807-1492. www. aveda.com. Subway: C/E to Spring St.

☆ **Bumble and bumble.University** `FREE`   The old-school butchers would never have believed it, but the Meat-Packing District is rapidly becoming style central in Manhattan. The slick new Bumble and bumble salon is right in the thick of it, but you can partake of the services for no money down. Their stylist training program offers model calls every Monday from 5:30 to 6:30pm.

You can register in advance or just walk in, where a screener will try and match you with a seminar. The appointments last between 1½ and 2 hours, and you'll have to wait between 1 and 4 weeks. Once you're in the program, however, you can stay tapped into the gravy train. Men can ask for a free cut every 8 weeks and women every 10 without going through the screening process. You must be willing to get more than a trim, though they'll consult with you first to figure out what works. Tips aren't even necessary. **415 W. 13th St., 6th floor, between Ninth Ave. and Washington St. ₡ 866/7-BUMBLE. www.bumbleandbumble.com. Subway: A/C/E or L to Eighth Ave./14th St.**

Charles Worthington London `FREE`   This Brit hairdresser keeps Yank heads trim in SoHo. Call to set up an appointment to model for a free haircut. They also offer color services for $10. **568 Broadway, Suite 101, at Prince St. ₡ 212/941-9696. www.cwlondon. com. Subway: N/R/W to Prince St.; 6 to Spring St.**

Clairol Product Evaluation Salon `FREE`   Become a product testing guinea pig here and you'll receive free Clairol hair coloring from a professional stylist. The first step is to get an appointment for a half-hour interview. Appointments are available Monday through Thursday from 9:30 to 11am and again from 1:30 to 4pm. I recommend calling ahead to schedule. If you're accepted, you can come back once a month—some people have been taking advantage for years. Only the stylist will know for sure. FINE PRINT Both men and women are accepted, but you have to be at least 18. **345 Park Ave., lobby level, between 51st and 52nd sts. ₡ 646/885-4200. Subway: 6 to 51st St.; E/V to Lexington–3rd Ave.**

Face Station `FREE`   This casual second floor salon holds training sessions throughout the year. Both cuts and coloring are covered here, for men and women. Call to see what their model needs are. **855 Lexington Ave., 2nd floor, between 64th and 65th sts. ₡ 877/815-FACE. www.facestation.com. Subway: F to Lexington Ave./63rd St.; 6 to 68th St.**

Matrix Technical Salon `FREE`   L'Oreal coloring and styling products are tested here, and if you make it through an interview, you can join in the experiment. Appointments are scheduled Monday through Thursday from 8 to 11am and 1 to 3pm. Women

Dirt Cheap Cuts

Barber colleges offer cut-rate cuts. The level of experience varies, however, from student to student, so I don't recommend going for anything too tricky.

American Barber Institute   Haircuts are only $3.99 here. Cuts are available Monday through Friday, and for men only on Saturday. 252 W. 29th St., between Seventh and Eighth aves. ✆ **212/290-2289.** Subway: 1/9 to 28th St.

Atlas Barber School   Both men's and women's stylings are only $5 at the Third Avenue location. At 10th Street they're even cheaper—$4 for both men and women. *34 Third Ave., between 9th and 10th sts.* ✆ **212/475-1360.** *80 E. 10th St., between Third and Fourth aves.* ✆ 212/475-5699. Subway: 6 to Astor Place; N/R/W to 8th St.

You can get cheap cuts from pros, too. The cuts will run you a bit more, but you can rest a little easier knowing the scissors are in experienced hands.

Chung Wah Barber Shop   This Chinatown cheap-chop shop offers $7 men's and $8 women's cuts. Note that those with straight hair may get the most reliable results. 19 Pell St., between Doyers and Mott sts. ✆ **212/267-4849.** Subway: J/M/N/R/Q/W/Z/6 to Canal St.

Lee Lee Beauty and Hair Salon   A regular cut is only $12, and you can augment for not much more at this Chinatown salon. The shampoo, style, and cut package is only $15. 12 Pell St., between the Bowery and Doyers St. ✆ **212/528-1381.** Subway: J/M/N/R/Q/W/Z/6 to Canal St.

Astor Place   The sprawling three-floor setup here has been consolidated to just a single basement, but you can still find a dizzying array of barbers and hairstylists. Cuts are professional, and more stylish than you might expect for $12. (Astor Place has had charge of my locks for years, and I look like a million bucks.) 2 Astor Place, between Broadway and Lafayette St. ✆ **212/475-9854.** Subway: N/R/W to 8th St.; 6 to Astor Place.

should have middle-length hair, and men are used for some studies. If you're accepted, you'll get a free coloring and follow-up visits if the study requires them. You can also sign up for the Consumer Expressions Research Center, where you can test L'Oreal from home. Participants get free gift bags of products at the end of the trial, although the test products have to be returned lest they fall into enemy hands. You'll also score a guest pass to shop at the L'Oreal company store, where beauty products (including the ever-popular Kiehl's) are offered at a big discount.

575 Fifth Ave., 3rd floor, at 47th St. © 212/984-4926. Subway: E/V to 5th Ave./53rd St.

MAKEUP

Just about any counter in a department store will dispense advice and a free sample or two. Some of them will even work up a quick makeover. If you're looking for more elaborate cosmetic giveaways, check out these smaller-scale operations.

IL-Makiage FREE   Volunteer for a workshop here and a student will give you a free makeover while practicing the techniques of the day. When you're all prettied up, you'll also walk away with a $25 credit for IL-Makiage products. Call first to sign up.

107 E. 60th St., Suite 2, between Madison and Park aves. © 800/722-1011. www.il-makiage.com. Subway: N/R/W or 4/5/6 to Lexington Ave./59th St.; F to Lexington Ave./63rd St.

Shiseido Studio FREE   You won't find a single cash register in this space—everything is free. You have to take a course to get at the Shiseido cosmetics samples, but the courses are free and you can come as often as you like. Check the online calendar for schedules. Once each calendar year you can also treat yourself to a free private makeup session. Sessions last an hour. Also once a year you can have your choice of a 45-minute customized facial or a 45-minute facial massage. These giveaways are understandably popular, so schedule as early as you can. If you have an appointment, show up on time, otherwise you'll have to reschedule.

155 Spring St., between Wooster St. and West Broadway. © 877/99-STUDIO. www.shiseidostudio.com. Subway: C/E to Spring St.

INSTANT MASSAGING

Massages are yet another bargain that can be found in New York's cheap alternative universe of Chinatown. There are a bunch of places that will work out your kinks, and a few of them can combine it with acupuncture, acupressure, and herbal medicine. One place I like is **Wu Lim Services,** which will knead away your cares for 10 minutes for $7. Each additional 10 minutes is another $7. 145 Grand St., between Crosby and Lafayette. ✆ **212/925-1276.** Daily 9am–11pm. Subway: J/M/N/R/Q/W/Z/6 to Canal St.

REIKI
Loving Touch Center–International School of Traditional Reiki FREE   Reiki is a form of healing (and massage) that works with transmitted energy. A light touch is all that's needed, and you don't even have to put on a robe. Skeptics can be converted during free healing circles at this school on Monday evenings, from 7:30 to 9:30pm.
172 Madison Ave., Suite 306, between 33rd and 34th sts. ✆ 800/LTCenter. www.reiki-ltc.org. Subway: 6 to 33rd St.

5 Recreation in the City

BIKE GANGS
Biking makes a virtue of New York's hard paved surfaces, turning our miles of roadway into recreational opportunities. One of the best ways to take advantage is by banding up with fellow riders. If you're not yet of the wheeled class, consider checking out **Recycle-A-Bicycle.** This nonprofit sells refurbished rides at low prices from two retail locations (see p. 189 in chapter 5).

Time's Up FREE   This environmental group sponsors several well-organized rides. The most well known is **Critical Mass,** held on the last Friday of every month and taking place simultaneously in over 300 cities worldwide. The ride is designed to raise consciousness about environmental alternatives and biker rights. It's fun for sidewalk spectators, too, who can watch every kind of bike and bike-rider pedal past to a chorus of perversely gratifying taxi horns. The route varies, but the meeting place is always the same, 7pm at Union Square Park North. Time's Up also hosts rides along tri-state rural routes, but the best trip to the country comes on the first Friday of the month. The **Central Park Moonlight Ride** shows off the water and trees and general tranquillity of the park at night. With guides riding point and taking up the rear, it's a safe and leisurely pedal. Rollerbladers with at least

FREE NYC's All Skate

The **Dead Road in Central Park** is one of my favorite spots in the city for a workout (well, an eyeball workout to be completely accurate). Watching dozens of expert roller skaters and bladers dancing and spinning to a jamming disco beat is a hypnotic sight. Some of the regulars have been rolling together for 2 decades and the skill level is very high, but if you're halfway competent you shouldn't feel intimidated. The scene is friendly and inclusive, so strap on some wheels and jump in. Even for non-skaters, this event is a highlight of the park. The DJs are great, especially now that the city has relented on its anti-beat campaign. (In 1995, music was temporarily banned from the park so skaters wore Walkmen all tuned to the same radio channel, creating a surreal silent choreography.) The outdoor roller disco is in session on Saturdays and Sundays in warm weather. The Dead Road is in the middle of the park, between 66th and 69th streets, just a little southwest of the Bethesda Fountain.

If skating in a boogielicious roller inferno is a little daunting to you, find safety in numbers with **Wednesday Night Skate** (www.weskateny.org), New York's biggest skating event, which wheels away from Union Square Park every Wednesday night. The routes vary from week to week, but generally you'll get to see a few miles' worth of NYC, say up Park Avenue, into Central Park, and back on over to Times Square. The event usually lasts 2 hours. The flock meets at the north end of Union Square Park between 7:30 and 8pm. FINE PRINT Helmets and wrist guards are required before you to turn yourself into a vehicle.

intermediate skills are welcome, too. The ride meets at 10pm at the southwest corner of Central Park, across from Columbus Circle. The trip is around 10 miles, and runs all 12 months of the year. Time's Up also helps sponsor **Bike New York** (see below).

☏ 212/802-8222. www.times-up.org.

Bike New York: The Great Five Boro Bike Tour FREE   The biggest event of its kind in the U.S., this mass ride brings 30,000 bipedal pedalists to NYC. Riders get to tour the city along 42 car-free miles in all five boroughs. Held the first or second Sunday in May, the tour begins in Manhattan usually along Church Street near Battery Park. On-site registration starts bright and early at 6:30am and runs until 7:45am. The event culminates with a party at Ford Wadsworth in Gateway National Recreation Area on Staten Island. Postparty, a fleet is on hand to ferry tired legs and bikes back to Manhattan. You can sign up by phone or online.

Bike New York Office: 891 Amsterdam Ave., between 103rd and 104th sts. ℂ 212/932-BIKE. www.bikenewyork.org.

Fast and Fabulous Cycling Club   Whether you're a fast rider or a fabulous rider, or both, this LGBT biking group will welcome you. Membership starts at $20 per year, but it'll get you invites to a series of rides around the city and out of town (say, a day trip to DIA Beacon). Intermediate cyclists are the target group. Meals and socializing often follow the rides.

ℂ 212/567-7160. www.fastnfab.org.

GYM NEIGHBORS

When hauling groceries and laundry up to your sixth-floor walk-up is no longer exercise regimen enough, it's time to hit a gym. The cheapest choice by far is signing up with the department of parks and recreation, though other options that don't much exceed $1 a day are available.

☆ **Department of Parks and Recreation**   On top of playing fields and courts, the city also runs 36 recreation centers. The amenity list is long and varied, including indoor and outdoor tracks, weight rooms, dance studios, and boxing rings. All of this can be yours for only $50 a year. If you want to join a center with a pool, it's an additional $25. (For seniors age 55 and over, it's only $10 a year with or without pools, and for under-18s it's all free.) Many centers also offer classes in Pilates, aerobics, karate, kickboxing, wrestling, swimming, and the like. Some centers even have personal trainers. Usually an extra fee applies for classes, say $5 for an hour of yoga instruction. The scene varies from rec center to rec center, but generally they're family friendly and community oriented. You won't find classic meat markets in most of these city-run facilities.

ℂ 212/360-8222. www.nycgovparks.org.

OTOM Gym Physical Culture   In addition to the Y, Green-point residents can take advantage of this large, affordable gym. Monday, Wednesday, and Friday mornings feature classes in kick-boxing, aerobics, and strength training. Classes are $5 for members and $10 for everyone else. A year's membership is $389. Night owls can take advantage of a late-night special, $269 per year for limited nighttime access Monday through Thursday and normal hours on the weekends.

169 Calyer St., between Lorimer St. and Manhattan Ave., Greenpoint, Brooklyn. ✆ 718/383-2800. www.otomgym.com. Subway: L to Bedford Ave. Open 24 hr., except closed from Fri midnight to Sat 7am and Sat midnight to Sun 7am.

24-7 Fitness Club   These round-the-clock clubs are a little rough around the edges, but they're hard to beat on both cost and convenience. There's a ton of machines, and they tend not to be overly crowded. The Chelsea gym (47 W. 14th St., between Fifth and Sixth aves.; F/V to 14th St., L/N/Q/R/W/4/5/6 to 14th St./Union Sq.; ✆ 212/206-1504) is $25 per month plus a $99 initiation fee if you commit for a full year. If you pay in full up front it's even cheaper, $352 for the year. To go month to month it's $30 initiation and $50 per month. The TriBeCa location (107 Chambers St., between West Broadway and Church St.; 1/2/3/9 or A/C to Chambers St.; ✆ 212/267-7949) is even cheaper. The $25 per month year's commitment only has a $28 initiation fee. Paying in full up front is $228 for a year, and for $287 you get three sessions with a personal trainer. You can go month to month for $50 per, with no initiation fee.

YMCA of Greater New York   The Y (✆ 212/630-9600; www.ymcanyc.org) runs 17 health and wellness centers in the city. The facilities vary from site to site, but the general roster includes gyms, pools, racquetball and handball courts, aerobics studios, exercise machines, steam rooms, and saunas. To have access to all locations is pretty steep, $993 per year plus a $125 initiation fee. It's cheaper if you only sign up for access to one location. Fees vary. The state-of-the-art facility is the new McBurney location (125 W. 14th St., between Sixth and Seventh aves.; F/V or L to 6th Ave./14th St., or 1/2/3/9 train to 14th St.; ✆ 212/741-9210). A 1-year membership is $912, plus the $125 initiation fee. To get fit at a less central location is a much better deal—the Greenpoint YMCA (99 Meserole Ave., between Leonard St. and

Manhattan Ave.; G to Nassau Ave. or Greenpoint Ave.; ✆ 718/ 389-3700) is only $462 for a year, with a $75 initiation fee.

POOLING RESOURCES

It costs $75 a year to use the city's indoor and outdoor pools (see "Gym Neighbors," above), but if you're a frequent crawler, the price turns out to be pretty reasonable. The indoor pools stay open year-round (unless they're superseded by an on-site outdoor pool), but the tubs under the sun synch up with the school year. Late June to Labor Day is the usual season, and you will find many, many kids taking advantage. In addition to the city pools (www.nycgovparks.org), the state runs an Olympic-size natatorium in Manhattan. Local favorites include:

Asser Levy An indoor and outdoor pool make this a great year-round swimming destination.

E. 23rd St. and Asser Levy Place, near the FDR Dr. ✆ 212/447-2020. Pool Mon-Fri 7am-9pm; Sat 8am-4:45pm; Sun 9am-4:45am. Subway: 6 train to 23rd St.

Carmine Recreation Center Another pool with indoor and outdoor bases covered, this rec center is a West Village fave.

1 Clarkson St., between Seventh Ave. South and Hudson St. ✆ 212/242-5228. Pool Mon-Fri 7am-10pm; Sat-Sun 9am-5pm. Subway: A/B/C/D/E/F/V to W. 4th St.

Hamilton Fish Despite its enormous size, this Lower East Side outdoor pool fills up quickly. Kids from the neighborhood splash while parents relax in the large adjoining plaza.

128 Pitt St., between E. Houston and Stanton sts. ✆ 212/387-7687. Pool Mon-Fri 7am-8:30pm; Sat 11am-7pm; and Sun 11am-7pm. Subway: F to Delancey; J/M/Z to Essex St.

Metropolitan Pool Williamsburg is kept buoyant at the indoor Met Pool, which still gleams from a recent multimillion-dollar renovation.

261 Bedford Ave., at Metropolitan Ave. ✆ 718/599-5707. Pool Mon-Fri 7am-9:30pm; Sat 7am-5:30pm. Subway: L to Bedford Ave.

Riverbank State Park This 28-acre park on the Hudson ably disguises its foundation, which is a wastewater treatment plant. The indoor pool here is run by the state, which charges $2 per visit.

679 Riverside Dr., at 145th St. ✆ 212/694-3665. www.nyspark.com. Pool Mon-Fri 6:30am-8:15pm; Sat 9am-3pm; 3:30-6pm. Subway: 1/9 to 145th St.

FREE Gotham's High-Tech Refuge

The **Three Jewels Refuge and Free Internet Cafe** ☆ community center is constructed on an East Village scale (tiny), but its selection of services is huge. Many events have a Buddhist angle. You can free your mind for free during morning meditations. The meditations last about an hour, starting at 7am Monday through Friday, and at 10am on Saturdays. In the back of the cafe you can find a free lending library with dharma-related texts and audio books, and in the front are computers offering free high-speed Internet access. You can also use the computers for free digital video editing. Workshops are scattered through the month, including Sunday programs for free software downloading and installation. Friday nights are home to a film series, from 8 to 10pm, where well-known movies of a spiritual bent like *Seven Years In Tibet* and *Groundhog Day* play for free. Saturday night from 8 to 10pm brings "Jazz at The Jewels," a no-cover, no-minimum music night. 211 E. 5th St., between Second and Third aves. ✆ **212/475-6650.** www. threejewels.org. Subway: 6 to Astor Place; N/R/W to 8th St.

OM MY GOODNESS: MEDITATION

In a town so loud it can be hard to hear one's own thoughts, the contrast of a quiet meditation space can be startling. Though just about any house of worship in the city will suffice, sometimes it's nice to get a little guidance for inner journeying.

Change Your Mind Day FREE   One extraordinary June day, the Buddhist magazine *Tricycle* sponsors a series of lectures and demonstrations. Music, chanting, and guided meditation are also part of the scene. I find this day totally inspiring. The speakers are fascinating and the crowd is responsive. If any 1-day experience in NYC can make a person more aware, this is the day. (At worst, you'll leave slightly relaxed and better informed.) The event, usually held the first Saturday of June, runs 12:30 to 5:30pm. If you're planning on watching a lot, a cushion or a blanket is probably a good idea.

The Great Hill in Central Park, 106th St. at midpark. ✆ **800/950-7008.** www.tricycle.com. Subway: 6 or B/C to 103rd St.

Shambhala   This Tibetan Buddhist group hosts open meditations in its two lovely meditation rooms. Beginners can learn more at the weekly introductory sessions, every Tuesday at 7pm. Suggested admission is $5 for half an hour of group meditation, followed by a talk.

118 W. 22nd St., 6th floor, between Sixth and Seventh aves. ℂ 212/675-6544. www.ny.shambhala.org. Subway: 1/9 or F/V to 23rd St.

Zen Center of New York City   Discover what one hand clapping sounds like at this Zen center in Brooklyn. Contributions are requested to participate in the meditation sessions (generally $3–$5), which are held almost every day. If you're new to zazen, you can attend an introductory session on a Sunday morning. Sessions start at 10am and last around 3 hours. Admission is by a suggested contribution of $7.

500 State St., between Nevins and Third Ave., Boerum Hill, Brooklyn. ℂ 718/875-8229. www.mro.org/firelotus. Subway: 2/3/4/5/B/Q to Atlantic Ave.; 4/5 to Nevins; D/M/N/R to Pacific; A/C/G to Hoyt-Schermerhorn.

WATERSPORTS

New York's waterways were once great recreational resources, but years of environmental laxity made much of the local liquid too toxic to touch. A handful of burgeoning groups are trying to speed along the rivers' rebounds with giveaways along the shore. The East River, Hudson, and Gowanus are all covered for seaworthy (or at least sea-curious) New Yorkers.

☆ **Downtown Boathouse** `FREE` If you know how to swim, you're eligible for free Hudson paddling. Out of the goodness of their hearts (and a desire to promote the Hudson as a recreational outlet), this group loans out kayaks and equipment all summer long. The trips are limited to 20 minutes in protected areas near three piers, but if you show up a few times and get into shape, you'll be eligible for a long paddle from Pier 26 into New York Harbor. This spectacular field trip lasts 3 hours, with unbelievable views all the way. Potential paddlers gather by 8am and wait to have names picked from a hat. On a nice day you've got about a 50-50 chance of going, though you can increase your odds by arriving on a day with cloud cover. The long trip season runs mid-June to mid-September. Pier 26 is open from 9am to 6pm on weekends and holidays, with kayaks available on select weeknights from mid-June until the end of August (call ℂ **646/613-0740** to check the daily status. In really lousy weather the kayaks stay docked). The Hudson is cleaner than it's been for decades, so getting splashed here and there no longer has any negative health consequences. *Note:* The boathouse's season runs from mid-May to mid-October.

Pier 26, between Canal and Chambers sts. ℂ **646/613-0375** for information. www.downtownboathouse.org. Subway: 1/2/3/9 or A/C trains to Chambers St. Pier 66a, at 26th St. 10am-5pm on weekends and holidays. Subway: C/E to 23rd St. 72nd St. at the Hudson. 10am-5pm weekends and holidays. Subway: 1/2/3/9 trains to 72nd St.

The Gowanus Dredgers Canoe Club `FREE` The Gowanus Canal is in a transitional phase between being the butt of jokes and serving as a genteel Brooklyn natural resource. A canoe trip here still leans toward the former, providing a surreal float through what is mostly a forgotten industrial wasteland. Equipment is loaned out for free on select weekends and holidays. Guided tours that run down to the Gowanus Bay are available by appointment. The season lasts from late March through the end of October. Pick up is near 2nd Street and Bond Street in Brooklyn, but check the calendar for availability details first. For landlubbers, the Dredgers also have a series of free bike tours. Canoe fever is contagious, with Long Island City, Queens, forming an offshoot of the Gowanus Dredgers. Check the website (www. hometown.aol.com/licboathouse/liccb.html) for updates on times and locations. `FINE PRINT` Donations are cheerfully accepted.

Gowanus Dredgers, Carroll Gardens, Brooklyn. ℂ **718/243-0849.** www. gowanuscanal.org. Subway: F/G to Smith-9th St.

Swim the Apple `FREE` The annual Manhattan Island Marathon Swim covers an amazing 28½ miles, circumventing the city (it's only possible because of the island's shifting currents). It's also a few hundred bucks to participate. Cheaper swimming is available from a fledgling group called Swim the Apple, which hosts day and night swims. The east and west sides of 23rd Street have spots to put in. *FYI:* The temperature of the Hudson in the summer is in the 70s. Log on to www.Columbia.edu/~mh22/swimtheapple for more info.

DOWNTOWN LIVING

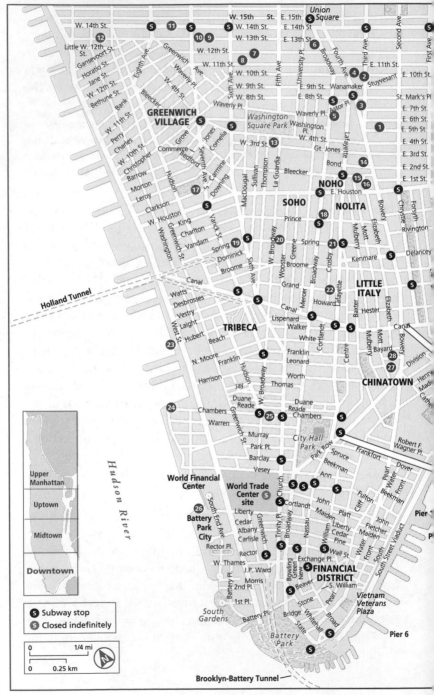

Upper Manhattan

Uptown

Midtown

Downtown

S Subway stop
S Closed indefinitely

0   1/4 mi
0   0.25 km

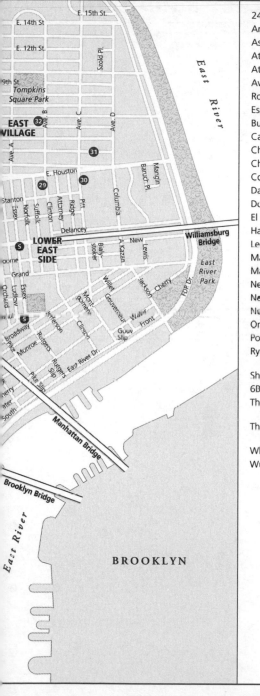

LIVING IN CHELSEA, THE FLATIRON DISTRICT, GRAMERCY & MIDTOWN

24-7 Fitness Club Chelsea **13**
Asser Levy **17**
Big Apple Hostel **3**
Bryant Park (fountain) **22**
Callen-Lorde Community Health
  Center **10**
Centro Maria **1**
Chelsea Center Hostel **4**
Chelsea International Hostel **9**
Clairol Product Evaluation
  Salon **24**
Downtown Boathouse Pier **6**
Eglise Français du St-Esprit **25**
Face Station **27**
Gay Men's Health Crisis **8**
Graduate Center at CUNY **21**
Henry George School **19**
IL-Makiage **26**
Loving Touch Center **20**
Matrix Technical Salon **23**
New York City Free Clinic/
  Sidney Hillman Clinic **14**
New York University College
  of Dentistry **18**
Pacific College of Oriental
  Medicine Clinic and
  Acupuncture Center **16**
Ryan Chelsea-Clinton
  Community Health Center **2**
Shambhala **11**
Sivananda Yoga Vedanta
  Center **7**
Teachers and Writers
  Collaborative **15**
YMCA (McBurney) **12**

UPPER WEST
SIDE

Lincoln
Center

CENTRA

West End Ave.
Amsterdam Ave.
Columbus Ave.
Central Park W.

West Drive

65th St

W. 67th St.
W. 66th St.
W. 65th St.
W. 64th St.
W. 63rd St.
W. 62nd St.
W. 61st St.
W. 60th St.
W. 59th St.
W. 58th St.
W. 57th St.
W. 56th St.
W. 55th St.
W. 54th St.
W. 53rd St.
W. 52nd St.
W. 51st St.
W. 50th St.
W. 49th St.
W. 48th St.
W. 47th St.
W. 46th St.
W. 45th St.
W. 44th St.
W. 43rd St.

Central Park S.
Columbus
Circle

THEATER
DISTRICT

MIDTOWN
WEST

TIMES
SQUARE

Port
Authority

DeWitt
Clinton
Park

Twelfth Ave.
Eleventh Ave.
Tenth Ave.
Ninth Ave.
Eighth Ave.
Broadway
Seventh Ave.

W. 42nd St.
W. 41st St.
W. 40th St.
W. 39th St.
W. 38th St.
W. 37th St.
W. 36th St.
W. 35th St.

Lincoln
Tunnel

Javits
Convention
Center

GARMEN
DISTRIC

W. 34th St.
W. 33rd St.
W. 32nd St.
W. 31st St.
W. 30th St.
W. 29th St.
W. 28th St.

Penn Station/
Madison Square
Garden

W 32nd

Tunnel
Entrance

Chelsea Park

W. 27th St.
W. 26th St.
W. 25th St.
W. 24th St.
W. 23rd St.
W. 22nd St.
W. 21st St.
W. 20th St.
W. 19th St.
W. 18th St.
W. 17th St.
W. 16th St.
W. 15th St.
W. 14th St.
W. 13th St.

West Side Hwy.
Eleventh Ave.
Tenth Ave.
Ninth Ave.
Eighth Ave.
Seventh Ave.

Hudson River

Chelsea Piers

CHELSEA

MEAT-PACKING
DISTRICT

UPPER EAST SIDE

E. 66th St.
E. 65th St.
E. 64th St.
E. 63rd St.
E. 62nd St.
E. 61st St.
E. 60th St.
E. 59th St.
E. 58th St.
E. 57th St.
E. 56th St.
E. 55th St.
E. 54th St.
E. 53rd St.
E. 52nd St.
E. 51st St.
E. 50th St.
E. 49th St.
E. 48th St
E. 47th St.
E. 46th St.
E. 45th St.
E. 44th St.
E. 43rd St.
E. 42nd St.
E. 41st St.
E. 40th St.
E. 39th St.
E. 38th St.
E. 37th St.
E. 36th St.
E. 35th St.
E. 34th St.
E. 33rd St.
E. 32nd St.
E. 31st St.
E. 30th St.
E. 29th St.
E. 28th St.
E. 27th St.
E. 26th St.
E. 25th St.
E. 24th St.
E. 23rd St.
E. 22nd St.
E. 21st St
E. 20th St.
E. 19th St.
E. 18th St.
E. 17th St.
E. 16th St.
E. 15th St.
E. 14th St.
E. 13th St.

PARK
The Pond
Central Park S.
ansverse
East Drive

Fifth Ave.
Madison Ave.

MIDTOWN EAST

Rockefeller Center

Sixth Ave. (Ave. of the Americas)
Fifth Ave.
Madison Ave.
Vanderbilt Ave.
Park Ave.
Lexington Ave.
Third Ave.

Grand Central Terminal

Bryant Park
New York Public Library

MURRAY HILL

Tunnel Exit
Tunnel Entrance

Queens Midtown Tunnel

United Nations

First Ave.
Second Ave.

Queensboro Bridge
Roosevelt Island Tram
From Lower Level
To Upper Level

Sutton Pl.
Sutton Pl. South
Beekman Place
Mitchell Place

Queens

Roosevelt Island

Queens-Midtown Tunnel

FDR Drive

East River

Empire State Bldg.

Broadway
Fifth Ave.
Madison Ave.
Park Ave. S.
Lexington Ave.

Madison Square Park

FLATIRON DISTRICT

Gramercy Park

GRAMERCY PARK

Union Square

Union Sq. W.
Union Sq. E.
Irving Pl.

Sixth Ave. (Ave. of the Americas)

Asser Levy Pl.
Ave. C

Peter Cooper Village

Stuyvesant Town

N.D. Perlman Pl.

🅂 Subway stop

0   1/4 mi
0   0.25 km

N

Upper Manhattan
Uptown
Midtown
Downtown

27
26
25
24
23
22
21
20
19
18
17
16
15
14
13

UPTOWN LIVING

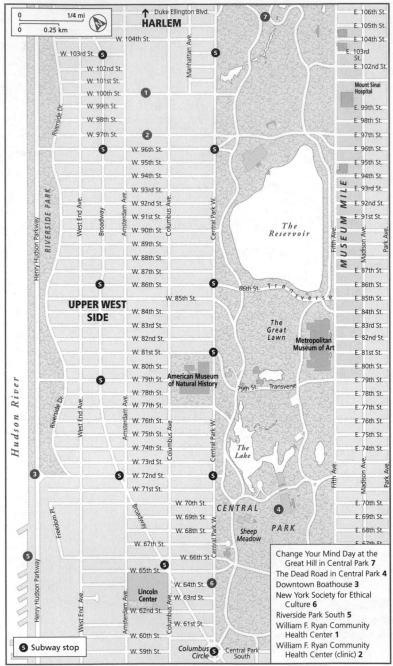

HARLEM

↑ Duke Ellington Blvd.

E. 106th St.
E. 105th St.
E. 104th St.
W. 104th St.
E. 103rd St.
W. 103rd St. ⓢ
E. 102nd St.
W. 102nd St.
Manhattan Ave.
W. 101st St.
W. 100th St. ❶
Mount Sinai Hospital
W. 99th St.
E. 99th St.
W. 98th St.
E. 98th St.
W. 97th St. ❷
W. 96th St. ⓢ
ⓢ E. 96th St.
W. 95th St.
E. 95th St.
W. 94th St.
E. 94th St.
W. 93rd St.
E. 93rd St.
W. 92nd St.
E. 92nd St.
W. 91st St.
E. 91st St.
W. 90th St.
W. 89th St.
W. 88th St.
W. 87th St.
W. 86th St. ⓢ
ⓢ E. 86th St.
W. 85th St.
E. 85th St.
UPPER WEST SIDE
W. 84th St.
E. 84th St.
W. 83rd St.
E. 83rd St.
W. 82nd St.
E. 82nd St.
W. 81st St. ⓢ
E. 81st St.
W. 80th St.
E. 80th St.
W. 79th St. ⓢ
E. 79th St.
W. 78th St.
E. 78th St.
W. 77th St.
E. 77th St.
W. 76th St.
E. 76th St.
W. 75th St.
E. 75th St.
W. 74th St.
E. 74th St.
W. 73rd St.
W. 72nd St. ⓢ
ⓢ
W. 71st St.
W. 70th St.
E. 70th St.
W. 69th St.
E. 69th St.
W. 68th St.
E. 68th St.
W. 67th St.
W. 66th St.
W. 65th St. ⓢ
W. 64th St. ❻
Lincoln Center
W. 63rd St.
W. 62nd St.
W. 61st St.
W. 60th St.
W. 59th St.
Columbus Circle ⓢ

Riverside Dr.
RIVERSIDE PARK
Henry Hudson Parkway
West End Ave.
Broadway
Amsterdam Ave.
Columbus Ave.
Central Park W.
Fifth Ave.
Madison Ave.
Park Ave.
MUSEUM MILE

Hudson River

The Reservoir

86th St. Transverse

The Great Lawn

Metropolitan Museum of Art

American Museum of Natural History

79th St. Transverse

The Lake

CENTRAL PARK ❹

Sheep Meadow

Central Park South

❸

❺

Freedom Pl.

0   1/4 mi
0   0.25 km

Change Your Mind Day at the
 Great Hill in Central Park 7
The Dead Road in Central Park 4
Downtown Boathouse 3
New York Society for Ethical
 Culture 6
Riverside Park South 5
William F. Ryan Community
 Health Center 1
William F. Ryan Community
 Health Center (clinic) 2

ⓢ Subway stop

168

On Sundays, any kind of clothing can be found for bargain-basement prices in the Lower East Side's "Bargain District." See p. 173 for more information.

SHOPPING

5

The last time my country friend came to visit I noticed him limping around the avenues of New York with a broken shoelace. I immediately tried to steer him into the nearest drugstore, but he demurred, telling me he didn't want to get slammed with those "big-city shoelace prices."

This memory still induces a chuckle whenever I'm scoring some crazy deal in the heart of NYC. Clothes, film, electronics, furniture, food, and, yes, even shoelaces, are available here for a fraction of their price in the sticks. Plus Gotham's refined taste is great news for the cost-conscious when it comes time for gowns and coffee tables to begin their second and third lives. New York thrift stores, flea markets, and curbside trash piles are all treasure troves for the patient and sharp-eyed, meaning savvy New Yorkers can finish off their cheap shopping lists better than anybody else in the US of A.

1 Dirt Cheap Shopping Zones

Maybe I was dozing through my Capitalism 101 classes, but I don't understand why New York stores of similar stripe all jam themselves into the exact same neighborhood. The Bowery is clogged with restaurant supply shops, and then suddenly every storefront is dedicated to lighting. A series of lampshade shops gathers on a couple of nearby side streets. Whatever the initial cause, the effect of the single-product density is bargaining power galore for the consumer. Don't like the price? Walk next door and see if you can't do a little better.

DOWNTOWN
THE FINANCIAL DISTRICT
Come lunchtime downtown, the streets fill with office workers scurrying around the cheap shopping outlets. **Fulton, Nassau,** and **Chambers streets** are big destinations, although there isn't anything here that can't be found in other places in the city. The two exceptions to that rule are the city's best electronics and best clothes stores, both near City Hall (see "Department Stores for Cheapskates" and "Electronics," later in this chapter).

Subway: J/M/2/3/4/5 to Fulton St.; A/C to Broadway Nassau.; R to Cortlandt St.; 6 to Brooklyn Bridge/City Hall.

CHINATOWN
A trip to Chinatown can feel like a visit to a foreign country. I like even better the way it can feel like a visit to a foreign economy. A vibrant, but still developing, economy, where prices are only a fraction of what's charged across the border in the city's various Americatowns. Dispersed around **Canal Street, between Lafayette and Mott streets,** you'll find a mind-numbing variety of knockoff versions of just about anything with a designer label, from Oakley sunglasses to Kate Spade bags. The area along **Allen Street between Division Street and East Broadway** doesn't attract many tourists, but locals take advantage of the abundance of cheap apartment-ware shops, where the best prices on appliances, furniture, knickknacks, and hardware can be found.

Subway: A/C/E/J/M/N/R/Q/W/Z/6 to Canal St.

THE BOWERY

Just to the west of Chinatown is the **Bowery.** Though a few of the famous flophouses and missions remain, the Bowery is now known for its profusion of restaurant- and kitchen-supply stores. Many are wholesalers, oriented toward industrial kitchens. Those that are open to the public often also have great deals on chairs, small tables, and stools. When you cross **Delancey Street** heading south, you'll be in the cheap-lighting district. Having so many dealers in one place gives the buyer a lot of leverage when it comes time to barter on the price.

Subway: J/M/Z to Bowery; F/V to Second Ave.

NoLITA & THE EAST VILLAGE

NoLita and the East Village are stylish boutique playgrounds. As such, bargains can be hard to find here. The good news is that low—if not dirt cheap—prices on haute couture can still be found in these neighborhoods, if you're willing to put in the legwork. NoLita's **Elizabeth, Mott, and Mulberry streets** (between Houston and Spring) are dotted with an ever-increasing number of fashionable boutiques, including one of the city's best consignment stores (see "Designer Consignment Stores" later in this chapter). In the Village, **East 9th Street,** between Second Avenue and Avenue A, is home to a slew of up-and-coming local fashion designers—for window shopping, if nothing else—and loads of small gift shops.

Subway: N/R/W to Prince St.; 6 to Spring St.

THE LOWER EAST SIDE

Street signs designate the chunk of Manhattan south of Houston and east of the Bowery as the "Bargain District." You can still find fabric, bedding, and some clothing, but expensive boutiques and trendy restaurants are crowding the bargains out. The state of flux makes it fun to visit, especially

L.E.S. Visitor Center

There's not much to see in the Lower East Side Visitor Center, 261 Broome St., between Orchard and Allen streets (© 866/224-0206 or 212/226-9010), but you can get maps and store guides. The website, www.lowereastside ny.com, has a form for a Go East card, which offers discounts at over 100 local shops and restaurants.

on Sundays. **Orchard Street** closes to traffic **between Delancey and Houston streets** and vendors lay out cheap goods on table-tops, in the spirit of the pushcarts that were once ubiquitous here. In the warmer months you may also get a free band, or a fashion show, usually on a stage at the corner of Orchard and Stanton streets. On the weekdays, you're more likely to hear the hard sell of a barker. Many of the shopkeepers will bargain, if that's in your skill set. Little hipster shops have infiltrated Orchard and can also be found scattered around **Ludlow and Stanton** and other nearby streets. Much cheaper goods are available on **Delancey Street,** which has a good selection of 99¢ stores and bargain-bin housewares.

Subway: F/V to Delancey St.; J/M/Z to Essex St.

ON BROADWAY

The stretches of **Broadway between Bleecker and Canal streets** are a fashion runway for New York youth. With cheap stores abounding, the streets stay packed into nightfall. Though it's some-times semiderisively referred to as the "Cheap Sneaker District," lower Broadway has a great selection of hip and affordable jeans, sweats, jackets, and, yes, sneakers. The area's traffic flow has only increased with the opening of a Bloomingdale's satellite in the dearly departed Canal Jeans' space. Thus far, fortunately, the high-profile addition hasn't priced out its cut-rate neighbors.

Subway: B/D/F/V to Broadway/Lafayette; 6 to Bleecker St.; N/R/W to Prince St.

CHELSEA

Proximity to Fifth Avenue's deep purses helped propel Chelsea's stretches of **Sixth Avenue and Broadway** to the top of Manhattan's shopping heap in the late 19th century. The deep purses moved uptown and the department stores followed, but not before leaving behind some lovely cast-iron architecture. Big discount chains have moved in, including a popular Old Navy. There's great thrift shopping along **17th Street between Fifth and Sixth avenues,** and the neig-borhood is also home to the photo district, the best place for photo-graphic supplies (soon to be digital-printing supplies, no doubt).

Subway: L to Sixth Ave.; A/C/E to 23rd St.

GRAMERCY

The residential enclave of Gramercy, sandwiched between hectic Midtown and East Village streets, is often overlooked as a shopping destination. That's great news for thrift aficionados, who can take advantage of less competition. Gramercy's almost total lack of hipster cred makes the hip clothing, furniture, and collectibles somewhat easier to come by than in picked-over East Village and NoLita stores. The stores along **23rd street between Second and Third avenues** are well stocked and the goods are priced low enough that they're continually flowing. For my money, this is the best place in the city to bargain hunt for thrift threads.

Subway: 6 to 23rd St.

MIDTOWN

THE GARMENT DISTRICT

The huge old buildings in **the 30s between Madison and Eighth avenues** still bear faded advertisements for the furriers and milliners whose shops and factories filled the lofts here. Although much of the manufacturing has moved to cheaper zip codes, the garment trade is still active in ground-floor showrooms. Most are wholesale only, particularly the stretch on **Broadway that runs into the 20s.** A few places are open to the retail public, but the majority of plastic gewgaws they sell aren't very desirable, on the express track for prime spots in landfills. Penn Station is a hub for light rail and subway trains, and the streets nearby are a natural mecca for shoppers. Several big discounters are stationed here, as is the largest store in the world, Macy's. For garment shopping, however, downtown is a better bet.

Subway: B/D/F/N/Q/R/V/W/1/2/3/9 to 34th St.

UPTOWN

Clustered on the Upper West and Upper East sides are some of the highest per capita incomes in the world. The big chains and department stores that cater to those big budgets dominate the local retail trade, though there are a few exceptions for discerning shoppers. For high-end fashions at low-end prices, the consignment shops on **Madison and Amsterdam avenues** are some of the best in the city.

Subway: 1/2/3/9 to 72nd St.; B/C to 72nd St.; 4/5/6 to 86th St.

2 Dirt Cheap Threads & More

THRIFT & VINTAGE

Used clothing falls into two categories in New York, "thrift" and "vintage." In a thrift shop you'll have to sort through racks of junk to find that one perfect shirt, but it won't set you back more than a few bucks. A good vintage proprietor will do the editing for you, but you'll pay for access to her good taste. For trendy items—like a '70s rock concert T-shirt—a couple of holes in the sleeve may not lower the $60 price tag. Uptown consignment shops will sell you a Chanel suit at a fraction of the original cost, but that's still going to be a several-hundred-dollar commitment. My favorites are shops that split the distance between thrift and vintage, selling used stuff that's still got some life left in it, but not at budget-busting prices. Many of the city's thrift shops are charitable nonprofits, so not only will you be getting a bargain, you'll also be helping out a worthy cause.

Note: Clothing isn't the only reason we tightwads love thrift stores. Most of the shops listed below also stock an impressive variety of used furniture, jewelry, electronics, books, records, and even art.

ON 17TH

Angel Street Thrift Shop
Angel Street does an impressive job of keeping its recycled goods au courant. The clothes are in good shape and most don't scream "just bought at a thrift shop." Some unused ringers like sealed sheets and unused electronics sneak into bric-a-brac and the small bedding section.

Easy Streets: 17th & 23rd Streets

Chelsea is home to a great series of thrift stores on **17th Street between Fifth and Seventh avenues.** Items here are priced to sell and they all have a dynamic shopping scene. Stocks turn over frequently, so if you don't see what you're looking for one day, come back the following weekend.

My favorite block to thrift shop is **23rd Street between Second and Third avenues.** The location in prosperous Gramercy ensures high-quality levels for discarded goods.

118 W. 17th St., between Sixth and Seventh aves. ✆ 212/229-0546. www.
angelthriftshop.org. Subway: F or C/E to 14th St.

★ **Housing Works Thrift Shop**   Housing Works has the city's
best thrift shops, with a constant stream of quality donations coming and going. Designer names pop up often on the clothes racks,
and the jewelry racks are filled with intriguing items. The real
draw, however, is the furniture. Although premium pieces end up
in the store windows (they're up for grabs in silent auctions),
many a well-preserved table or chair finds its way to the sales floor.
Note the DJs flipping through the record stacks (disks $1 each, or
during sales, 10 for $1).

143 W. 17th St., between Sixth and Seventh aves. ✆ 212/366-0820. www.
housingworks.org/thrift. Subway: F to 14th St. **Other locations:** *202 E. 77th
St.*, between Second and Third aves. ✆ 212/772-8461. Subway: 6 to 77th St.;
306 Columbus Ave., between 74th and 75th sts. ✆ 212/579-7566. Subway:
B/C to 72nd St.; *157 E. 23rd St.*, between Third and Lexington aves. ✆ 212/
529-5955. Subway: 6 to 23rd St.

17@17   The UJA (United Jewish Appeal) runs a solid thrift shop,
with great prices on groovy art and assorted bric-a-brac. Though
the furniture can be dated (the '80s just haven't aged very well),
the clothes stay current. Frequent sales knock already-low prices
in half.

17 W. 17th St., between Fifth and Sixth aves. ✆ 212/727-7516. www.thrift
shopscharity.org. Subway: F or C/E to 14th St.

On 23rd

City Opera Thrift Shop   Locals sing the praises of this lovely
shop, with its balconies full of deals on art, books, and bric-a-
brac. Prices for furniture are excellent. Costumey looks dominate
the clothing selection, including some pieces that look like they
just left the stage.

222 E. 23rd St., between Second and Third aves. ✆ 212/684-5344. Subway: A/C/E to 23rd St.

Goodwill   Compared to the Salvation Army next door, this place
feels spacious. There's about the same volume of goods here, but
prices are a tad higher, and the fashion quota is pretty low. But
then if it were easy all the time, it wouldn't be treasure hunting.

220 E. 23rd St., between Eighth and Ninth aves. ✆ 212/447-7270. www.
goodwillny.org. Subway: A/C/E to 23rd St. **Other locations:** *2196 Fifth Ave.*,

A Sample Plan

New York's top fashion designers can't sell just everything they lay their scissors to. Sample outfits made specially for store buyers end up sitting on a rack, along with canceled orders, overstock, and items whose day in the fashion sun has come and gone. When it's time for these garments to leave the warehouse, they go to sample sales, NYC's cheapest way of nabbing haute couture.

These websites can help you track down time and locations of sample sales throughout the city (you have to sign up for all of them, but membership is free):

● **www.lazarmedia.com**   This site maintains an extensive list of monthly sales and sample sales. Entries are detailed, with information on credit card and check policies.

● **www.nysale.com**   Store openings and bridal events augment the sale and sample sale information provided when you register here.

● **www.dailycandy.com**   The e-mail newsletter generated by this site is hugely popular, meaning events advertised here can be crowded. The website is well organized, with whimsical graphics and listings of all manner of city events, including food and drink choices. The sample sale listings are detailed and include indicative prices.

at 135th St. ℂ 212/862-0020; *217 W. 79th St.*, between Broadway and Amsterdam Ave. ℂ 212/874-5050; *512 W. 181st St.*, at Audubon St. ℂ 212/923-7910; *1704 Second Ave.*, between 88th and 89th sts. ℂ 212/831-1830.

OFF 23RD
The Vintage Thrift Shop   The selection here is very well chosen, with most items in good enough shape to make this feel more like a boutique than a thrift shop. Cheap glassware, scarves, and shirts can all be found. There isn't room for much furniture, but what's here is priced to sell.

286 Third Ave., between 22nd and 23rd sts. ℂ **212/871-0777.** www.thelowereastside.org/oldisnew. Subway: 6 to 23rd St.

● **www.clothingline.com**   This site provides information on the SSS Sample Sale. Designers change every week but the location stays the same, 261 W. 36th St., 2nd floor, between Seventh and Eighth aves, ℂ **212/947-8748.** Days of the week and hours vary, usually opens 10am. Subway: 1/2/3/9/A/C/E to 34th St.

Note: Designers have to tiptoe around their retail buyers, who are getting bypassed in the sample system. Rather than flaunt customer-filching, they make their sales low-key. Few are advertised widely, and many of them subsist on word of mouth alone. Keep your eyes open in retail neighborhoods, especially the Garment District; many sample sales take place in vacant storefronts, rented out for only a single weekend's sale.

Tips: Wear elbow pads if you're going at peak hours, especially during weekday lunches. A lot of sales don't take credit cards. Even if they do, cash is still a good idea because sometimes they'll let the sales tax slide. Dressing rooms are few and far between at sample sales, so be prepared to try things on over your clothes. Also, don't expect a lot of latitude for sizes, it's all catch as catch can. Finally, items go "as is," so check carefully for stains and rips before you cash out.

IN BROOKLYN

Beacon's Closet   Hipsters delight in the well-stocked palaces of Park Slope's Beacon's Closet. They buy clothes from the public so you can clean out your closet and turn it into cash. Or you can pick up 25% more by getting store credit so you can put all those newly empty hangers to use. Both locations have extensive collections of clothes and shoes.

220 Fifth Ave., between President and Union sts., Park Slope, Brooklyn. ℂ **718/230-1630.** www.beaconscloset.com. Subway: R to Pacific St., exit at Union St.

Domsey's   Huge selection means that with agile hanger shuffling you can come up with real finds here. As Williamsburg continues to boom, however, so does your hanger-shuffling competition.

431 Broadway, between Hewes and Hopper sts., Williamsburg, Brooklyn. ℭ 718/384-6000. www.domsey.com. Subway: J/M to Hewes St. **Other location:** *Ridgewood, Queens:* 1609 Palmetto St., at Myrtle Ave. ℭ 718/386-7661. Subway: L to Myrtle Ave.; M to Wyckoff Ave.

DESIGNER CONSIGNMENT STORES

It's not that hard to look like a million bucks in NYC, even if your clothes budget tops out at a substantially smaller number. New York's best consignment shops carry loads of preowned, vintage, and overstock garments in near show-room condition. The clothes are by no means dirt cheap, but for the high end of design, the prices are as low as they come.

Allan & Suzi   From the window this looks like a shop targeting transvestites, but there's consignment for all tastes inside. Heavy hitters like Halston and Versace mix with one-off numbers and the rest of the best of 20th-century design.

416 Amsterdam Ave., at 80th St. ℭ 212/724-7445. www.allanandsuzi.net. Mon–Sat 12:30–7pm; Subway: 1/9 to 79th St.; B/C to 81st St.-Museum of Natural History.

Encore   For resale women's wear, the Upper East Side is the place to be. Encore is the best of the best, chock-full of big, big names on two floors. A lot of it costs a fortune the first time around and it's still not cheap, but periodic sales can bring luxury into reach.

1132 Madison Ave., between 84th and 85th sts., 2nd floor. ℭ 212/879-2850. www.encoreresale.com. Subway: 4/5/6 to 86th St.

Ina   When *Sex and the City's* wardrobe department sold off its leftovers, of course it turned to Ina. This designer consignment shop has a solid reputation for carrying the height of style, including the likes of Halston, Prada, and Daryl K. The racks are filled with both vintage and current items, and they're always in excellent shape. Shoes and accessories are here as well, and everything is marked way, way down (though outside of the sales, it's still not cheap). A new men's store on Mott Street caters to the burgeoning metrosexual class.

NoLita: 21 Prince St., between Mott and Elizabeth sts. ℭ 212/334-9048. www.inanyc.com. Subway: N, R, W to Prince St.; 6 to Spring St. *SoHo:* 101 Thompson St., between Prince and Spring sts. ℭ 212/941-4757. Subway:

N/R/W to Prince St.; 6 to Spring St. *Men's store:* 262 Mott, between Prince and Houston. ℂ 212/334-2210. Subway: N/R/W to Prince St.; 6 to Spring St. *Uptown:* 208 E. 73rd St., between Second and Third aves. ℂ 212/249-0014. Subway: 6 to 68th.

Michael's   Designer wear for women is the focus of this much-loved consignment boutique. The names are familiar—Chanel, YSL, Prada, and Gucci—but the prices are barely recognizable. The bridal salon is a great find, also specializing in top-shelf quality at rock-bottom prices.

1041 Madison Ave., between 79th and 80th sts., 2nd floor. ℂ **212/737-7273.** www.michaelsconsignment.com. Subway: 6 to 77th St.

Tokyo Joe   When hipsters need the good stuff, they turn straight to this designer consignment shop. Cramped quarters can make for tough browsing, but the clothes themselves are in excellent shape. Don't miss the big section of lightly used and new shoes, going for a fraction of their cost Uptown.

334 E. 11th St., between First and Second aves. ℂ 212/473-0724. Subway: L to First Ave. **Other location:** *240 E. 28th St.,* between Second and Third aves. ℂ 212/532-3605. Subway: 6 to 28th St.

TRÉS CHEAP RETAIL FASHIONS

H&M   Swedish discounter Hennes & Mauritz knocks out the latest looks at low, low prices. They specialize in hip looks for women and men, and as such they're a big hit with the teens. Durability is not the greatest, though it is about what you'd expect for these prices.

Herald Sq.: 1328 Broadway, at 34th St. ℂ **646/489-8777.** www.hm.com. Subway: B/D/F/N/R/V/W to 34th St./Herald Sq. **Other locations:** *640 Fifth Ave.,* at 51st St. ℂ 212/656-9305. Subway: E/V to Fifth Ave.; *558 Broadway,* between Prince and Spring sts. ℂ 212/343-0220. Subway: N/R to Prince St.

Loehmann's   When the original Barneys faltered, longtime discount fave Loehmann's was quick to fill much of the square footage. Casual wear comes in at one-third to two-thirds off the department store prices, and you can reel in even deeper discounts on the likes of Donna Karan and Versace inside the "Back Room." Great prices for women's shoes, too, and there's an underpublicized men's floor.

101 Seventh Ave., between 16th and 17th sts. ℂ **212/352-0856.** www.loehmanns.com. Subway: 1/9 to 18th St.

Weiss & Mahoney   Camouflage patterns are still in fashion locally, though we find it a little ironic, given that green-shaded organics are about the worst ways to camouflage oneself in NYC (a series of large gray and black squares would better do the trick). Weiss & Mahoney has been outfitting the city for decades in camouflage, not to mention peacoats and berets. Work clothes are just at normal prices, but surplus and camping goods are much lower, and quality new tees come in at three for $20.

> ### For Fashion DIYers
>
> The fabric selection in **Harry Zarin Company's** upstairs warehouse goes the whole nine yards, with an almost overwhelming selection of textures and styles. Deep discounts get even deeper for overruns and closeouts. *Warehouse:* 72 Allen St., at Grand St. ✆ **212/226-3492.** *Storefront:* 318 Grand St., between Ludlow and Orchard sts. ✆ 212/925-6112. Subway for both locations: B/D to Grand St.; F/V to Delancey St.; J/M/Z to Essex St.

142 Fifth Ave., at 19th St. ✆ **212/675-1915.** www.wmarmynavy.com. Subway: 6 to 23rd St.

Rainbow Shops   When the new women's and girl's clothes lines come out, Rainbow wastes no time in coming up with affordable copies. Urban styles predominate, with the target audience well under 25. Cheap shoes and accessories, and lots for plus sizes, too.

110-114 Delancey St., between Essex and Ludlow sts. ✆ **212/254-7058.** www.rainbowshops.com. Subway: F to Delancey St.; J/M/Z to Essex St. **Other locations:** *90 John St.,* between Gold and Pearl sts. ✆ 212/227-2896. Subway: A/C to Broadway-Nassau; *380 Fifth Ave.,* between 35th and 36th sts. ✆ 212/947-0837. Subway: B/D/F/NQ/R/V/W to 34th St.; *320 W. 57th St.,* near Eighth Ave. ✆ 212/333-5490. Subway: A/B/C/D/1/9 to 59th St.-Columbus Circle. Several locations in Brooklyn, too.

Village Style   Excellent selection for the lads, tees come in around $8 and button-downs $15. Shoes, cowboy boots, and a women's section, too.

111 E. 7th St., between First Ave. and Ave A. ✆ **212/260-6390.** Subway: F/V to Second Ave.; L to First Ave.

Treasure Trends NYC   The premium rock T-shirts are over $20, but there's a ton of cheaper tees in the $3 to $7 range as well as cool jackets and pants. Up front you can find a $2 rack, and should you wish to walk a mile in someone else's shoes you can find a big $5-each selection in the back. Stock rotates quickly to reward repeat visits.

204 First Ave., between 12th and 13th sts. ℭ **212/777-5514.** Subway: L to First Ave. **Other location:** *25 St. Marks Place,* between Second and Third aves. ℭ 212/614-8981. Subway: 6 to Astor Place.

SHOE INS & OUTS

All the miles New Yorkers log as pedestrians help explain the occasional obsessive bent applied to our shoe shopping. My two favorite shoe-shopping clusters can be found downtown. **Lower Broadway beneath 4th St. and down to Canal** has some great street options. **West 8th Street between Fifth and Sixth avenues** is another excellent mini district, with the stylish and all-too-stylish intermixed. NYU undergrads haunt both areas, and prices often accommodate student budgets.

ON BROADWAY

Juno   The regular prices here are no great shakes, but during the frequent half-off and two-for-one sales you can shod your hooves for $40 or $50. The designs are interesting and in step with the latest style.

543 Broadway, between Prince and Spring sts. ℭ **212/625-2560.** www.junoshoes.com. Subway: N/R to Prince St.; 6 to Spring St. **Other location:** *426 W. Broadway,* between Prince and Spring sts. ℭ 212/219-8002. Subway: C/E to Spring St.

Tip Top Shoes   This Uptown shop is tops for walking shoes, which are essential equipment in New York. Rockport, Mephisto, and Ecco are among the brands represented here, sold at reasonable prices. They also carry shoes of a less practical nature for those who prefer form to function.

155 W. 72nd St., between Broadway and Columbus Ave. ℭ **800/WALKING** or 212/787-4960. www.tiptopshoes.com. Subway: 1/2/3/9 to 72nd St.

Shoe Mania   This popular discount store has a wide-ranging selection, putting Kenneth Coles sole to sole with Doc Martens, Birkenstocks, and Mephistos. Whether you go for style or comfort, you'll find a good price on it here.

853 Broadway, at 14th St. ℂ **212/245-5260.** Subway: 4/5/6/L/N/R/Q/W
to 14th St./Union Sq. *Also at 331 Madison Ave.*, between 42nd and 43rd sts.
ℂ 212/557-6627. Subway: 4/5/6/7/S to 42nd St./Grand Central.

ON 8TH

Village Shoe Revue   Frequent clearance sales here make this
store worth frequent visits. The stock is kept up-to-date, with the
latest footware often on hand. The best bargains lurk in the back
section, where $50 is often enough for a $100 pair of shoes.

29 W. 8th St., between Fifth and Sixth aves. ℂ **212/529-1800.** Subway:
A/B/C/D/E/F/V to West 4th St.

Da'Vinci   Shoppers here should be alert for on-the-spot discounts.
With a little bargaining savvy, you can get great prices on all the
modern looks.

37 West 8th St., between Fifth and Sixth aves. ℂ **212/674-4746.** Subway:
A/B/C/D/E/F/V to West 4th St.

3 Flea New York

New Yorkers seeking free stimuli can certainly do worse than
whiling away a few hours at a flea market. The rows of tables can
function as touchable museums, and the sheer width and breadth
of available stuff is stunning. Prices for goods are generally not as
cheap as they should be given the low-overhead locales, but
there are ways to tip the scales in your favor. Sunday, as closing
time approaches, the last thing a dealer wants to do is reload that
half-ton armoire back into the truck. Likewise, a sudden rain can
make parting with a wooden antique or a suede jacket more
sweetness than sorrow. Use the elements to your advantage when
it's time to haggle.

Chelsea Antiques Building   Twelve stories of dealers offer
plenty of variety in this permanent flea market. The 20th-century
collectibles can be spendy, but with some luck and persistence
bargains can be found.

110 W. 25th St., between Sixth and Seventh aves. ℂ **212/929-0909.** Subway: F/V/1/9 to 23rd St.

The Garage   Imagine a series of yard sales jammed up right on
top of each other and you'll have an idea of the scene at The Garage.
Lots of art, loose photos, and other oddball junk, and the prices
are in the same stratosphere as you'd find on a suburban lawn.

112 W. 25th St., between Sixth and Seventh aves. ℂ **212/243-5343.** Subway: F/V/1/9 to 23rd St.

Annex Antiques Fair & Flea Market   Hundreds of vendors and thousands of browsers make for a great scene in this Chelsea parking lot. On the weekends commuter cars are banished and row after row of indispensable junk is put out on display. Setting up new apartments is made easy (well, easier) with a strong selection of vintage housewares and furniture.

Sixth Ave., at 26th St. ℂ 212/243-5343. www.annexantiques.citysearch. com. Admission $1. Subway: F/V to 23rd St.; 1/9/N/R to 28th St.

Greenflea   This bustling indoor/outdoor fair is a favorite way to spend a Sunday afternoon on the Upper West Side. The antiques tend to be priced fairly, marginalized as they are by dealers offering contemporary imports, crafts, and clothes. The latter also line the nearby strip of Columbus Ave.

W. 76th St., at Columbus Ave. ℂ 212/877-7371. Subway: B/C to 72nd St.; 1/9 to 79th St.

Come Sale Away

When out-of-towners gawk and marvel that anyone would pay what's printed on a New York price tag, they aren't taking into account that most locals won't throw money away on the full retail price. The key to dirt cheap shopping in the Big Apple is timing the sales. Stores trumpet their markdowns in window displays, newspapers, and flyers, and sales fever is contagious. If one shoe store is doing two-for-one, the rest of the block often isn't far behind. Season ends, like just before back-to-school and just after Christmas, are routinely great for bargain hunters. Buy your sundresses and air conditioners in August, and wait until February to pick up that new winter coat. If your tastes run to vintage or barely used, try looking around in January, when a fresh crop of nonreturnable items get consigned. A good way to keep abreast of the action is in the **"Sales and Bargains"** section of *New York* magazine, or on the website at www.newyorkmetro.com. **"Check Out"** in *Time Out* is another good source, as is **NYSale,** www.nysale.com.

4 Department Stores for Cheapskates

New York traditionally makes it hard for big franchises and chains to survive. The city is competitive to an extreme and there just isn't enough profit margin to pay a bunch of middle management salaries. Though there are a few chains sprinkled through these pages, for the most part we avoid the national retailers. They don't give enough bang for your buck.

☆ **Century 21** Nearly destroyed on 9/11, Century 21 has risen from the ashes to reclaim its place as the top clothes shopping destination in the city. Fancy labels are fully represented here, sans the fancy prices. Expect designer goods at less than half the prices they carry in other department stores. Great deals on sunglasses, linens, and housewares, too. Avoid peak hours at lunch and on the weekends if possible. Don't be intimidated by long lines for the women's dressing room; the queue moves quickly.

2 Cortlandt St., between Broadway and Church St. ℂ **212/227-9092.** www.c21stores.com. Subway: J/M/2/3/4/5 to Fulton St.; A/C to Broadway Nassau; R to Cortlandt St. *Also at 472 86th St.*, between Fourth and Fifth aves., Bay Ridge, Brooklyn. Subway: R to 86th St.

Tax-Free Week

In the long-ago boom years, New York could afford to look the other way on sales tax. Clothes and shoes under $100 per item were sold out of the goodness of the Big Apple's heart, not for any pecuniary interest. Jerseyians flooded to the city, strolling up and down Broadway and putting their Mall at Short Hills' cash into Gotham's retail coffers. During the doldrums of late January you can relive those glory days of retail when the city offers a tax-free shopping week. (Only items $110 and less are included.) Check the city's website, as at least one other week a year is often offered. Many stores sweeten the deal by having major sales coincide with the tax-free window. www.nyc.gov/html/dof/html/salestax.html.

Daffy's Daffy's never seems as crowded as it should be, given how cheap the clothes are. The merchandise usually isn't big names, and you have to sort through some cheesy-looking Italian designs, but patient shopping always reveals gems. Excellent for staples for men, and New Yorkers are just starting to discover the great kids' selection. The Herald Square location is comprehensive.

1311 Broadway, at 34th St. ℂ **212/736-4477**. www.daffys.com. Subway: 1/2/3/9 to 34th St. **Other locations:** *111 Fifth Ave.*, at 18th St. ℂ 212/529-4477. Subway: 4/5/6/L/N/R/Q/W to 14th St./Union Sq.; *462 Broadway*, at Grand St. ℂ 212/334-7444. Subway: N/Q/R/W to Canal St.; *335 Madison Ave.*, at 44th St. ℂ 212/557-4422. Subway: 4/5/6/7/S to 42nd St./Grand Central; *125 E. 57th St.*, between Park and Lexington aves. ℂ 212/376-4477. Subway: 4/5/6 to 59th St.

Kmart   The words *Kmart* and *inspiring* are rarely found in the same sentence, but for us every trip to Astor Place's K is a

Take an Unböring Trip to Ikea

Ikea gives Manhattanites a free lift to the massive mother-ship furniture store in Elizabeth, New Jersey. Unfortunately the bus only runs on weekends, and weekends at Ikea are *insane*. The children of a thousand scattered tribes stream through tasteful simulations of living rooms and kitchens. Parents fondle vaguely cheap-looking Swedish furniture. The checkout lines wind into infinity. Ikea's labyrinth layout also means you can't just dash in, get want you want, and get right back out. That said, the prices are pretty amazing. Nobody else in the tri-state can compete for decent-looking postdorm furniture. The big basket racks are often filled with amazingly cheap items; I'm still using the complete kitchen knife set I bought for $3 a few years back. There's an in-store cafeteria should you need a break from the action, with affordable food (including meatballs, of course). The views from the cafeteria of Newark Airport runways are spectacular, almost enough on their own to make this interstate excursion worthwhile. Port Authority, Eighth Avenue at 42nd Street. Buses leave every half-hour between 10am and 2:30pm and return from Jersey every half-hour between noon and 6pm. The trip takes about 30 minutes each way (ℂ **800/BUS-IKEA;** www.ikea-usa.com). *Note:* There's room to stow your new possessions on the ride back, as long as they're not too big to carry.

thrilling reminder of NYC's awesome cultural diversity. Students, yuppies, outer-borough homemakers, and Japanese hipsters all rub shoulders as they prowl the long aisles for cheap clothing, housewares, furniture, and even food. The hardware and paint departments have great deals, and there's an excellent plant department behind the cash registers. Direct access to the subway makes it easy to drag your haul home. Even the view down Broadway from the cut-rate upstairs cafeteria is inspiring, although the food is at least a few stars short of four.

770 Broadway, between 8th and 9th sts. ℂ 212/673-1540. www.kmart. com. Subway: 6 to Astor Place; N/R/W to 8th St. **Other location:** *250 W. 34th St.,* between Sixth and Seventh aves. ℂ 212/760-1188. Subway: A/C/E or 1/2/3/9 to 34th St.

Conway's This chain of stores is stuffed with housewares, health and beauty products, and cheap clothing. If you've ever wondered what became of name brands like Botany 500 and Lada, they're alive and well at Conways. Prices are crazy low, but then polyester is cheaper to grow than cotton. Better buys can be found on linens, towels, small appliances, and other apartment necessities. The kids' shopping is good, too, with toys and backpacks priced absurdly low.

201 E. 42nd St., at Third Ave. ℂ 212/922-5030. www.conway stores.com. Subway: 4/5/6/7/S to 42nd St./Grand Central Station. Several other locations around the city; check the website for details.

Macy's (One-Day Sales) Covering 10 stories and an entire city block, this megalith has just about everything, including at any given time a large chunk of the metropolitan shopping population. The key is to buy during the frequent sales. The famous One-Days are the best, usually held on

> ### Macy's Flower Show
>
> Outside of sales, the big department stores aren't much help for the budget-minded. For free entertainment, though, they hold their own. Window displays make great theater and floor after floor of regal goods makes for great browsing. The first 2 weeks of April bring some serious spectacle when Macy's goes nuts for flowers. The store is transformed by over a million blossoms in 18 gardens. Free tours run every half-hour from 11 to 4. www. macys.com. Flower hot line ℂ 212/494-4495.

Wednesdays, with the occasional Saturday thrown in. Check the *New York Times* for Macy's full-page advertisements, which sometimes include clip-out coupons for additional 10% to 15% discounts.

At Herald Sq., W. 34th St. and Broadway. (℮ **212/695-4400.** www.macys.com. Subway: A/C/E or 1/2/3/9 to 34th St.

Pearl River   This mini-department store brings Chinatown prices to SoHo ambience. The inventory favors Asian classics like paper lanterns, silk pajamas, and sequined slippers. Glazed bowls and other housewares make for inexpensive kitchen outfitting.

477 Broadway, between Broome and Grand sts. (℮ **212/431-4770.** www.pearlriver.com. Subway: N/Q/R/W to Canal St. Also at 200 Grand St., between Mott and Mulberry sts. (℮ 212/966-1010. Subway: B/D to Grand St.

5 Dirt Cheap Shopping: A to Z

ANTIQUES

See "Flea New York," earlier in this chapter.

BIKES

Recycle-A-Bicycle   The organization that runs these shops promotes biking in the city by selling rehabbed bikes at reasonable prices. Prices start at a kid's BMX model for $15. A top-of-the-line bike could set you back as much as $500 (a fraction of its cost new, however), though you'd be helping out a worthy cause.

75 Ave. C, between 5th and 6th sts. (℮ **212/475-1655.** www.recycleabicycle.org. Subway: L to First Ave.; F to Second Ave. *DUMBO, Brooklyn location:* 55 Washington St., between Front and Water sts. (℮ 718/858-2972. Subway: F/V to Second Ave.

BOOKS

The Strand   The Strand is as legendary for its 8 miles of books as it is for its 5 inches of aisle space to maneuver in. The big crowds are a testament to the great prices. Review copies of recent books share space with art books at 85% off list and used fiction hardbacks that go for under $5. Bibliophiles with small apartments beware because that 8 miles is reputed to be up to 16 now; it's hard to leave empty-handed.

828 Broadway, at 12th St. (℮ **212/473-1452.** www.strandbooks.com. Subway: L/N/Q/R/W/4/5/6 to 14th St./Union Sq. There's also a smaller, less

crowded **Strand Annex** at 95 Fulton St., between William and Gold sts. ℂ 212/732-6070. Subway: J/M/Z/2/3/4/5 to Fulton St.; A/C to Broadway-Nassau St.

Gryphon Bookshop   This tiny, charming shop has the best used books Uptown. Browsers delight in the broad selection of literary and historical works. The occasional reviewer's copy can also be found, at discounted prices.

2246 Broadway, between 80th and 81st sts. ℂ 212/362-0706. Subway: 1/9 to 79th St.

12th Street Books   This is a great place to look for used and rare books. The selection runs especially strong in history, psychiatry, art, and theater. Most fiction comes in for under $10. In front of the store the sales racks have great prices (under $1), though it may take some serious scrounging to find something you really want to read.

11 E. 12th St., between Fifth Ave. and University Place. ℂ 212/645-4340. Subway: 4/5/6/L/N/R/Q/W to 14th St./Union Sq.

EDIBLES

Cooking at home is an obvious way of cutting costs, but a trip to the corner deli for necessities can feel like a shakedown by the time you step away from the cash register. Most NYC grocery stores aren't much better, but a couple of specialty shops do offer bargains.

GROCERIES

Deluxe Food Market, Inc.   Several buffets have recently opened in Chinatown, offering some variety of four dishes over rice for $4. The best by far can be found inside this bustling grocery store. You can get three dishes served over rice for $2.75. The selection changes every day, and the food is always fresh and delicious. In addition to the buffet line you can find supercheap savory take-aways, and a bakery section where three big sugared dough twists are only $1. The rest of the real estate here is dedicated to regular grocery store goods. Fish, meats, and greens are all rock bottom. You can also load up on frozen specialties, like big packs of dumplings, for amazingly low prices. There's limited seating for cafeteria food.

79 Elizabeth St., between Hester and Grand sts. ℂ 212/925-5766. Subway: N/R to Prince St.; 6 to Spring St.

☆ **East Village Cheese Store**   For gourmet on the cheap, nothing else in the city comes even close to this East Village gem. You can get bread, crackers, pâtés, pickles, and other side items here, but the real jaw-dropping prices are on the cheeses. In the front refrigerators, goat cheese tubes and boursin packages go for $1 and big brie wedges are $1.50. Behind the counter you can find tons of specials on fancy goudas and cheddars for $2.99 a pound. The give-away prices aren't indicative of quality, either. It's not second-rate goods, just items picked up when some importer added a mistaken zero to an order. This mom and pop store is uniquely equipped to get rid of it all in a hurry.

40 Third Ave., between Ninth and Tenth aves. ℂ 212/477-2601. Subway: 6 to Astor Place; N/R/W to 8th St.

Essex St. Market   When the city squeezed the pushcarts off the Lower East Side 50 years ago, it built a garagelike city market as a replacement. The market now functions like a low-rent shopping mall, frequented by Spanish and Chinese locals, who love the low prices. **Best Farms** (ℂ 212/533-5609), a huge Korean deli, has taken over the north end of the market. They sell just about everything, but the best deals are on fresh fruit and vegetables. A huge container with a blend of gourmet lettuces is just $1.99, fruit salads are $1.50, and when the mangos are ripe they're two for $1. The middle of the market has butchers, fish sellers, and a botanica. In the back you'll find **Batista Grocery** (ℂ 212/254-0796), a shop with great prices on Goya and other dry goods. Cafe tables are available if you want to make a picnic (on nice days you can take it down to the East River, assuming the city finally finishes fixing up the park). At the south end of the market is a good little dumpling stand. Veggie side dishes are only $1 each and a fish sandwich is $1.25. I particularly like the veggie dumplings, cooked in almost fluorescent green skins, eight for $2.50. Since this is downtown, there's even the **Cuchifritos** art gallery tucked away in the very back (ℂ 212/598-4124; www.artistsai.org/cuchifritos; Mon–Sat 10am–5pm). On your way out, grab a $5 bottle of kosher wine from longtime neighborhood presence **Schapiro's,** or save $5 and just try a free sample (ℂ 212/832-3176; www.schapiros-wine.com; Mon–Thurs 10am–6pm, Fri 9am–4pm).

120 Essex St., between Rivington and Delancey sts. ℂ 212/312-3603. www.essexstreetmarket.com. Subway: F train to Delancey St.; J/M/Z trains to Essex St.

Café du Monde: The Anti-Starbucks

For me, one of the least appealing aspects of modern American society is the $3.49 cup of coffee. Instead of being gouged every morning, I make my own cup for just pennies. **Café Du Monde** of New Orleans produces some of the finest grounds in the country. The chicory-flavored tins hold a real 15 ounces, packed all the way to the lid, without the 3 or 4 ounces of air you find in the containers of other brands. The coffee itself is dark and dense, so you only use about a third of the usual amount of grounds. If you go straight to the source and order online from Café Du Monde (www.cafedumonde.com), it'll cost you $4.60, plus shipping. In New York's Chinatown, however, you can pick up a big orange tin for $3.49. I use **Eastern Supermarket** (335 Grand St., at Ludlow St.; B/D trains to Grand St.; ℂ 212/625-8920).

May Wah Healthy Vegetarian Food, Inc.   Sometimes a vegetarian needs a break from the bean sprout and tofu regimen. The Chinese are fake meat experts, and this little Chinatown shop has a massive selection. A big package of frozen unchicken nuggets is only $3.55, and the citrus spare ribs are an even better deal at $2.90.

213 Hester St., between Centre St. and Centre Market Place. ℂ 212/334-4428. www.vegieworld.com. Subway: J/M/N/R/Q/W/Z/6 to Canal St.

Sahadi's   This brightly lit and perennially mobbed Brooklyn grocery store is a great source for Middle Eastern cooking staples. Dozens of varieties of olive oil are available, as are nuts, dried fruits, olives, lentils, chickpeas, and of course top quality *maleb* (the Lebanese seasoning made from the insides of cherry pits).

187-189 Atlantic Ave., between Court and Clinton sts., Boerum Hill, Brooklyn. ℂ 718/624-4550. www.sahadis.com. Subway: M/R to Court St.; 2/3/4/5 to Borough Hall.

SWEETS

Economy Candy   The Lower East Side of the '30s was littered with small specialty shops like this one, which remains a family business almost 70 years later. With the other shops gone, Economy Candy has taken on their responsibilities, selling everything from coffee to nuts to dried fruit. Oh yeah, they also sell a little candy. From floors to rafters the store is packed with lollipops, gum drops, halvah, gourmet candy bars, bulk chocolate, and pretty much anything else sweet you can think of. Prices are very reasonable, especially when you buy by the pound.

108 Rivington St., between Essex and Ludlow sts. ℂ 212/254-1531. www. economycandy.com. Subway: F to Delancey St.; J/M/Z to Essex St.

ELECTRONICS

J&R Music World/Computer World   I'm constantly surprised how often an online search for discounted electronics brings up J&R as the cheapest supplier out there. Save the shipping cost by coming in to the bustling block-long series of stores. The staff is knowledgeable and not too brusque (at least by New York standards). The prices on cameras, stereos, computers, and software are excellent, and there's good CD and DVD shopping as well. There's even a store for closeout specials at 33 Park Row. Check the paper or the website for dates on the frequent sales.

Along Park Row, at Ann St., opposite City Hall Park. ℂ 800/426-6027 or 212/238-9000. www.jandr.com. Subway: 2/3 to Park Place; 4/5/6 to Brooklyn Bridge/City Hall.

GIFTS & OTHER CURIOSITIES

Daily 235   For gift shopping, this tiny, creative shop has plenty of tiny, creative gifts for under $10.

235 Elizabeth St., between Prince and Houston sts. ℂ 212/334-9728. Subway: N/R to Prince St.; 6 to Spring St.

Extraordinary   This gallery-like space holds a small world of international gifts. The items show a sensitivity to design, along with whimsical tendencies. You won't pay through the nose for that appealing combination—prices are lower here than at comparable NYC boutiques.

251 E. 57th St., just west of Second Ave. ℂ 212/223-9151. Subway: 4/5/6 to 59th St. Subway: 4/5/6 to 59th St.; N/R/W to Lexington Ave.

House of Cards and Curiosities   A jam-packed Victorian-style shop, this West Village favorite is a great place to browse. Oddball gifts and gizmos share space with an excellent collection of cards.

23 Eighth Ave., between 12th and Jane sts. ℂ 212/675-6178. Subway: A/C/E to 14th St.; L to Eighth Ave.

HOUSEWARES

Leader Restaurant Equipment & Supplies   Take us to Leader for great prices on kitchenware, especially Asian appointments like chopsticks, bowls, and plates.

191 Bowery, between Spring and Delancey sts. ℂ 800/666-6888 or 212/677-1982. Subway: J/M/Z to Bowery; F/V to Second Ave.

Fishs Eddy   You can reel in remainders of custom china here. Prices are relatively low, certainly the best you'll do on a plate marked "Blue Plate Special." You can also find retro designs, including soda fountain glasses and vintage-looking flatware.

889 Broadway, at 19th St. ℂ 212/420-9020. www.fishseddy.com. Subway: 4/5/6/L/N/R/Q/W to 14th St./Union Sq. **Other locations:** *2176 Broadway,* at 77th St. ℂ 212/873-8819. Subway: 1/9 to 79th St.; *1388 Third Ave,* at 79th St. ℂ 212/737-2844. Subway: 6 to 77th St.

Broadway Panhandler   Pan reviews consistently put this place at the top. For restaurant-quality cookware and kitchen tools, you can't find a better combo of selection, price, and service.

477 Broome St., between Greene and Wooster sts. ℂ 212/966-3434. Subway: C/E to Spring St.

Flower Power

Two green thumbs go up for the selection of plant and flower stores on **28th Street between Sixth and Seventh avenues,** and overflowing onto Sixth Avenue. (For those with brown thumbs, there's a great selection of plastic plants, too.) The stores are a mix of wholesale and retail, with the best prices going to bulk buyers. Small purchasers can also reel in good buys, especially at **Starbright Floral Design** (150 W. 28th St., between Sixth and Seventh aves.; N/R trains to 28th St.; ℂ 800/520-8999; www.starflor.com).

Lighting by Gregory   Great selection and good prices on lighting, plus a big collection of ceiling fans. The latest lighting trends can always be found.

158 Bowery, between Delancey and Broome sts. ℂ 888/811-FANS or 212/226-1276. www.lightingbygregory.com. Subway: J/M/Z to Bowery; F to Second Ave.

Pearl Paint   Pearl Paint has the city's best art supply prices and selection, in a sprawling compound tinted by an air of genial disarray. Specialty stores on the rear block (Lispenard) back up five floors of supplies in front (Canal). Frames, papers, canvas, and incidentals like day-planners and portfolios all carry the lowest prices in the city.

308 Canal St., between Broadway and Mercer St. ℂ 212/431-7932. www. pearlpaint.com. Subway: A/C/E or 1/9 to Canal St. *School of Visual Arts location:* 209 E. 23rd St., at Third Ave. ℂ 212/592-2179. Subway: 6 to 23rd St.

National Wholesale Liquidators   Almost anything you would want inside a house—from batteries to cosmetics to water filters—can be found here at absurdly low prices. The upstairs clothing section is often overlooked, though it's just as cheap.

632 Broadway, between Bleecker and Houston sts. ℂ 212/979-2400. Subway: F/S/V to Broadway-Lafayette Ave.

Industrial Plastics   Whenever I'm in the mood for some industrial plastics, I make a beeline for Canal Street and my favorite store. Acrylic rods! Acrylic tubes! Vinyl hemispheres! Disco balls! Though there isn't much practical to buy here, there's a wealth of great art supplies, to say nothing of the excellent plastic fruit selection. To browse alone is worth a visit.

309 Canal St., at Mercer St. ℂ 212/226-2010. www.yourplasticssupermarket. com. Subway: N/Q/R or 6 to Canal St.

LUGGAGE, LEATHER & HANDBAGS

Jobson's   For 50-some years, Jobson's has been selling luggage and leather at only 10% above cost. Discount shoppers mingle with professional travelers here.

666 Lexington Ave., between 55th and 56th sts. ℂ 212/355-6846. Subway: 6 to 51st St.

Altman Luggage   This old-time LES classic has wheeled luggage galore, in addition to businessperson sundries like pens, wallets, and watches. Already deep-discounts get even deeper for closeouts and items that have been too long on the showroom floor.

135 Orchard St., between Rivington and Delancey sts. ℂ 212/254-7275. www.altmanluggage.com. Subway: F to Delancey St.; J/M/Z to Essex St.

Knock It Off

By lore, the first major New York swindle was Dutch settlers trading $24 worth of beads and baubles for the island of Manhattan. There's some question as to who was scamming whom in that arrangement (it's likely the natives didn't think the land could be bought or sold), but it set a karmic pattern that's still in place today. Tourists buy a Movado watch or a Chanel purse or Armani sunglasses, giggling as they leave $18 with some sucker of a vendor. It's not until the cheap knockoff disintegrates 3 days later that they realize which side of the con they were actually on. If the price seems too good to be true, it certainly is. **Orchard Street** on the Lower East Side has decent fakes, but the real action is in the stalls of Chinatown. The designer purses and bags are pretty convincing and they'll survive a little wear and tear. Along **Canal Street between Lafayette and Mott** you can also find decent wallets, scarves, perfume, and a surfeit of counterfeit Von Dutch. My favorite point of attack is in the scrum in the middle of the sidewalk on the **northwest corner of Broadway and Canal.** Dealers distracted by the dizzying traffic offer the widest latitude when it comes to fine bargaining on the Vuittonesque and Burberryish.

MUSIC

Between burning, shredding, and downloading, it's almost unnecessary to actually go to brick and mortar to shop for music. New York still has a bevy of CD shops, but few of them can match the prices of cut-rate Internet retailers like **www.alldirect.com,** and they definitely can't compete with free.

If you take your music hard, a broad selection of used CDs can be found on and around St. Marks Place between Second and Third avenues in the East Village.

Mondo Kim's   This minimall with eclectic taste is the best place to find a used CD you might actually want to listen to. A long rack of electronica dominates the ground floor, but all kinds of stuff can be found, usually for $7 and under. DJs riffle through the vinyl racks upstairs. The music in the small 99¢ section at the entrance doesn't have much of a future outside of Fresh Kills.

6 St. Marks Place, between Second and Third aves. ☏ **212/598-9985.** Subway: 6 to Astor Place; N/R/W to 8th St.

Norman's Sound & Vision   Upstairs at Norman's you can find a surprisingly broad collection of sounds and styles, but bargain hunters head straight for the basement. Every CD belowground is $2, with a lot to choose from, though as far as musical desirability goes the picking can be pretty slim. The vinyl selection is much better, strong in punk and blues, though the archaic medium fetches higher prices ($5–$10).

67 Cooper Sq., between E. 7th St. and St. Marks Place. ☏ **212/473-6610.** Subway: 6 to Astor Place; N/R/W to 8th St.

Vinyl Aisle: The WFMU Record Fair

If you've got an issue with piracy, or album art is a must, old-fashioned vinyl is the way to go. Thrift stores top out at $2 per disk, though DJs assure there's slim pickings outside of classical. For record fanatics, there are two paramount weekends every year, when the **WFMU Record Fair** comes to town. WFMU's free-form radio is one of New York's greatest cultural assets, and the record fair brings an incredible array of dealers. The show costs $5 to enter, but that fee includes free live bands, screenings in an AV room, and table after table of cheap CDs and vinyl. I ignore the $70 collector disks and head straight for the boxes under the table, where the 2 for $1 disks are most likely to be found. The fair is held over the first weekend in May and the first weekend in November, and it takes place at the **Metropolitan Pavilion** (125 W. 18th St., between Sixth and Seventh aves.; 1/9 trains to 18th St.). For more information, call ☏ **201-521-1416,** ext. 243, or log on to www.wfmu. org/recfair. *Tip:* Sunday afternoon is the best bargain-hunter's time. Buyers are burned out and dealers are doing everything they can to keep from hauling all that obsolete technology back home.

Joe's CDs Prices for used CDs here come in around $10. The selection is good, though, with more rarities than clunkers.

11 St. Marks Place, between Second and Third aves. ② 212/673-4606. Subway: 6 to Astor Place; N/R/W to 8th St.

PHOTO

Adorama Photo pros flock to Adorama, which has unbelievably low prices for film, paper, and sundry items like blank cassettes. Also, a decent collection of used lenses and bodies in the back.

42 W. 18th St., between Fifth and Sixth aves. ② 212/675-6789. www. adorama.com. Subway: 1/9 to 18th St.; F/V to 14th St.; L to Sixth Ave.

B&H A bustling 35,000-square-foot space holds B&H's massive inventory of film, digital equipment, lighting, DVD players, home theater systems, and a host of other photo-related products. Prices are very competitive, especially for used cameras and accessories.

420 Ninth Ave., between 33rd and 34th sts. ② 800/606-6969 or 212/444-6615. www.bhphotovideo.com. Subway: A/C/E to 34th St.

VIDEO

Sure, you pay money to rent videos. You can even drop a few bucks buying them. The best deal in town, however, is free. Browse New York's libraries for an extensive collection of videos that go on loan for no money at all. See p. 59 for more info.

6 From The Sidewalks of New York: Free Furniture

My apartment would be an exercise in minimalism if it weren't for the generosity of the sidewalks of New York. Lamps, chairs, end tables, and even the lovely beveled mirror in the kitchen have all been harvested from the bounty of the curbs. With the economy a little out of sorts lately, the pickings have been slimmer, but I still see couches with plenty of life left in them just begging for new homes. The key is to strike without hesitation because good stuff doesn't lay around the streets for long.

A good place to start is the Department of Sanitation's website (www.nyc.gov./html/dos), where you can find out the current collection schedule for any address in any of the boroughs. Unless you're a van owner, you'll probably want to target places that are

MANHATTAN SIDEWALK GIVE-AWAY/TRASH PICKUP DAYS

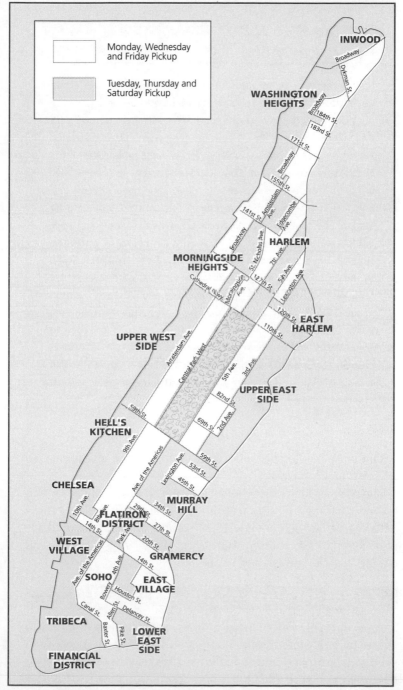

Monday, Wednesday and Friday Pickup

Tuesday, Thursday and Saturday Pickup

INWOOD

WASHINGTON HEIGHTS

Broadway
Dyckman St.
Broadway
184th St.
183rd St.
171st St.
Broadway
155th St.
141st St.
Amsterdam Ave.
Edgecombe Ave.

HARLEM

MORNINGSIDE HEIGHTS

St. Nicholas Ave.
7th Ave.
5th Ave.
Lexington Ave.
Cathedral Pkwy.
Morningside Ave.
127th St.
120th St.
110th St.

EAST HARLEM

UPPER WEST SIDE

Amsterdam Ave.
Central Park West
5th Ave.
3rd Ave.
82nd St.
2nd Ave.
69th St.
59th St.

UPPER EAST SIDE

HELL'S KITCHEN

9th Ave.
Ave. of the Americas
Lexington Ave.
59th St.
53rd St.
45th St.

CHELSEA

10th Ave.
Broadway
14th St.
Park Ave.
34th St.
29th St.
27th St.
20th St.

MURRAY HILL

FLATIRON DISTRICT

WEST VILLAGE

Ave. of the Americas
Bowery
4th Ave.
14th St.

GRAMERCY

SOHO

Houston St.
Canal St.
Allen St.
Delancey St.

EAST VILLAGE

TRIBECA

Baxter St.
Pike St.

LOWER EAST SIDE

FINANCIAL DISTRICT

Getting Free & Dirt Cheap Furniture Online

It's no secret that bargains galore can be found in the ether. Collectibles, clothes, even subway maps end up on the online auction block. If you're in the market for furniture in New York City, you may have an advantage over your midwestern and West Coast rivals. Many of New York's eight million residents live in tiny spaces, and **Ebay** (www.ebay.com) is loaded with our local treasures. But dressers, desks, and other pieces with heft can cost several hundred dollars to ship, doubling or tripling the cost of an Ebay purchase. When you're doing your bidding keep an eye out for New York zip codes—you may be the only person who can get a Man with a Van to take it home for a reasonable price. In addition to Ebay, **Craig's List** (www.craigslist.org) is another site worth scoping. A whole section of postings is reserved for free items. Ugly furniture, moving boxes, pit bulls, boa constrictors, and computers are easy to come by, as well as less essential items like box turtles, hermit crab shelters, and 12-packs of nonalcoholic beer, purchased in error. Check back frequently because the free mosaic is constantly shifting.

within close hauling distance. (Trash-picking pros invest in small wheeled hand trucks.)

Late May, at the end of the school year, is an excellent time to go out searching. The streets around NYU and Columbia overflow with abandoned student goods. Though much of what you'll see is better suited to a dorm than your swanky digs, with careful culling you can always find gems.

7 Pet Project

Sure, your loyal, vicious Yorkie saves you thousands of dollars a month in bodyguards and private security services, but you don't want to turn around and sink all that cash into an expensive pet-care proposition. Fortunately, New York has a couple of places that provide veterinary support without robbing you blind. Don't yet have that mouse-killing tabby in the house? NYC has pets available at low, low costs.

American Society for the Prevention of Cruelty to Animals Subsidized pet care is available at the Berg Memorial Animal Hospital & Clinic, run by this legendary group. An appointment for an exam with a vet costs $55, and an emergency visit is $75. They also provide shots, $20 for rabies and $25 for distemper. If you need to get a pet before you can start worrying about pet care, the ASPCA also has adoption services. The cost covers several necessities, including "pet Lojack"—a microchip should your new best friend make a break for freedom. Cats and dogs are about $75, puppies and kittens $125, more for purebreds.

424 E. 92nd St., between First Ave. and York St. © 212/876-7700. www. aspca.org. Subway: 4/5/6 to 86th St.

Bide-A-Wee The name of this century-old charitable organization derives from the Scottish for stay awhile, though they'd just as well put cats and dogs through the revolving door as quickly as possible. Adoptions here can be had for under $100, which covers a host of services. When it's time for follow-up, Bide-A-Wee's veterinary clinic is subsidized and the most affordable in the city. An exam is just $32.50 and an emergency visit is $42.50.

410 E. 38th St., 2nd floor, between First Ave. and the FDR. © 212/532-5884. www.bideawee.org. Subway: 4/5/6/7/S to 42nd St./Grand Central Station.

The Brooklyn Animal Resource Coalition Love dogs, but not ready for the full-out commitment of daily walking and feeding? Billburg's BARC will let you test-drive a pooch. You'll be helping the shelter out by giving one of their minions some exercise, you'll have a handy conversation-starter, and who knows? Maybe you'll form a bond. Allow a couple of hours if you want to walk or adopt.

253 Wythe Ave., at N. 1st St., Williamsburg, Brooklyn. © 718/486-7489. www.barcshelter.org. Subway: L to Bedford Ave.

SHOPPING DOWNTOWN

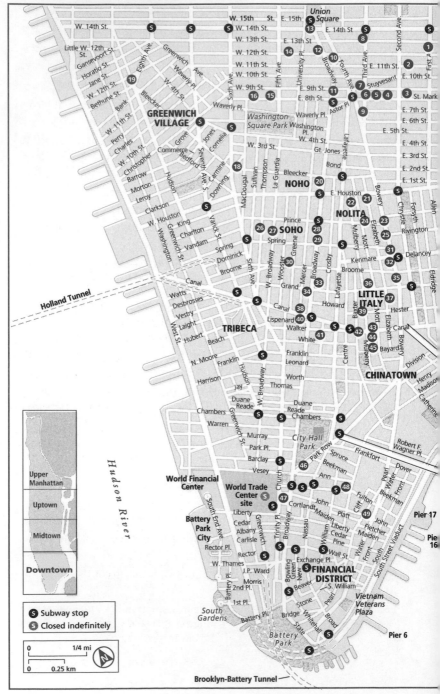

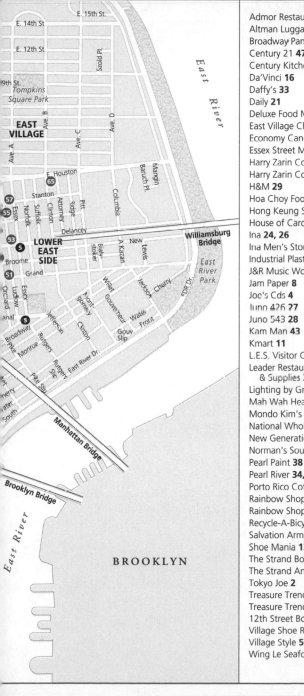

SHOPPING IN CHELSEA, THE FLATIRON DISTRICT, GRAMERCY & MIDTOWN

17@17 **14**
Adorama **12**
Angel Street Thrift Shop **8**
Annex Antiques Fair
  & Flea Market **26**
B&H **6**
Bide-A-Wee **34**
C & M Farms **28**
Chelsea Antiques Building **24**
City Opera Thrift Shop **23**
Conway's **35**
D Shoe Mania **36**
Daffy's **16, 31, 37, 40**
Extraordinary **41**
Fabrics Garden **3**
Fishs Eddy **17**
Goodwill **22**
H&M **32, 38**
Housing Works Thrift Shop **10, 18**
Jam Paper **11**
Jobson's **39**
Kmart **5**
Loehmann's **9**
Macy's **30**
Paper Productions **13**
Pearl Paint **20**
Rainbow Shops **1**
Rainbow Shops **33**
Salvation Army **2, 21**
SSS Sample Sale **4**
Starbright Floral Design **27**
The Garage **25**
The Vintage Thrift Shop **19**
Tokyo Joe **29**
Weiss & Mahoney **15**

SHOPPING UPTOWN

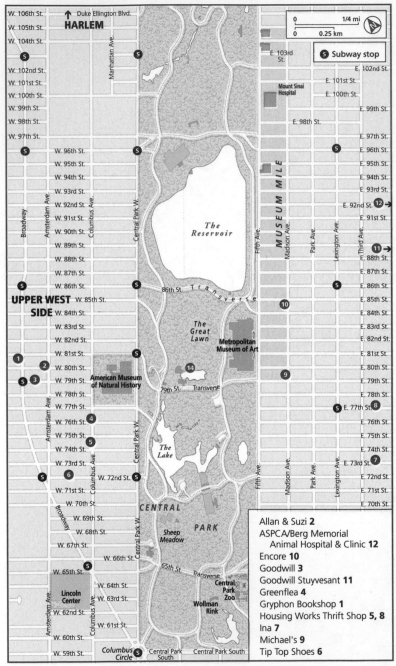

W. 106th St.

↑ Duke Ellington Blvd.

HARLEM

W. 105th St.
W. 104th St.
W. 102nd St.
W. 101st St.
W. 100th St.
W. 99th St.
W. 98th St.
W. 97th St.
W. 96th St.
W. 95th St.
W. 94th St.
W. 93rd St.
W. 92nd St.
W. 91st St.
W. 90th St.
W. 89th St.
W. 88th St.
W. 87th St.
W. 86th St.

Manhattan Ave.

E. 103rd St.
E. 102nd St.
E. 101st St.
E. 100th St.
E. 99th St.

Mount Sinai Hospital

E. 98th St.
E. 97th St.
E. 96th St.
E. 95th St.
E. 94th St.
E. 93rd St.
E. 92nd St. **12** →
E. 91st St.
E. 88th St. **11** →
E. 87th St.
E. 86th St.

The Reservoir

MUSEUM MILE

Fifth Ave.
Madison Ave.
Park Ave.
Lexington Ave.
Third Ave.

Broadway
Amsterdam Ave.
Columbus Ave.
Central Park W.

UPPER WEST SIDE

W. 85th St.
W. 84th St.
W. 83rd St.
W. 82nd St.
W. 81st St.
W. 80th St.
W. 79th St.
W. 78th St.
W. 77th St.
W. 76th St.
W. 75th St.
W. 74th St.
W. 73rd St.
W. 72nd St.
W. 71st St.
W. 70th St.
W. 69th St.
W. 68th St.
W. 67th St.
W. 66th St.
W. 65th St.
W. 64th St.
W. 63rd St.
W. 62nd St.
W. 61st St.
W. 60th St.
W. 59th St.

86th St. Transverse

The Great Lawn

Metropolitan Museum of Art

10

E. 85th St.
E. 84th St.
E. 83rd St.
E. 82nd St.
E. 81st St.
E. 80th St.
E. 79th St.
E. 78th St.

9

E. 77th St. **8**

E. 76th St.
E. 75th St.
E. 74th St.
E. 73rd St. **7**
E. 72nd St.
E. 71st St.
E. 70th St.

American Museum of Natural History

14

79th St. Transverse

The Lake

Central Park W.
Columbus Ave.
Amsterdam Ave.
Broadway

CENTRAL PARK

Sheep Meadow

65th St. Transverse

Central Park Zoo

Wollman Rink

Lincoln Center

Columbus Circle

Central Park South

Central Park South

0 Subway stop

0 —— 1/4 mi
0 —— 0.25 km

Allan & Suzi **2**
ASPCA/Berg Memorial
  Animal Hospital & Clinic **12**
Encore **10**
Goodwill **3**
Goodwill Stuyvesant **11**
Greenflea **4**
Gryphon Bookshop **1**
Housing Works Thrift Shop **5, 8**
Ina **7**
Michael's **9**
Tip Top Shoes **6**

THE ASTOR LIBRARY
FOUNDED BY
JOHN JACOB ASTOR
FOR THE
ADVANCEMENT OF USEFUL KNOWLEDGE
MDCCCXLVIII

THE LENOX LIBRARY
FOUNDED BY
JAMES LENOX
DEDICATED TO HISTORY
LITERATURE AND THE FINE ARTS
MDCCCLXX

THE
SAMU
TO SER
SCIENCE A

THE NEW YORK PUBLIC LIBRAR

A haven of elegant, Beaux Arts architecture, the Humanities and Social Sciences Library offers a wealth of free exhibits. See p. 229 for more information.

EXPLORING
NEW YORK

New Yorkers have so many amazing culture options that it's probably inevitable we start to take them a little for granted. We sometimes forget that many of the world's great treasures have found their way to our little island and its surrounding boroughs. New York is in a constant state of transformation, but miraculously a lot of history has survived, too, in houses, churches, and museums. Foundations and galleries protect New York's cutting-edge reputation, putting on thousands of risk-taking avant-garde art shows every year. What's most amazing, given the out-of-control nature of New York rents, is how easy it is to access these jewels on the cheap. Many museums let the public in for free, and many more either have special pay-what-you-wish times or admission prices that are only suggestions. If it all seems a little overwhelming, you can get a professional to guide you through the cultural minefield—New York has a bushel of free tours as well.

1 Museum Peace

Museum admission prices in New York are working their way sky-ward, with inflation running higher than even our outrageous movie tickets. The big institutions are no longer shy about stepping over the $10 barrier—the MoMA has stepped right up to a $20 regular admission (and that's despite recent shows that seemed more like corporate advertising ops than art, such as motorcycles and Armani). It's a good thing that New York's cultural resources run deep. Below you'll find almost forty places that never charge, 16 that have select times when the museum is free, and 6 museums that only suggest their admission prices. NYC has an embarrassment of cut-rate culture riches—go take advantage.

ALWAYS FREE

American Bible Society **FREE**   Dedicated to the dissemination of the Good Book, the ABS maintains galleries in its Midtown headquarters. Shows range from biblical archaeology to contemporary artwork. Pagans and Satanists may tire quickly here, as shows are limited to Judeo-Christian expressions. Three to four exhibits come through annually.

1865 Broadway, at W. 61st St. ⓒ 212/408-1500. www.americanbible.org. Mon-Wed, Fri 10am-6pm; Thurs 10am-7pm; Sat 10am-5pm. Subway: A/B/C/D/1/9 to 59th St./Columbus Circle.

American Folk Art Museum Eva and Morris Feld Gallery
FREE   The main Folk Art collection has moved to 53rd Street to rub shoulders with newly renovated MoMA, leaving not much in this original location. New acquisitions and a smattering of selections from the permanent collection fill the galleries. A sign at the security desk notes that there's a $3 suggested donation, but nobody hits you up as you go in.

2 Lincoln Sq., Columbus Ave., between 65th and 66th sts., across from Lincoln Center. ⓒ 212/595-9533. www.folkartmuseum.org. $3 suggested donation. Tues-Sun 11am-7:30pm; Mon 11am-6pm. Subway: 1/9 to 66th St.

Audubon Terrace FREE   Broadway, between 155th and 156th streets, boasts a complex of educational and cultural institutions, housed around a central courtyard with an odd, oversized statue of El Cid. The sedate classical structures are highly unexpected in the middle of a colorful Harlem neighborhood, so unexpected that few people make the trek this far north. As a result, Audubon Terrace has been hemorrhaging institutions at a rapid pace. All but two have flown south.

Audubon Terrace, Broadway, between 155th and 156th sts. ℭ 212/926-2234. www.hispanicsociety.org. Tues-Sat 10am-4:30pm; Sun 1-4pm. Subway: 1 to 157th St.

The Hispanic Society of America FREE   Hispanic treasures ranging from Bronze Age tools to Goya portraits, seemingly assembled at random, fill this musty but intriguing museum. Don't miss the intricate marble chapel sculptures on the first floor and the gorgeous arabesque tiles upstairs.

Audubon Terrace, Broadway, between 155th and 156th sts. ℭ 212/926-2234. www.hispanicsociety.org. Tues-Sat 10am-4:30pm; Sun 1-4pm. Subway: 1 to 157th St.

American Academy of Arts and Letters FREE   This prestigious century-old organization extends membership to the cream of the nation's writers and artists. In the spring and fall exhibits highlight the works of these artists, as well as the recipients of Academy prizes. There are three exhibits every year.

Audubon Terrace, Broadway, between 155th and 156th sts. ℭ 212/368-5900. Open when exhibitions are up, Tues-Sun 1-4pm. Subway: 1 to 157th St.

Art Students League of New York Gallery FREE   This independent art school, founded in 1875, is a New York legend. A host of big names started out here, including Norman Rockwell and Georgia O'Keeffe, who left behind work in the league's permanent collection. The galleries exhibit portions of that collection along with art by current students, members, and other contemporaries.

215 West 57th St., between Broadway and Seventh Ave. ℭ 212/247-4510. www.theartstudentsleague.org. Mon-Fri 10am-8:30pm; Sat 9:30am-4pm; Sun 1-4:30pm. Subway: N/R/Q/W to 57th St.; B/D/E to Seventh Ave.

Austrian Cultural Forum FREE   The architecture of the new Austrian Cultural Forum has garnered more eyebrow raises than critical praise. I find the exterior ominous, like a dagger looming over the street. The interior is more attractive, with sleek touches compensating for a cold quality. The multilevel spaces accommodate several galleries. Austrian and European-themed shows rotate through.

11 E. 52nd St., between Fifth and Madison aves. ℂ 212/319-5300. www.acf ny.org. Mon-Fri 8am-4pm. Subway: E/V to 53rd St.

Carnegie Hall FREE The Rose Museum recounts the practice, practice, practice it takes to get to this storied music hall. A chronology and memorabilia are on view, in addition to occasional temporary exhibits on Carnegie legends like the Gershwins, Tchaikovsky, or Leonard Bernstein.

154 W. 57th St., between 6th and 7th aves., 2nd floor. ℂ 212/903-9629. www.carnegiehall.org. Daily 11am-4:30pm; and to ticket holders during concerts. Subway: A/B/C/D/1/9 to 59th St.-Columbus Circle.

Center for Jewish History FREE Beautiful new galleries document the Jewish experience. Photos, prints, and portraits are the primary mediums. See p. 272 in chapter 7 for a full review.

15 W. 16th St., between 5th and 6th aves. ℂ 212/294-8301. www.cjh.org. *Reading Room and Genealogy Institute:* Mon-Thurs 9:30am-4:30pm; Fri by appt. *All other galleries:* Mon-Thurs 9am-5pm; Fri 9am-2pm; Sun 11am-5pm. Subway: L/N/Q/R/W/4/5/6 to 14th St./Union Sq.

Fashion Institute of Technology Museum FREE This museum on FIT's campus is long on historical fashion, specializing in the 20th century. Fashion showoffs complement surprisingly sophisticated students shows. Other exhibits display items from the special collections, like accessories or sketches.

The southwest corner of 7th Ave., at 27th St. ℂ 212/517-5800. www.fitnyc. suny/edu. Tues-Fri noon-8pm; Sat 10am-5pm. Subway: 1/9 to 28th St.

Federal Hall National Memorial FREE A former customs house, this columned Wall Street museum now recounts the long history of the site. See p. 284 in chapter 7 for a full review.

26 Wall St., at Nassau St. ℂ 212/825-6888. www.nps.gov/feha. Mon-Fri 9am-5pm. Subway: 2/3/4/5 to Wall St.

Federal Reserve Bank FREE In addition to the gallery of the American Numismatic Society on the ground floor here, advance sign-up will give you the chance to glimpse a little of the building. It's basically a tour of a bank. A bank with the largest gold cache in the world, but still a bank. Along the way you'll see two short videos, one weirdly defensive about the employees of the currency-processing division, and one weirdly defensive about the employees working with the gold. Five stories beneath the street you'll get to see the vault itself, which resembles a gym locker room, only with $90 billion in gold shimmering behind the bars. As a reward for your attention, you'll get a free $1,000 in cash. Shredded cash. Call 1 to 2 weeks in advance to reserve a space.

33 Liberty St., between William and Nassau sts. ℂ 212/720-6130. www. newyorkfed.org. Tours weekdays 9:30am, 10:30am, 11:30am, 1:30pm, and 2:30pm (they last about an hour). Subway: A/C/J/M/Z/2/3/4/5 to Fulton St./ Broadway Nassau.

Fisher Landau Center for Art FREE   Though this museum has been around for almost 15 years, few New Yorkers know about its 25,000-square-foot exhibition and study center. The galleries, which show painting, sculpture, and photography from 1960 to the present, are huge and well lit. You'll find three floors of viewing pleasure, usually modern art icons.

38-27 30th St., between 38th and 39th aves. ℂ 718/937-0727. www.flcart. org. Mon–Sun 10am–5pm; extended Fri until 7:45pm. Subway: N/W to 39th Ave.

☆ **Forbes Magazine Galleries** FREE   Wind through well-maintained displays of Malcolm Forbes' idiosyncratic fancies in this whimsical boutique museum. See p. 273 in chapter 7 for a full review.

62 Fifth Ave., at 12th St. ℂ 212/206-5548. www.forbes.com/forbescollection. Tues–Wed and Fri–Sat 10am–4pm (hours can vary, call ahead). Subway: L/N/ Q/R/W/4/5/6 to 14th St./Union Sq.

General Grant National Memorial FREE   Manhattan is home to the nation's largest mausoleum, the graceful 1897 structure that houses the remains of General Ulysses S. Grant. For punch-line sticklers, Mrs. Julia Grant is interred here as well. The hushed interior conveys peaceful repose. There's a small on-site museum where you'll be surprised to discover what a big deal Grant's funeral was in New York. The tomb itself was once a huge attraction, but tourists have found more pressing enticements and the memorial feels secluded, nearly forgotten.

Riverside Dr., at 122nd St. ℂ 212/666-1640. www.nps.gov/gegr. Daily 9am–5pm. Subway: 1/9 to 125th St.

Hall of Fame for Great Americans `FREE`   You'd think a gigantic monument designed by Sanford White with tablets by Tiffany Studios, memorializing American heroes like Mark Twain, Abe Lincoln, and Susan B. Anthony, would be a major draw, but this oddball attraction is sadly overlooked. The distant location, on the Bronx Community College campus, might be part of the problem. If you're in the area don't miss out because the open colonnade with its 102 bronze busts and classical architecture is a wonderful surprise.

Hall of Fame Terrace, 181st St. and University Ave., the Bronx. ☏ 718/289-5161. www.bcc.cuny.edu/halloffame. Daily 10am–5pm. Subway: 4 to 183rd St.

Hamilton Grange National Memorial `FREE`   Federalist Paper author and first secretary of the treasury Alexander Hamilton started construction on his country home in 1800. Once part of a 32-acre estate, Hamilton Grange is now crowded by an undistin-guished apartment building and an impudent church balcony. The National Park Service has well-maintained exhibits inside, including a scale model of the yellow Federal-style house as it looked when it was surrounded by the hills and trees of a van-ished Harlem.

287 Convent Ave., between W. 141st and W. 142nd sts. ☏ 212/283-5154. www.nps.gov/hagr. Fri–Sun 9am–5pm. Subway: 1/9 to 137th St.; A/B/C/D to 145th St.

Hebrew Union College–Jewish Institute of Religion, Brookdale Center `FREE`   Multiple galleries here display assorted Judaica and contemporary artwork of a Jewish bent. The curatorial team doesn't seem particularly discerning—clunkers and standouts are given equal prominence. Exhibitions change pretty regularly, with 8 to 10 moving through each year. `FINE PRINT` A photo ID is required to enter.

1 W. 4th St., between Broadway and Mercer St. ☏ 212/824-2205. www.huc. edu/museums/ny. Mon–Thurs 9am–5pm; Fri 9am–3pm; selected Sundays. Subway: N/R/W to 8th St.; 6 to Astor Place.

Irish Hunger Memorial `FREE`   This recent addition to the down-town Hudson waterfront memorializes the Irish famine of 1845–52. The center of the installation is a famine-era cottage moved stone by stone from the old country, resting on a field of blackthorn and heather. Take the path to the memorial's top and you'll be treated to sublime views of the Statue of Liberty and Ellis Island.

Vesey St. and North End Ave. www.batteryparkcityparks.org. Subway: 1/2/3/9/A/C to Chambers St.

John M. Mossman Lock Collection FREE When you first enter this room you think "well, it's just a bunch of old locks." Inevitably, though, as you learn more about the evolution of keys and vaults you get drawn in. The exhibit includes 4,000-year-old Egyptian devices, Renaissance locks with elaborate tracery, and spectacularly crafted 19th-century time locks. Sign in with the guard on the ground floor and you'll be taken to the exhibit, on a second-floor balcony overlooking the landmark General Society of Mechanics and Tradesmen library.

20 W. 44th St., between Fifth and Sixth aves. (©) 212/921-1767. www.general society.org. Sept-Mar Mon-Thurs 9am-7pm, Fri 9am-5pm; Apr-Aug Mon-Thurs 9am-6pm, Fri 9am-5pm. Closed July. Subway: 7 to 5th Ave.; B/D/F/V to 42nd St.

Museum of American Illustration FREE Illustrators never seem to get their proper respect as visual artists, constantly upstaged by showoff painters and photographers. The two galleries maintained by the Society of Illustrators strive to remedy that situation. Contest winners and works of society members can be found on the walls, along with classics from the permanent collection (the Society was formed in 1901, so there's a lot to fall back on). Exhibits change frequently.

28 E. 63rd St., between Park and Lexington aves. (©) 212/838-2560. www. societyillustrators.org. Tues 10am-8pm; Wed-Fri 10am-5pm; Sat noon-4pm. Subway: N/R/W/4/5/6 to 59th St.

★ **National Museum of the American Indian** FREE Housing Native American treasures in a former arm of the federal government seems a bit of a cruel irony, but the overall effect is of reverence for endangered arts. This Smithsonian branch augments its exhibits with films and videos; check the schedule at www. nativenetworks.si.edu. There's programming for kids, too, including storybook readings and workshops. Everything is free, though craft workshops can have material fees of up to $25. Some events require reservations. See also p. 288 in chapter 7.

1 Bowling Green, between State and Whitehall sts. (©) 212/514-3700. www. americanindian.si.edu. Daily 10am-5pm; Thurs until 8pm. Subway: 4/5 to Bowling Green; 1/9 to South Ferry.

The New York City Police Museum `FREE`　This museum borders on hagiography, but plenty of good little nuggets can be found here, including a 1933 letter from a private citizen suggesting police cars adopt "sirens." See p. 285 in chapter 7 for a full review.

100 Old Slip, between Water and South sts., 2 blocks south of Wall St. ℂ 212/ 480-3100. www.nycpolicemuseum.org. Suggested admission of $5 is not enforced. Tues–Sat 10am–5pm. Subway: 2/3 to Wall St.; J/M/Z to Broad St.

New York Unearthed `FREE`　A tiny branch of the South Street Seaport Museum, with brief glimpses of urban archaeology. See p. 286 in chapter 7 for a full review.

17 State St. Enter off Pearl St., between Whitehall and State sts. ℂ 212/748-8628. www.southstreetseaportmuseum.org. Mon–Fri noon–5pm. Subway: R/W to Whitehall St.

Nicholas Roerich Museum `FREE`　One of New York's least-known museums showcases the Russian scholar and painter Nicholas Roerich. A genteel Riverside Drive town house holds three floors of galleries, cluttered with Roerich's paintings. The images favor Russian icons and Himalayan landscapes, and though the bright colors and stylized lines border on the cartoonish, the overall effect is impressive. Objects gathered in Roerich's Asian explorations are scattered throughout the museum and a subtle spiritual air pervades. The museum's motto *Pax Cultura* (Peace Through Culture) gets expressed in a full schedule of free concerts and poetry readings. Music plays Sundays at 5pm; check online for other dates and times.

319 W. 107th St., between Riverside Dr. and Broadway. ℂ 212/864-7752. www.roerich.org. Subway: 1/9 to 110th St.

Onassis Cultural Center `FREE`　Aristotle Onassis—or as most of us know him, Mr. Jackie O.—was the man behind this Midtown institution, which supports Hellenic art and culture. Rotating exhibits and a long-term display of rare casts of Parthenon marbles can be found here. There's also a pleasant indoor waterfall to rest for a spell.

The Olympic Tower atrium, 641 Fifth Ave., entrance just east of Fifth on 51st or 52nd sts. ℂ 212/486-4448. www.onassisusa.org. Subway: E/V to 53rd St.

Pratt Galleries `FREE`　The fruits of Pratt Institute's prestigious arts and design programs can be found in the galleries the school runs. Current student shows are mixed in with alumni and faculty exhibitions, plus other artistic innovators.

144 W. 14th St., between Sixth and Seventh aves. ℂ 212/647-7778. www.pratt.edu. Tues-Fri 10:30am–5:30pm; Sat noon–5pm. Subway: 1/2/3/9 and F/V to 14th St.; L to 5th Ave. *Schafler Gallery on Pratt's campus:* 200 Willoughby Ave. Ft. Greene, Brooklyn. ℂ 718/636-3517. Mon-Fri 9am–5pm. Subway: G to Clinton-Washington aves.

★ **SculptureCenter** FREE

Though this institution has been supporting and showcasing modern sculpture since 1928, its new home in a former Queens trolley repair shop can make a visitor feel like he's come to a start-up. Maya Lin's industrial-chic design is of the moment, but many of the touches are timeless. Ceilings soar 40 feet in the main room, and the basement project spaces are like minimalist catacombs. The rough edges haven't been disguised, but the overall effect is still refined, a perfect backdrop for the contemporary sculptures and installation art exhibited here. I love this place—it's a miniature version of what the Tate Modern in London should have been.

FREE **Socrates Sculpture Park**

Among the most glamorous of New York's former industrial dumps, Socrates Sculpture Park brings large-scale modern art to the banks of the East River. Apropos for the location, the work here has an organic quality. It's certainly much less slick looking than what one finds on the Manhattan side. The park is roomy and the views are spectacular. 32-01 Vernon Blvd., at Broadway. Long Island City, Queens. ℂ 718/956-1819. www.socratessculpturepark.org. Daily 10am–sunset. Subway: N/W trains to Broadway. Walk 8 blocks along Broadway toward the East River.

44-19 Purves St., off Jackson Ave., Long Island City, Queens. ℂ 718/361-1750. www.sculpturecenter.org. Thurs-Mon 11am–6pm. Some shows have a $5 suggested donation, not enforced. Subway: E/V to 23rd St./Ely. G to Court St. 7 to Court House Sq.

Sony Wonder Technology Lab FREE Sony sucks in new generations of technology addicts with this four-level supermodern demonstration center. Kids can try their hands at robotics, medical imaging, and video game design, among other expensive toys. Free movies round out the stimuli; see p. 54 in chapter 2. FINE PRINT Reservations should be made in advance, up to 2 weeks ahead. Call on Monday, Wednesday, or Friday between 11am and 4pm. Otherwise, you may not get in, or you may get in at a less convenient hour later in the day.

550 Madison Ave., at 56th St. (✆ **212/833-8100,** or 212/833-5414 for reservations. www.sonywondertechlab.com. Tues–Wed and Fri–Sun 10am–6pm; Thurs 10am–8pm; last entrance 30 min. before closing. Subway: E/N/R/V/W to Fifth Ave.; 4/5/6 to 59th St.

Storefront for Art and Architecture FREE   Designed with odd panels that expand into the street, this idiosyncratic institution does a lot with its very narrow space. Always intelligent exhibits explore architecture, art, and design.

97 Kenmare St., between Mulberry St. and Cleveland Place, near Lafayette St. (✆ **212/431-5795.** www.storefrontnews.org. Tues–Sat 11am–6pm. Subway: 6 to Spring St.; N/R/W to Prince St.

Tibet House U.S. FREE   This institution presents Tibetan art through a small permanent collection and spacious temporary exhibits. See p. 272 in chapter 7 for a review.

22 W. 15th St., 2nd floor, between Fifth and Sixth aves. (✆ **212/807-0563.** www.tibethouse.org. Suggested admission $2, not enforced. Subway: L/N/Q/R/W/4/5/6 to 14th St./Union Sq.

Urban Center FREE   The landmark 1882 Villard Houses on Madison Avenue have an exclusive look, but the north side is actually open to the public. Enter the central courtyard, designed like an Italian palazzo by McKim, Mead & White, and take the door on your left. The Municipal Art Society and the Architectural League of New York both keep galleries here, with rotating exhibits detailing a love of the city. While you're here, check out the bookstore's huge selection of urban planning and architecture tomes.

The Municipal Art Society. (✆ **212/935-3960.** www.mas.org. *Urban Center Books:* (✆ 212/935-3592. www.urbancenterbooks.com. *Architectural League of New York:* (✆ 212/753-1722. www.archleague.org. Mon–Wed and Fri–Sat 11am–5pm. Subway: 6 to 51st St.

Visual Arts Museum FREE   With a little imagination, you can guess the focus of the School of Visual Arts' museum. Exhibitions start with student portfolios and go on to digital salons and masters' series, highlighting visual art superstars.

209 E. 23rd St., at Third Ave. ✆ 212/592.2010. www.schoolofvisualarts. edu. Mon-Wed and Fri 9am-6:30pm; Thurs 9am-8pm; Sat 10am-5pm. Subway: 6 to 23rd St.

Whitney Museum of American Art at Altria FREE This tiny Whitney outpost shows contemporary artists. The lobby is often adorned with large-scale modern sculpture. See p. 278 in chapter 7 for a full review.

120 Park Ave., southwest corner at 42nd St., opposite Grand Central Terminal. ✆ 917/663-2453. www.whitney.org. Gallery Mon-Wed and Fri 11am-6pm; Thurs 11am-7:30pm. Sculpture Court Mon-Sat 7:30am-9:30pm; Sun and holidays 11am-7pm. Extended hours for performances and lectures. Subway: 4/5/6/7/S to Grand Central.

SOMETIMES FREE

Several museums that won't give up their goods for free do set aside special hours and days where you can pay what you wish. If you're feeling energetic, you can link up multiple stops. Thursday nights are popular admission by donation nights in Manhattan. Although many of the Bronx's attractions are spread far afield, Wednesday is a clearinghouse day when many of them relax their entrance policies. Beware the last free day before an exhibition ends. More than a few procrastinators call New York home, and you can find what looks like all of them taking advantage of a final free window of opportunity.

American Folk Art Museum Recently relocated, the new folk art building has generated some serious architectural buzz for its slender modern design. It's too bad that the high-tech slick finishes aren't harmonious with the rustic works on display. Rotating exhibitions complement the permanent collection, which represents some amazing oddball autodidacts.

45 W. 53rd St., between 5th and 6th aves. ✆ 212/265-1040. www.folkart museum.org. Regular admission $9; free Fri after 6pm. Tues-Sat 10am-6pm; Fri until 8pm. Subway: E/V to Fifth Ave./53rd St.

Asia Society John D. Rockefeller III founded the Asia Society in the midfifties to encourage cultural exchanges and understanding between Asians and Americans. The newly renovated headquarters building has beautiful galleries, showing off parts of Rockefeller's collection in addition to rotating exhibits. The interior architecture is impressive, especially the sleek new staircase that looks like a snake's skeleton wandering up the floors.

Sometimes Free (or Pay-What-You-Wish) Museums

Wednesday	Thursday	Friday	Saturday	Sunday
The Bronx Museum of the Arts (Wed noon-9pm)	Children's Museum of the Arts (Thurs 4-6pm)	American Folk Art Museum (Fri 6-8pm)	Brooklyn Museum of Art (First Sat 11am-11pm)	Museum for African Art (Sun 2-6pm)
	Dahesh Museum of Art (First Thurs 6-9pm)	Asia Society (Fri 6-9pm)	The Studio Museum in Harlem (First Sat 10am-6pm)	
	El Museo Del Barrio (Thurs 4-8pm)	Guggenheim Museum (Fri 6-8pm)		
	Jewish Museum (Thurs 5-8pm)	MoMA (Fri 4-8pm)		
	Museum of Arts & Design (Thurs 6-8pm)	Museum of Chinese in the Americas (Fri noon-7pm)		
		New York Hall of Science (Fri 2-5pm, Sept-June)		
		Whitney Museum of American Art (Fri 6pm-9pm)		

725 Park Ave., at 70th St. ℭ 212/288-6400. www.asiasociety.org. Regular admission $7; free Fri 6-9pm. Tues-Sun 11am-6pm; Fri extended until 9pm. Subway: 6 to 68th St./Hunter College.

Bronx Museum of the Arts   This hulk of modernity plunked down amid the Art Deco restraint of the Grand Concourse puts on adventurous shows. Most of the artists who get exhibited here have logged time as Bronx residents. If not, they'll represent some aspect of New York's cultural diversity. Entrance is by a suggested admission, though the suggestion gets dropped all day Wednesdays, which are completely free.

1040 Grand Concourse, at 165th St., the Bronx. ℭ 718/681-6000. www.bxma.org. Suggested admission $5; free Wed all day. Wed noon-9pm; Thurs-Sun noon-6pm. Subway: B/D/4 to 161st St./Yankee Stadium.

Brooklyn Museum of Art   The second-largest art museum in the US of A, the Brooklyn Museum is as spruced up and thriving as the borough that hosts it. With a glorious new entryway, remodeled exhibitions, and a building with over half a million square feet, there are several days' worth of exploring to be done here. The Egyptian collection is world-class and beautifully displayed, with informative, well-written notes accompanying each object. The fourth floor's period rooms are definitely worth a peek. Don't miss the Jan Schenck House, a touch of Dutch in old Breuckelen that somehow survived on the edge of Jamaica Bay from 1675 to 1952.

200 Eastern Pkwy., at Washington Ave., Brooklyn. ℭ 718/638-5000. www. brooklynmuseum.org. Suggested admission $6; free 1st Sat of the month 11am-11pm. Wed-Fri 10am-5pm; 1st Sat of the month 11am-11pm; each Sat thereafter 11am-6pm; Sun 11am-6pm. Subway: 2/3 to Eastern Pkwy./ Brooklyn Museum.

Children's Museum of the Arts   This institution, on an industrial stretch between SoHo and Chinatown, is dedicated to getting kids involved with art. Kids 12 and under and families roll up their sleeves for informative workshops, which cover everything from puppet making to computer drawing. On the walls you'll find selections from the museum's permanent collection, including some great WPA pieces, or rotating exhibits of kid-friendly artists

☆ Date Night: First Saturdays at the Brooklyn Museum

One of New York's best cheap date opportunity comes once a month at the Brooklyn Museum. **Every first Saturday** `FREE` the museum transforms itself into a house party on a massive scale. The crowd is more diverse than the U.N. General Assembly, with a dizzying range of ages, cultures, and castes represented. The museum keeps most of its galleries open for your perusal. When you run low on witty commentary, distractions like films and lectures beckon. Dance performances can be found, too, or if the date is going particularly well, you might let your feet work the floor yourself. The live music performances tend to be upbeat and very danceable. There's no charge for any of this and nobody hits you up for a donation. The night is so festive that your date may not even notice just how cheap it's been. See the Brooklyn Museum review above for address and subway directions.

like Keith Haring. Call or check the website for the current exhibition and activities schedule.

182 Lafayette St., between Broome and Grand sts. (C) 212/941-9198. www. cmany.org. Regular admission $6, but pay what you wish Thurs 4-6pm. Wed and Fri-Sun noon-5pm; Thurs noon-6pm. Subway: 6 to Spring St.

Dahesh Museum of Art   This small museum presents the cream of classicist art, the academic school dedicated to European art before the academy was tainted by Impressionism. Renaissance, baroque, and rococo traditions play out on elaborate canvases documenting historical subjects and pastoral life. The Dahesh recently upgraded to three expansive floors in an office building, and in the process they abandoned their no-fee admissions. It now costs $9 to enter, though the first Thursday of every month has extended hours and a pay-what-you-wish policy.

580 Madison Ave., at 57th St. (C) 212/759-0606. www.daheshmuseum.org. Regular admission $9; pay what you wish first Thurs of every month 6-9pm. Tues-Sun 11am-6pm; until 9pm the first Thurs of every month. Subway: F to 57th St.; E/V to 53rd St./Fifth Ave.; N/R/W to 59th St./Fifth Ave.

El Museo del Barrio   A school classroom display was the genesis for this Museum Mile institution, the only U.S. museum dedicated to Puerto Rican, Caribbean, and Latin American art. The artistic history of the region from pre-Columbian origins to the present is recounted in a permanent installation. Changing exhibitions cover contemporary subjects and artists.

1230 Fifth Ave., at 104th St. (C) 212/831-7272. www.elmuseo.org. Regular admission $7; free Thurs 4-8pm. Wed and Fri-Sun 11am-5pm; Thurs 11am-8pm. Subway: 6 to 103rd St.

Guggenheim Museum   Artists complained bitterly (of course) about the curved walls that spiral up seven stories, but Frank Lloyd Wright knew what he was doing and flat art mounts on the walls of the Guggie just fine. You'll feel like you're climbing through a nautilus shell as you view the latest temporary installation in the central atrium, recently tending toward low-art crowd-pleasers like motorcycles and Norman Rockwell. A tower alongside the spiral hosts a permanent collection stocked with Chagalls, Matisses, van Goghs, and Picassos.

1071 Fifth Ave., at 88th St. (C) 212/423-3500. www.guggenheim.org. Regular admission $15; pay as you wish Fri 6-8pm. Sun-Wed and Sat 10am-5:45pm; Fri 9am-8pm. Subway: 4/5/6 to 86th St.

The Jewish Museum   Four thousand years of Jewish history for this? Absolutely. A Gothic-style mansion on the Upper East Side holds these remarkable collections, which chronicle the twists and turns of the Jewish experience. Everything from ancient artifacts to Borscht Belt ruminations from television's Golden Age can be found under this roof.

1109 Fifth Ave., at 92nd St. © 212/423-3200. www.thejewishmuseum.org. Regular admission is $8 adults, but it's pay what you wish Thurs 5-8pm. Sun 11am-5:45pm; Mon-Wed 11am-5:45pm; Thurs 11am-8pm; Fri 11am-3pm. Subway: 4/5 to 86th St.; 6 to 96th St.

Museum of Modern Art (MoMA)   Van Gogh's *Starry Night,* Picasso's *Les Demoiselles d'Avignon,* and Mondrian's *Broadway Boogie-Woogie* have given up the charms of Queens for the comfort of home. MoMA is back in Midtown after 2 years with QNS appended to the name. Painting and sculpture fans will be joined by architecture lovers, eager to check out Yoshio Taniguchi's $650-million redesign of the 53rd Street space. Taniguchi has doubled the amount of exhibition space, so there will be plenty of new places to pack in the crowds, which are certain to be legion. Check the website for upcoming exhibitions.

11 W. 53rd St., between Fifth and Sixth aves. © 212/708-9400. www.moma. org. Regular admission $20; seniors $16; students $12; pay what you wish Fri 4-8pm. Wed-Mon 10:30am-5:30pm; Fri 10:30am-8pm. Subway: E/V to Fifth Ave.

Museum for African Art   Traditional African arts are displayed in two galleries in this stylish temporary home (the museum is eventually headed to the Museum Mile back in Manhattan). In addition to the gorgeous masks and jars you'd expect, temporary exhibits also cover contemporary African art and culture.

36-01 43rd Ave., at 36th St., 3rd floor, Long Island City, Queens. © 718/ 784-7700. www.africanart.org. Regular admission $6; free Sun 2-6pm. Mon and Thurs-Fri 10am-5pm; Sat-Sun 11am-6pm. Subway: 7 to 33rd St. Walk north to 36th St., turn left and go 1 block to 43rd Ave.

Museum of Arts and Design   Craft design gets its 15 minutes of fame at this small, stylish Midtown museum. Exhibits often focus on emerging artists and new ideas of form, especially as the latter follows function. Clay, glass, wood, metal, and fiber are among the materials represented. For big spenders, the artisans on display often have their wares available in the shop.

40 W. 53rd St., between Fifth and Sixth aves. ℂ **212/956-3535**. www. americancraftmuseum.org. Regular admission $9; pay what you wish Thurs 6-8pm. Tues-Wed and Fri-Sun 10am-6pm; Thurs 10am-8pm. Subway: E/V to 53rd St./Fifth Ave.

Museum of Chinese in the Americas This small museum in an old public school building is dedicated to the Chinese immigrant experience. Oral history projects, photo shows, and art installations all have a place here.

70 Mulberry St., at Bayard St., 2nd floor. ℂ **212/619-4785**. www.moca-nyc. org. Regular admission $3; free all day Fri. Tues-Thurs and Sat-Sun noon-6pm; Fri noon-7. Subway: J/M/N/Q/R/W/Z/6 to Canal St.

New York Hall of Science Nominally a hall of science, this place is really a big playground. The exhibits are hands on, letting kids get engulfed by a giant soap bubble, float on air in an antigravity mirror, and retrieve astronomical images from the depths of outer space. In summer the huge Outdoor Science Playground provides jungle gyms, slides, seesaws, and spinners to help the physics medicine go down.

47-01 111th St., in Flushing Meadows-Corona Park, Queens. ℂ **718/699-0005**. www.nyhallsci.org. Regular admission $9; free Fri 2-5pm (Sept 1-June 30 only). July-Aug Mon 9:30am-2pm; Tues-Fri 9:30am-5pm; Sat-Sun 10:30am-6pm. Sept 1-June 30 Tues-Thurs 9:30am-2pm; Fri 9:30am-5pm; Sat-Sun noon-5pm. Subway: 7 to 111th St.

The Studio Museum in Harlem Dedicated to the art of African Americans, with a sideline on the African Diaspora, this small museum has gathered together a terrific permanent collection. Exhibits rotate frequently and the calendar is packed with freebies. There are poetry readings, dance, forums, and open studios for the A-I-R program, which shows off the Artists in Residence that the Studio Museum helps support.

144 W. 125th St., between Lenox Ave. and Adam Clayton Powell Blvd. ℂ **212/864-4500**. www.studiomuseuminharlem.org. Suggested admission $7; free on first Sat of the month. Sun and Wed-Fri noon-6pm; Sat 10am-6pm. Subway: 2/3 to 125th St.

Whitney Museum of American Art Behind somewhat imposing Bauhaus walls on Madison Avenue lies a spectacular collection of 20th-century art. The Whitney is rich in Edward Hopper, Louise Nevelson, and Georgia O'Keeffe, and they're good about rotating the permanent collection through their galleries. Shows of contemporary artists on other floors tend to be surprisingly cutting edge for a big Uptown institution.

945 Madison Ave., at 75th St. © 212/570-3676. www.whitney.org. Regular admission $12; pay what you wish Fri after 6pm. Tues-Thurs and Sat-Sun 11am-6pm; Fri 1-9pm. Subway: 6 to 77th St.

SUGGESTED ADMISSIONS

Many New York institutions let in visitors on the basis of a "suggested admission." The price you have pay isn't set in stone; it's set by the dictates of your own conscience. Before you decide how much to give remember that you're already giving if you pay local taxes. We working stiffs support the NYC Department of Cultural Affairs, the largest agency of its kind in the U.S. In 2004, the agency had $118 million set aside for expenses and $250 for its capital budget. Cultural Affairs helps fund dozens of local institutions, many of which are owned by the city (and by extension, you and me). Sometimes $1 seems like the right amount to be spending on one's own museum. That's not to say if you're flush you should be stiffing these institutions. If you've got a spare couple of bucks, by all means toss it in the hat.

The Cloisters   This Met subsidiary is one of the city's most unlikely treasures. Situated on a Hudson cliff side, the Cloisters is a Frankenstein-esque amalgamation of medieval architecture: a Romanesque chapel, a 12th-century Spanish apse, and portions of cloisters from five different monasteries. Its treasures include the Unicorn Tapestries, the Les Belles Heures du Duc de Berry illuminated manuscript, and the 12th-century Bury St. Edmunds cross. The building is surrounded by tranquil gardens.

At the north end of Fort Tryon Park. © 212/923-3700. www.metmuseum. org. Suggested admission $12. Nov-Feb Tues-Sun 9:30am-4:45pm; Mar-Oct Tues-Sun 9:30am-5:15pm. Subway: A to 190th St., then a 10 mln. walk north along Margaret Corbin Dr., or pick up the M4 bus at the station (1 stop to Cloisters). Or take the M4 Madison Ave. to Fort Tryon Park-The Cloisters.

The Metropolitan Museum of Art   On the Upper East Side, tucked away just off Central Park, you can find this undiscovered little gem of a collection. Allow yourself a good 10 minutes to see everything they've got. Yeah, well, the Met is the 800-pound gorilla of New York's museum scene, and it's not hiding from anybody. If it's not the greatest museum in the world, it must be damn close, and it's all right there for the price of a suggested admission.

Fifth Ave., at 82nd St. ℂ **212/535-7710.** www.metmuseum.org. Suggested admission $12. Tues-Thurs 9:30am-5:30am; until 9pm Fri-Sat, closed Mon. Subway: 4/5/6 to 86th St.

Museum of the City of New York   Exhibits here trace NYC from the windmills of its Dutch colonial days up to its present status as the undisputed capital of the world. Lovely period rooms and a collection of theatrical memorabilia are highlights of the collection.

Fifth Ave., at 103rd St. ℂ **212/534-1672.** www.mcny.org. Suggested admission $7. Wed-Sat 10am-5pm; Sun noon-5pm. Subway: 6 to 103rd St.

New York City Fire Museum   FDNY Engine Co. 30's former home holds an impressive collection of fire-service memorabilia. Exhibits range from the 18th century to the present, where the most poignant materials are. During the 9/11 attacks, 343 firefighters gave their lives just a few blocks to the south of the museum.

278 Spring St., between Varick and Hudson sts. ℂ **212/691-1303.** www.nyc firemuseum.org. Suggested admission $4. Tues-Sat 10am-5pm; Sun 10am-4pm. Subway: C/E to Spring St.

☆ **P.S. 1 Contemporary Art Center**   School is out, replaced by art that's inside this 19th-century former public school. The Renaissance Revival building has been beautifully converted, with avant-garde shows rotating through the former classrooms. Now affiliated with MoMA, P.S. 1 does a terrific job of bringing fresh, intriguing art to Queens.

22-25 Jackson Ave., Long Island City, Queens. ℂ **718/784-2084.** www. ps1.org. Suggested admission $5. Thurs-Mon noon-6pm. Subway: E/V to 23rd St./Ely Ave.; 7 to 45th Rd./Court House Sq.

Queens Museum of Art   This museum has reproductions of Greek marbles and some nice Tiffany glass, but the real draw is The Panorama of New York City, the world's largest scale model. Every single building in the five boroughs is represented, in addition to every street and bridge, and even airplanes that take off and land at a tiny LaGuardia. The Museum is located in Corona Park, on the site of the legendary 1964 World's Fair. Don't miss the nearby Unisphere, a highlight of the fair and the largest representation of Earth that we humans have cooked up yet. Twelve gleaming stories high, the Unisphere will give you a good idea of what the planet looks like from 6,000 miles in space.

Next to the Unisphere in Flushing Meadows-Corona Park, Queens. ✆ 718/
592-9700. www.queensmuse.org. Suggested admission $5. Tues-Fri 10am-
5pm; Sat-Sun noon-5pm. Subway: 7 to Willets Point/Shea Stadium, follow
signs through the park.

DIRT CHEAP

Fraunces Tavern Museum   A small museum above the tavern
and restaurant shows off the building's illustrious history along with
scattered relics of colonial life. See p. 287 in chapter 7 for a full
review.

54 Pearl St., near Broad St. ✆ 212/425-1778. www.frauncestavernmuseum.
org. Admission $3. Tues-Fri 10am-5pm; Thurs until 7pm; Sat 11am-5pm. Sub-
way: J/M/Z to Broad St.; 2/3 to Wall St.

Museum of American Financial History   Though affiliated
with the Smithsonian, this tiny basement space is more advertor-
ial than enlightener. Photos, busts, and numismatic matters make
up most of the collection, but the gift shop occupies nearly as
much space as the museum proper. Admission is only $2, but the
purchase of a *Wall Street Journal* and a cup of coffee would be a
more informative investment of time and money.

28 Broadway, just north of Bowling Green Park. ✆ 212/908-4601. www.
financialhistory.org. Admission $2. Tues-Sat 10am-4pm. Subway: 4/5 to
Bowling Green; J/M/Z to Broad St.

Scandinavia House   The Nordic Center in America has a stylish
new Midtown building. You can check out the cafeteria and gift
shop for free, but they ask for $3 for the third-floor gallery. The
space isn't very big, but the rotating exhibits are well presented,
with a wealth of informative notes. *Note:* There are occasional
free gallery talks; check the website.

58 Park Ave., between 37th and 38th sts. ✆ 212/879-9779. www.
scandinaviahouse.org. Suggested donation $3. Mon-Fri noon-5pm. Subway:
4/5/6/7/S to 42nd St./Grand Central; 6 to 33rd St.

Theodore Roosevelt Birthplace   Though not the original
birthplace, this historic site is a deft reproduction of the place
where T. R. spent his first 14 years. See p. 275 in chapter 7 for a full
review.

28 E. 20th St., between Broadway and Park Ave. S. ✆ 212/260-1616. www.
nps.gov/thrb. Admission $3. Mon-Fri 9am-5pm (tours hourly 10am-4pm).
Subway: N/R to Broadway/23rd St.; 6 to 23rd St.

This Old House

I find it amazing than anything can survive for long in NYC, especially old houses that don't do anything except clog up prime real estate. The Historic House Trust of New York City has information on 21 surviving dwellings, spread across all five boroughs. Admissions are usually $2 or $3, which is not bad for the opportunity to step into a relic and travel back a couple of hundred years. Recorded information from the Trust is available at ⓒ **212/360-3448**, and you can request a brochure at ⓒ 212/360-8282; www.preserve.org/hht.

The Morris-Jumel Mansion   One of Manhattan's coolest surprises is coming upon the grounds of the Morris-Jumel Mansion in the midst of monolithic Harlem apartment buildings. This genteel Palladian wonder is the oldest house in Manhattan, built in 1765 as a summer getaway. There isn't much land left on the plot, but what remains is pleasant to stroll around. You have to pay to enter the house, which provides a fascinating snapshot of its era. *Tip:* Don't miss picturesque Sylvan Terrace across the street (just west of the mansion), one of the city's last blocks of wooden workers' row houses. 65 Jumel Terrace at 160th St., east of St. Nicholas Ave. ⓒ **212/923-8008.** www.morrisjumel.org. Admission $3. Wed–Sun 10am–4pm. Subway: C to 163rd St.

Edgar Allan Poe Cottage   Happy-go-lucky author E. A. P. moved to the Bronx in 1846, hoping that the country air would be good for his tubercular wife. She died the next year, and Poe himself checked out 2 years later. The cottage is now an anomaly among brick high-rises. The interior has period furnishings and Poe exhibits. 2460 Grand Concourse at E. Kingsbridge Rd. ⓒ **718/881-8900.** www.bronxhistoricalsociety.org. Admission $3. Sat 10am–4pm; Sun 1–5pm. Subway: D/4 to Kingsbridge Rd.

FREE EXHIBITS AT THE LIBRARIES

Free books are just the beginning with New York's libraries. In addition to our free classes (p. 139) and free films (p. 57), Gothamites also get free exhibitions. The libraries really care about their material, which comes through in the surprisingly well-crafted displays.

Brooklyn Public Library FREE The galleries here present everything from painting to installation art to rare books. The works and the artists often have a local connection.

Grand Army Plaza. ℂ 718/230-2100. www.brooklynpubliclibrary.org. Tues-Thurs 10am-9pm; Fri-Sat 10am-6pm; Sun 1-6pm. Subway: 2/3 to Grand Army Plaza.

☆ **Donnell Library Center** FREE Many local fans of the writer A. A. Milne don't realize that Winnie-the-Pooh has been a fellow Manhattan resident for 50 years. Pooh and friends Piglet, Eeyore, Kanga, and Tigger are all on display in the Central Children's Room in Midtown. These are Christopher's actual stuffed animals, instantly recognizable from their portrayals on the page. Though they look a little forlorn for being stuck behind glass, they've held up pretty well for 80-year-olds. Take the elevator to the third floor and you'll see the animals on your right. Nearby display cases show off children's books from the collection.

20 W. 53rd St., between Fifth and Sixth aves. ℂ 212/621-0618. www.nypl. org. Mon, Wed, and Fri noon-6pm; Tues 10am-6pm; Thurs noon-8pm; Sat noon-5pm; Sun 1-5pm. Subway: E/V to 53rd St. B/D/F to Rockefeller Center.

☆ **Humanities and Social Sciences Library** FREE The book- and manuscript-themed exhibits here are lovingly displayed and as well written as you'd expect from a library. See p. 280 in chapter 7 for a full review.

Fifth Ave., at 42nd St. ℂ 212/869-8089 exhibits and events, or 212/661-7220 library hours. www.nypl.org. Mon and Thurs-Sat 10am-6pm; Tues-Wed 11am-7:30pm. Subway: B/D/F/V to 42nd St.; 7 to Fifth Ave.; 4/5/6/S to Grand Central.

New York Public Library for the Performing Arts FREE This library branch is a performance clearinghouse, conveniently located near the arts central that is Lincoln Center. Performing arts exhibitions can be found in the Donald and Mary Oenslager Gallery.

40 Lincoln Center Plaza, between 64th and 65th sts. ℂ 212/870-1630. www.nypl.org. Tues-Wed and Fri-Sat noon-6pm; Thurs noon-8pm. Subway: 1/9 to 66th St.

Schomburg Center for Research in Black Culture FREE The massive collection of books and art gathered by bibliophile

Moving Views

Straphangers get treated to a few spectacular scenes in exchange for their swipes. I love the **7 line** as it approaches Manhattan from Queens. The track twists and turns like a slo-mo roller coaster with the Midtown skyline in the background. The **J/M/Z ride across the Williamsburg** has great views from windows north and south. The Manhattan Bridge is back to full train capacity and B/D/N/Q riders can enjoy dramatic East River vistas.

One lesser-known public transportation thrill is the **Roosevelt Island Tram** (✆ **212/832-4543**, ext. 1). As you dangle in the air over the East River you get the East Side skyline, plus the U.N., plus great sightlines on the engineering marvels of the East River bridges. The trip between 60th Street and Second Avenue and Roosevelt Island takes about 4 minutes. It's $2 each way, though if you're on an unlimited Metrocard plan, you can get back via the F train's Roosevelt Island stop, just a few blocks away. The Tram operates daily 6am to 2am; until 3:30am on weekends.

Arturo Alfonso Schomburg is housed at this research branch of the New York Public Library. The Exhibition Hall, the Latimer/Edison Gallery, and the Reading Room all host exhibits related to black culture. Talks and performing arts are also part of the program here. Call or check online for scheduling details.

515 Malcolm X Blvd., at Lenox Ave., between 135th and 136th sts. ✆ **212/ 491-2200**. www.nypl.org. Gallery Mon–Sat 10am–6pm; Sun 1–5pm. Subway: 2/3 to 135th St.

2 Gallery Scene

Art galleries may be Gotham's greatest free cultural resource. Not only do these minimuseums provide us with works of inspiration, they also give us free booze and snacks at their openings. Don't be shy about barging into a show with million-dollar pieces. Gallery owners are almost as happy raising the profiles of their artists as they are closing a sale; both are essential for upping the prices they charge. We should also take a moment to be thankful for the dot.com boom. Not only did we all make a killing on our stock options, the dot.com boom made it possible for scruffy people in jeans and sneakers to be stealth millionaires. Gallery owners and employees can no longer easily distinguish between the underemployed and walking gold mines, meaning that our presence in galleries is not merely tolerated, but actively sought and desired.

If you want invites to openings, you have a couple of options. You can sign in whenever you visit a gallery and they'll keep you informed, or you can check online. Douglas Kelly keeps an amazingly comprehensive list of gallery openings at http://dks.thing.net. Most galleries are open Tuesday through Saturday from 10am to 6pm. Many openings are on Thursday nights. Summers can be pretty dead in the art world, and many galleries keep shorter hours, often closing on Saturdays.

> **Sources**
>
> The local papers provide rundowns on the higher profile shows. The *Village Voice* has good listings, which can also be perused online (www.villagevoice.com). Other sources include the "Art Guide" in the Friday "Weekend" section of the *New York Times* or the Sunday "Arts & Leisure" section; the "Cue" section of *New York* magazine; the "Art" section in *Time Out New York;* and the *New Yorker*'s "Goings on About Town."

IN CHELSEA

New York's big money art scene has put most of its eggs in one basket by clustering galleries **between 10th and 11th avenues.** For the gallery fan, this means you can visit hundreds of shows without ever leaving **the lower West 20s.** The geography also rewards the serendipitous, allowing for quick pop-ins at random-selected spaces. Not interested in a bunch of paint splotches on a pile of brillo pads? Pop right back out. My favorite strategy is to write down some interesting-sounding shows from the listings in the *Voice* and then hit a few of their unlisted neighbors. With floor after floor of galleries in the old warehouse buildings here, you're bound to find something of interest.

Subway: C/E to 23rd St.

FREE Watching the Auction Action

Sure, you know all about New York's auction scene, the way you follow a stranger in, take an inconspicuous seat off to the side, and try to suppress a sneeze just as a gavel comes down to announce you're the proud owner of a $50,000 Ming vase. But there's more to New York auction houses than expensive misunderstandings and antitrust violations. Viewings and sale previews are excellent chances to treat upcoming lots as museum exhibits. The current top house is **Christie's,** at 20 Rockefeller Plaza, 49th Street between Fifth and Sixth avenues (✆ **212/ 636-2000;** www.christies.com), and at 219 E. 67th St., between Second and Third avenues (✆ 212/606-0400). **Sotheby's** runs a close second on the Upper East Side, 1334 York Ave., at 72nd Street (✆ **212/606-7000;** www.sothebys.com). There are two often-overlooked smaller houses that sell equally intriguing artifacts. **Guernsey's,** 108½ E. 73rd St., between Park and Lexington avenues (✆ **212/794-2280;** www.guernseys.com), focuses on modern collections and memorabilia. The city's oldest privately owned house is **Tepper Galleries** at 110 E. 25th St., between Park and Lexington avenues (✆ **212/677-5300;** www.teppergalleries. com). Fine and decorative arts shows and estate sales are the specialties of the house.

Full calendars for all houses are available online.

David Zwirner FREE One of many recent SoHo refugees, Zwirner shows a range of interesting, inventive art.

525 W. 19th St., between 10th Ave. and West St. ✆ 212/727-2070. www. davidzwirner.com.

Gagosian Gallery FREE Perhaps the heaviest hitter around, this gallery puts on major shows in a space large enough to accommodate sculptures by Richard Serra.

555 W. 24th St., between 10th and 11th aves. ✆ 212/741-1111. www.gagosian. com.

Matthew Marks Gallery FREE Matthew Marks has built a miniempire in west Chelsea. His three galleries show top-tier painting, photography, and sculpture.

523 W. 24th; 522 W. 22nd; 521 W. 21st, all between 10th and 11th aves. © 212/243-0200. www.matthewmarks.com.

DOWNTOWN

In the early and mid-'80s, the headquarters of New York's avant-garde was the East Village. Tiny galleries dotted the landscape and helped break the era's big names. The stock market crash of '87 put an abrupt end to frivolous spending and most of the galleries withered away. It's taken more than a decade, but galleries are just now starting to come back. Throughout the **East Village** and **Lower East Side,** and even into **Chinatown,** store-front operations are coming to life. SoHo, conversely, continues to atrophy as an art scene. The galleries can't afford the rents and every year there are fewer and fewer hanging on. A few institutions are firmly embedded in the area, and they put on some of the best shows.

Subway: N/R/W to Prince; C/E to Spring.

FREE Photo Ops

Two of my favorite photo galleries can be found at **535 W. 22nd St., between 10th and 11th avenues.** This building has a bunch of interesting galleries for spontaneous pop-ins, plus a great book organization on the ground floor (see "Printed Matter," p. 89). **Julie Saul** (© 212/627-2410; www.saul gallery.com) brings in up-and-coming contemporary photography, while **Yancey Richardson** (© 646/230-9610; www.yanceyrichardson. com) represents an impressive stable of big names and new innovators.

Artists Space FREE   Young artists get exposure on the walls of this SoHo collective.

38 Greene St., between Broome and Grand sts., 3rd floor. © 212/226-3970. www.artistsspace.org.

The Drawing Center FREE   This downtown institution supports the often-overlooked discipline of drawing. Two spaces across the street from each other present simultaneous shows.

35 Wooster and 40 Wooster St., between Broome and Grand sts. © 212/269-2166. www.drawingcenter.org.

FREE SoHo's Secret Installations

The DIA Foundation for the Arts maintains a pair of hidden galleries with eccentric conceptual works by Walter De Maria (✆ 212/989-5566; www.diacenter.org).

☆ **New York Earth Room** As the name suggests, it's a room full of dirt. Really—140 tons of soil filling up a SoHo loft to a depth of almost 2 feet. It's an oddly compelling sight in the middle of the city, and the rich earthy scent is almost refreshing. 141 Wooster St., between Houston and Prince sts. www.earthroom.org.

The Broken Kilometer A few blocks away you can find a gallery floor covered with orderly rows of solid brass rods. Placed end to end, the 500 rods would stretch exactly—yup, 1km. (Its sister piece is in Germany, a sculpture with identical, unbroken brass rods buried vertically in the ground.) www.brokenkilometer.org. 393 West Broadway, between Spring and Broome sts.

Both galleries are open from Wednesday to Sunday, noon to 6pm (closed 3–3:30pm). Closed in summer.

Deitch Projects FREE SoHo standby Deitch puts up inventive shows, often of a conceptual variety.

76 Grand St., between Wooster and Greene sts. ✆ 212/343-7300.

Swiss Institute FREE The artists shown here usually have a Swiss connection. Innovative project ideas include the Institute's "Extension 17 project" featuring audio art (most recently by Sonic Youth's Kim Gordon)—just call the Institute and dial ext. 17.

495 Broadway, between Broome and Spring sts., 3rd floor. ✆ 212/925-2035. www.swissinstitute.net

MIDTOWN/UPTOWN

With the avant-garde ensconced downtown and in Brooklyn, the galleries that breathe the rarified air of the **Upper East Side** tend toward the staid side. Art here is of a classic bent, though the definition of classic is pretty elastic these days. Expect to see master works from the Renaissance up to the last couple of decades. And if you thought the asking prices were wacky downtown, wait until you see these . . . .

Subway: 6 to 68th St.; F to 63rd St.; N/R/W or 4/5/6 to 59th St.

Americas Society Art Gallery `FREE`   The Americas, from Canada all the way down to Patagonia, are the focus of art shows here.

680 Park Ave., at 68th St. ✆ 212/249-8950. www.americas-society.org. Wed–Sun noon–6pm.

Hirschl & Adler Galleries `FREE`   Five floors of galleries display 18th- to 20th-century European and American painting and decorative arts in an exquisite landmark town house.

21 E. 70th St., between Fifth and Madison aves. ✆ 212/535-8810. www. hirschlandadler.com.

Pace Wildenstein `FREE`   Modernism is now classicism, and this gallery specializes in the best of it.

32 E. 57th St., between Fifth and Madison aves. ✆ 212/421-3292. www. pacewildenstein.com. Also a new Chelsea location: 534 W. 25th St., between 10th and 11th aves.

Richard L. Feigen & Co. `FREE`   Master works of the last few centuries are the focus here.

34 E. 69th St., between Park and Madison aves. ✆ 212/628-0700. www. rlfeigen.com.

Wildenstein `FREE`   This gallery has over a century's experience in handling huge-ticket items. Renaissance and Impressionism treasures are a specialty.

19 E. 64th St., between Fifth and Madison aves. ✆ 212/879-0500. www. wildenstein.com.

WILLIAMSBURG

Recently Williamsburg's orthodox Jewish population distributed petitions asking for help from above to stem the "plague of the artists" that encroaches on their community. There's been no immediate response from G-d, but I'd bet that the plague continues to rage for the foreseeable future, as artists flock to Brooklyn and overrun Bedford's hipster boundaries. Though it's still more DIY and low-budget than Manhattan's galleries, the scene here is catching up rapidly. The only drawback is that the spaces are spread far afield. To make a full tour here be prepared to trek some blocks. *Note:* Brooklyn galleries keep different hours from the Manhattan side; many are open from Friday to Monday.

Subway: L train to Bedford Ave. or Lorimer St.; J/M/Z to Marcy Ave.; G train to Metropolitan Ave.

Dollhaus FREE Welcome to one of Williamsburg's more eclectic spaces, representing art from out in left field. Look for the occasional free film screening on Sunday night, too.

37 Broadway, between Wythe St. and Dunham Place. ℂ 718/384-6139. www. dollhaus.org.

Pierogi 2000 FREE The best painting I've seen in Brooklyn has been hanging in this small, well-established gallery.

177 N. 9th St., between Bedford and Driggs aves. ℂ 718/599-2144. www. pierogi2000.com. Fri-Mon noon-6pm.

Roebling Hall FREE One of the oldest and best of the Brooklyn galleries, Roebling Hall has bucked a trend by opening an offshoot space in SoHo. Look for really great paintings by young artists in both locations.

390 Wythe, between S. 4th and S. 5th sts. ℂ 718/599-5352. www.brooklyn art.com. *SoHo "Satellite" location:* 94 Prince St., at Mercer St. ℂ 212/966-9043.

31Grand FREE A solid crop of young artists shows their painting and photos here.

31 Grand St., at Kent Ave. ℂ 718/388-2858. www.31grand.com.

Williamsburg Art and Historical Center FREE Housed in an amazing 1867 bank building, this community center is always good for an intriguing art exhibit or two.

135 Broadway, at Bedford St. ℂ 718/486-7372. www.wahcenter.org. Sat-Sun noon-6pm.

3 Open Studios & Art Fests

Run-down industrial neighborhoods beget artists populations, as the creatively minded come in for cheap, raw studio space. In the old days a few neighbors would open their doors one weekend, to show off their work to friends and their floor-mates' friends. With the explosion of New York's artist population, things have become more organized than the old flier-on-a-light-post invitation system. Several neighborhoods now offer full-blown arts festivals, with music, installations, theater, and gallery events supplementing open studios.

EFA Studio Center `FREE` The Elizabeth Foundation for the Arts provides 110 artists with subsidized workspaces in Midtown. At least half the artists show off their work at the annual open studios. The third weekend in October.

323 W. 39th St., between Eighth and Ninth aves. ℭ 212/586-5896. www. efacenter.org. Thurs 5-8pm; Fri 5-8pm; Sat 1-5pm.

Gowanus Artists Studio Tour `FREE` Gowanus Canal boosters claim the neighborhood is destined to be New York's answer to Venice. We're confident there's a few decades left to enjoy things just as they are now, with crumbling brick warehouses and factories and row house back streets instead of marble palaces and singing gondoliers. The arts scene here leans toward the artsy-craftsy, but there's definitely some talent, and the spaces are great. The tour is held on the fourth weekend of October. The studio territory lies between Park Slope and Red Hook and Carroll Gardens, but the distances can be shortened by taking advantage of the free shuttle bus. The bus makes eight area stops starting at 1pm; check the map online.

Gowanas Canal and surrounding areas, in Brooklyn. ℭ 718/789-7243. www. gowanusartists.com. 1-6pm. Subway: F/G to Carroll St.

Hoboken Open Studios `FREE` The Garden State offers open studios in Hoboken, New Jersey, which is part of this "mainland America" thing we've heard so much about. On the third Sunday in October you can investigate the creativity of over 100 artists while enjoying more than a few sweet views of Manhattan. On the day of the show you can get free tour maps from City Hall.

City Hall, 94 Washington St., between 1st and Newark sts., 2 blocks from the Path, Hoboken, New Jersey. ℭ 201/402-2207. www.hobokennj.org. Noon-6pm. PATH train to Hoboken, from 33rd, 23rd, 14th, 9th, or Christopher sts.

See Williamsburg: Central Williamsburg Arts Festival `FREE` Scenesters abound in Billburg, which is by far the hippest 'hood for playing artiste. Despite wannabe proliferation, there's plenty of top-notch new art to be found here. On the first weekend in May, the galleries and studios around the Lorimer Street subway station come together for open studios, with group and gallery exhibitions, film, music, and a party or two thrown into the mix.

FREE Mi Casa Es Su Casa: Open House New York

Some of the most mysterious spaces in the city open their doors during this annual architecture celebration. The second weekend in October brings New Yorkers access to envy-inducing private residences and awe-inspiring public structures. When else are you going to get a peek at Chelsea's Grand Lodge of the Masons, or the grounds of the Roosevelt Island Smallpox Hospital? Locales are scattered across all five boroughs and you'll have to come up with a schedule, or limit your targets to a few spots. Obviously, intriguing spaces in central locations will have the longest lines. You will need to do a little ground-work. Some 45,000 of the curious took advantage of the first Open House. Certain venues limit the number of guests, so for personal must-sees sign up early on the website (www.ohny. org; 𝄞 917/626-6869).

www.williamsburgartscentral.org. Sat-Sun noon-5pm. Subway: G/L to Lorimer St.

Third-Fridays Late-Night Gallery Tour FREE Working folks get a chance to look at art once a month when Williamsburg's art purveyors keep extended hours. Two dozen representatives of the neighborhood's burgeoning gallery scene participate, making this a great time to mix bar and art crawling. A map is available online.

www.williamsburggalleryassociation.com. Noon-9pm. Subway: L to Bedford St.

Washington Square Outdoor Art Exhibit FREE This Depression-era idea for helping artists get their work out there is now safely into its 8th decade. Streets near Washington Square Park become a gigantic open-air art gallery, where you can browse through the works of some 200 artists and artisans. The show is juried, so even the crafts have standards to meet. Pick up a free map at the intersection of 8th St. and University.

Show covers University Place between 3rd and 12th sts., and spills over to Washington Place between Green St. and Washington Sq., and LaGuardia between Bleecker and E. 4th. 𝄞 212/982-6255. Noon-7pm; Sat-Mon on

Memorial Day weekend and Sat–Sun the following weekend, Sat–Mon on Labor Day weekend and Sat–Sun the following weekend. Subway: N/R/W to 8th St.; A/B/C/D/E/V to W. 4th St.

4 Free Tours

SPONSORED TOURS

New York's Business Improvement Districts (BIDs) started off as coalitions of local merchants who were mostly concerned with picking up trash and herding the homeless into neighborhoods without BIDs. Now fully established, they've taken on cultural roles in their communities, sponsoring concerts and public art. Always eager to boost their 'hoods, a few now offer free tours. There's always something new to learn about New York, although don't expect to hear many critical words about the neighborhood or its friendly, hardworking BID.

The Alliance for Downtown New York FREE   Every Thursday and Sunday at noon the Alliance shows off lower Manhattan during the Wall Street Walking Tour. You'll wander by Wall Street icons that include the New York Stock Exchange, Trinity Church, and Federal Hall. Tours meet on the steps of the National Museum of the American Indian at 1 Bowling Green. The tour runs about 1½ hours. Reservations not required.

© 212/606-4064. www.downtownny.com. Thurs and Sat noon, rain or shine. Subway: 4/5 to Bowling Green.

8th Street Walking Tour FREE   8th Street, and its East Village equivalent St. Marks Place, are among the city's most colorful commercial strips. Get the inside dirt on the area courtesy of The Village Alliance. Tours meet on the Northwest corner of Second Avenue and St. Marks.

© 212/777-2173. www.villagealliance.org. Select Sat at 11:30am. Tours late May to early Oct.

Orchard Street Bargain District Tour FREE   The Lower East Side is a bottomless well of history and lore. The neighborhood's current incarnation is marked by a revival of its commercial fortunes, which you will see in detail on this tour. Learn about stores ancient and ultramodern as you wander the narrow streets between the tenements. Reservations not required.

Meet up with the guide in front of Katz's Delicatessen, 205 E. Houston St., at Ludlow St. ✆ **866/224-0206** or 212/226-9010. www.lowereastsideny. com. Apr-Dec 11am, rain or shine. Subway: F/V to 2nd Ave.

Sidewalk Surprises in Lincoln Square FREE   Lincoln Square is on the cusp of major changes, with new buildings going up left and right and an overhaul of Lincoln Center in the offing. Learn more about the area and its overlooked historical sites courtesy of the Lincoln Square BID. Meet at the Maine Monument at Merchant's Gate in Columbus Circle, across from the fountain.

✆ **212/581-3774.** www.lincolnbid.org. Sat 11am; usually June–Nov, rain or shine. Subway: A/B/C/D/1/9 to 59th St./Columbus Circle.

34th Street Tour/Penn Station Tour FREE   The 34th Street Partnership presents two tours of their insanely crowded corner of the city. Every Thursday at 12:30pm the tour meets in the lobby of the world's most famous building (the Empire State), 350 Fifth Ave. at 34th Street, for the 34th Street tour. (In case of rain call ✆ **917/438-5123** to make sure it's on.) New Yorkers still lament the murder of the old Penn Station. Tours of the new include many references to the old. The tours happen on the fourth Monday of each month from 12:30 to 2pm. Meet up in the rotunda of the main station, near the tourist information booth at Seventh Avenue between 32nd and 33rd streets.

✆ **212/719-3434.** www.34thstreet.org. Subway: A/C/E to 34th St.-Penn Station.

INDEPENDENT TOURS

Battery Park City FREE   Battery Park is justifiably proud of its beautiful landscaped grounds. With the parks restored to pre-9/11 showroom condition, the area is eager to show itself off. On select Thursdays you can get a 1-hour tour from a real live horticulturalist. Locations and times vary so check online. On select weekend days you can take a 2pm public art tour, surveying the mixed bag of public installations down here.

✆ **212/267-9700.** www.bpcparks.org. Subway: 1/9 to Rector St.; 4/5 to Bowling Green.

Big Apple Greeter FREE   These New York boosters roll out the red carpet in an attempt to make their own enthusiasm for the city infectious to visitors. Visitors can pick any neighborhood they like, and the greeters will find a knowledgeable volunteer to tour them around for 2 to 4 hours. An unlimited 1-day Metrocard Fun Pass is even thrown in for free. FINE PRINT Reservations should be made at least a week ahead of time.

© 212/669-8159. www.bigapplegreeter.org.

Brooklyn Brewery FREE More of a lecture than a tour, this popular Saturday event entails a visit to a room full of silver beer vats followed by a trip to the company store. Your attention is rewarded with two complimentary drink tickets, which will let you sample a couple of half-pints of Brooklyn's tasty brews. Tours run on the hour between 1 and 4pm. Doors open at noon and close at 5pm.

79 N. 11th St., between Wyeth and Levit sts. © 718/486-7422. www. brooklynbrewery.com. Subway: L to Bedford Ave.

Central Park Conservancy Walking Tours FREE Central Park's rich history and hidden nuggets are explored in these hour-long walks. Themes range from landscaping, to Revolutionary War sites, to the rugged Ramble. Check the website because times and dates and locations vary. The tours run frequently. Also look out for the Conservatory Garden lunchtime tours, which take you through Manhattan's most beautiful garden.

© 212/794-6564. www.centralparknyc.org.

Evergreens Cemetery Tour FREE This boneyard on the Brooklyn/Queens border seems to stretch forever. As the final resting place for over half a million people, it's a good thing there's ample space (225 acres to be exact). Lovely rolling hills and vegetation galore make a lush contrast to the city. Guided walking tours of this historic site are held on select Saturdays at 11am.

1629 Bushwick Ave., at Conway St., Brooklyn. © 718/455-5300. www. theevergreenscemetery.com. Tours assemble at the main entrance, Bushwick Ave. and Conway St. Subway: A/C/J/L/Z to Broadway Junction.

John J. Harvey Fireboat FREE It's a spectacular scene when this retired fire department mainstay shoots its many hoses into the air. In service between 1931 and 1994, the fireboat remains an impressive piece of engineering. Free public tours of the boat run sporadically, often in concert with other riverfront-themed events, and occasional free excursions leave from the Pier 63 dock. Check the website for details and to sign up for a tour.

Pier 63, at 23rd St. on the Hudson. No phone. www.fireboat.org. Subway: C/E to 23rd St.

The Lower East Side: Birthplace of Dreams `FREE` Modern technology comes to the ancient streets of the Jewish Lower East Side on this new tour, which requires a cellphone. Dial in to the toll-free number to listen to George's dad (sorry, Ben), Jerry Stiller, whose voice has the perfect undulcet tones for a stroll through the old neighborhood. The tour takes about an hour. (Also look for the new Lower Manhattan/Ground Zero tour.)

© **800/644-3545.** www.talking street.com. Maps are available at the Lower East Side Visitor's Center, 261 Broome, between Allen and Orchard sts., or download one from the website. Subway: F to Delancey; J/M/Z to Essex St.

Privately Owned Public Space Walking Tour `FREE` This tour comes with an agenda: to inform the public about city zoning laws, and to point out places where building owners come up short. If this is a topic of interest for you, you'll probably be able to handle the full 90 minutes of it. Tours are about once a month, on Saturdays at 3pm, usually leaving from One Worldwide Plaza, on 49th (between 8th and 9th aves.). Check the website for info.

www.walkingtoursnyc.com. Subway: C/E to 50th St.

Prospect Park Discover Nature Tours `FREE` My favorite tour here leads into the wilds of Brooklyn, where you can see a newly rehabbed ravine, waterfalls, and Brooklyn's last forest. It's just like the Adirondacks—only less driving and better proximity to ethnic food when it's over. Tours run on the weekends and Monday holidays at 3pm, March through November. Check the website for other destinations, like nearby Green-Wood

---

Dirt Cheap Tours Worth Checking Out

With so many free tours around, it seems silly to plunk down money, but **Adventure on a Shoestring** (© **212/ 265-2663**) is worth every penny. Urban historian Howard Goldberg has been providing the behind-the-scenes story on New York nabes for over 40 years, and you're guaranteed to learn something new. Tours follow themes like the "Haunted East Village," "Salute to Sinatra," or "Marilyn Monroe's Manhattan." At $5, they're an inexpensive way to load up on New York lore. Tours last 1½ hours and take place rain or shine. Call for more information.

Cemetery. Meet at the Audubon Center, just inside the Lincoln Road/Ocean Avenue entrance.

℃ **718/287-3400. www.prospectpark.org. Subway: B/Q/S to Prospect Park.**

Shorewalkers FREE   Shorewalkers sure know how to hoof it. This environmental walking group makes some huge treks around the city, usually keeping close to water. FINE PRINT A $3 donation is requested.

℃ **212/330-7686. www.shorewalkers.org.**

Take a Walk, New York! FREE   The Listen to your Heart Campaign endeavors to slow the widening of New York waists through a series of guided urban walks. The walks are scheduled for weekends in all five boroughs and last 2 to 3 hours. Go fight the good fight against cardiovascular disease! Check online for current schedules.

℃ **212/379-8339. www.walkny.org.**

5 Green Peace: Community Gardens

It's just not healthy for humans to spend too much consecutive time without a break from the concrete jungle. New York has some great parks, but the space tends to be pretty cultivated. Our community gardens are nice, too, but they're small and usually don't let the public in for more than a couple of hours a week. Botanical gardens are the best way to inhale fresh country air, and they're closer than you might think. Time your visit right, and they're also completely free.

Brooklyn Botanic Garden   Fifty-two acres of cherry trees, roses, formal gardens, and ponds in the heart of Brooklyn is nothing short of a miracle. This is the city's most popular botanic garden and it's spectacular almost year-round. May is particularly worth noting, with bright green leaves on the trees and the cherry blossoms rioting. Don't miss the Fragrance Garden, designed for the blind, and the world's oldest and largest collection of bonsai. The regular admission is $3, but Tuesdays are free, as are Saturday mornings from 10am to noon. In winter, you can add Wednesdays, Thursdays, and Fridays to the free list (mid-Nov to mid-Mar).

1000 Washington Ave., at Eastern Pkwy., Brooklyn. ℃ 718/623-7200. www. bbg.org. Tues-Fri 8am-6pm; Sat-Sun 10am-6pm; closes at 4:30 Oct-Mar.

Subway: 2/3 to Eastern Pkwy./Brooklyn Museum; B/Q to Prospect Park. S to Botanic Garden.

Queens Botanical Garden `FREE`   This little-known park is an oasis in the heart of busy Flushing. Formal gardens are joined by a rose garden, a bee garden, a Victorian garden, and a 21-acre arboretum. Spring is the natural time to visit—the entire garden is awash with color.

43-50 Main St., at Dahlia St., Flushing, Queens. ℭ **718/886-3800.** www. queensbotanical.org. Mar Tues-Sun 8am-4:30pm; Apr-Sept Tues-Fri 8am-6pm, Sat-Sun 8am-7pm. Subway: 7 to Main St. Flushing.

☆ **New York Botanical Garden**   Visions of the Bronx don't conjure up uncut forests, rhododendron valleys, waterfalls, ponds, and wetlands. As unlikely as it may seem, though, for over a century the Bronx has been home to one of America's premier public gardens. With over 250 acres of rolling hills and land-scaped gardens, if it's flora you can probably find it. Admission is

`FREE` Parking It

Parks are among the city's best freebies, and we're fortunate to be in an era of expansion. Some 550 acres (!) of new park-land have just opened up along the piers near Chelsea. The city did a gorgeous job with these urban beaches, including planting some actual slender-leaved vegetation called "grass." Across town, restoration continues on the **East River Park.** When it's finally completed, epic Brooklyn views will comple-ment benches, ball fields, and a wide jogging path. Everyone knows about the great Manhattan views from the Brooklyn Promenade, but Queens has an equally impressive skyline van-tage that many New Yorkers have never seen. The **Gantry Plaza State Park** in Long Island City is fitted out with long piers that jut out over the East River, with the U.N. and Empire State Building standing out among Midtown's architectural jumble. The park has been newly fixed up and expanded on its northern end, with a swath of grass and comfy seats for chill-ing out. 49th St. and East River Dr., Queens. ℭ **718/786-6385.** Subway: 7 train to Vernon Jackson, walk west to the river.

$6 to the grounds, but all day Wednesday and Saturday morning from 10am to noon you can get in for free.

200th St. and Southern Blvd., the Bronx. ✆ **718/817-8700.** www.nybg.org. Metro North (✆ 800/METRO-INFO or 212/532-4900; www.mta.nyc.ny.us/ mnr) runs from Grand Central Terminal to the New York Botanical Garden station; it's a 20-min ride. Apr–Oct Tues–Sun and Mon holidays 10am–6pm; Nov–Mar Tues–Sun and Mon holidays 10am–4pm. Subway: B/D/4 to Bedford Park, walk southeast on Bedford Park Blvd. 8 blocks.

Staten Island Botanical Gardens `FREE` Staten Islanders have gardens galore nestled inside the Snug Harbor Cultural Center. The center is 2 miles from the ferry terminal, so getting here is a bit of a haul from the other boroughs. The grounds are open daily from dawn to dusk. They're free, but a couple of the gardens inside have fees ranging from $2 to $5. Connie Gretz's Secret Garden is well worth its $2 charge—it has a maze and a castle with a moat. They'll even waive the $2 if you've got a child in tow.

1000 Richmond Terrace, Staten Island. ✆ **718/273-8200.** www.sibg.org. S40 bus from the ferry to Snug Harbor.

Wave Hill Some of the city's most gorgeous acreage can be found in Riverdale, in the Bronx, where Wave Hill's breathtaking views take in the panorama of the Hudson and the Palisades. Thousands of plant species are spread across the 28 acres here, originally the grounds of a private estate. The plant curious can educate themselves in the carefully labeled herb and flower gardens. Horticultural, environmental, and forestry programs provide further edification. Regular admission is $4, but the grounds are free in winter. In summer, Tuesdays are free, as are Saturday mornings from 9am to noon.

675 W. 252nd St., at Independence Ave., the Bronx. ✆ **718/549-3200.** www. wavehill.org. Tues–Sun 9am–4:30pm, with extended hours in summer (call ahead). Subway: 1/9 to 231st St., then take the Bx7 or Bx10 bus to the 252nd St. stop; or A to 207th St. and pick up the Bx7 to 252nd St. From the 252nd St. stop, walk west across the parkway bridge and turn left; at 249th St., turn right. Metro North (✆ 212/532-4900) travel from Grand Central to the Riverdale station; from there, it's a pleasant 5-block walk to Wave Hill.

6 Zoo York

New York has plenty of fauna to go with its flora, though it isn't always cheap to check out. The mini zoos in the major Brooklyn, Queens, and Manhattan parks charge $5 to $6 admission. The

☆ A Midnight Elephant Walk

When the pachyderms visit the big town, they arrive on a train that takes them only as far as the Long Island City yards. They can't exactly get a lift to the gig from a black car, so they have to hoof it, through the Queens-Midtown Tunnel and down the streets of Manhattan. Watching the elephants emerge from the tunnel is an amazing spectacle. They walk in a file of trunks holding tails, with clown escorts all around. Often other hoofed beasts like zebras and camels come along for the stroll. The walk goes all the way to the elephants' five-story ramp at Madison Square Garden, but the best scene is at the tunnel entrance on 34th Street. There's a fun-loving crowd, including some of the freaks that events in Manhattan always seem to bring out, and a coterie of animal rights protesters. The procession hits the Manhattan side of the tunnel around 11:30pm. Be sure to be on time because the whole thing goes surprisingly quickly. The **elephant walk** FREE takes place at the beginning of the circus' annual stand (usually late winter); check the weekly update on the website for the exact date and time. ℂ **212/465-6741.** www.ringling.com/weekly. Subway: 6 to 33rd. St.; A/C/E or 1/2/3/9 to 34th St.

Bronx Zoo asks for $11. Fortunately, there are alternatives. The Bronx has a pay what you wish policy 1 day a week, and the city's parks are rich with other opportunities for getting close to critters.

Bronx Zoo Wildlife Conservation Park   Yankee Stadium isn't the only place in the Bronx where you can find 4,000 wild animals running around in their natural habitat. The Bronx Zoo is the largest city zoo in the country, and one of New York's greatest assets. Gibbons, snow leopards, red pandas, Western lowland gorillas, okapi, and red river hogs are just a few of the famous residents. With 265 acres to explore, it's easy to wander away a full day here. For summer visits, try to get here early or late, as the midday heat often finds the animals sleepy in their enclosures. Admission is $11, but Wednesdays are on a contribution basis (suggested admission is $11, but pay what you wish). Nominal additional charges ($2 or so) may apply for some exhibits.

185th St. and Southern Blvd. ℂ **718/367-1010.** www.wcs.org/zoos. Nov-Mar daily 10am-4:30pm (extended hours for Holiday Lights late Nov to early Jan); Apr-Oct Mon-Fri 10am-5pm; Sat-Sun 10am-5:30pm. Subway: 2 to Pelham Pkwy., Metro North to Fordham Rd. (then Bx9 bus); BxM11 Liberty Line bus (ℂ 212/652-8400).

FREE BIRDS

A dearth of rest stops on the Eastern Seaboard makes New York parks essential for avian travelers. Three New York parks loan out equipment for better boning up on our most welcome tourists.

Battery Park City FREE Eighty different bird species pass through the lush tip of Manhattan. At the Wagner Park pavilions binoculars and field guides are loaned out for free. Select Wednesdays, Thursdays, and Saturdays; check online as times vary.

ℂ **212/267-9700.** www.bpcparks.org. Subway: 1/9 to Rector St.; 4/5 to Bowling Green.

Central Park FREE Birdsong fills the thickets of the Ramble, an unexpectedly rural stretch of the park. You can take a closer look at the warbling set with a kit available from the Belvedere Castle. The kit is a backpack with binoculars, reference materials, and a map. The Castle is open Tuesday to Sunday from 10am to 5pm. FINE PRINT Two pieces of ID are required.

Midpark at 79th St. ℂ **212/772-0210.** Subway: B/C to 81st St.

Falconry Extravaganza FREE The falcon has landed: One day a year the birds of prey uncloak in Central Park. All manner of raptors swoop through the air above the East Meadow under the close supervision of the Urban Park Rangers. Leave the Chihuahuas at home. Meet at the East Meadow on the east side of the park at 97th Street.

ℂ **212/360-1311.** Mid-Oct Sat 1-4pm. Subway: 6 to 96th St.

Prospect Park FREE During spring's annual northward migration, hundreds of different bird species pass through here. To get some expert assistance in figuring out what's what, take the Saturday tour from noon to 1pm. To catch the worm-getting birds, you'll have to get up earlier. On the first Sunday of every month join the Early Bird Walk as it ambles through the park from 8am

FREE What Up, Dog?

Being trapped in small, dark apartments is just as hard on dogs as it is on us. Fortunately, dogs have their own release valves in the form of dog runs. The human and canine interactions make great free public theater. The Tompkins Square dog run is my favorite. Both the four-legged and two-legged regulars have a ton of character, and their friendships and rivalries are fascinating to observe. Watching a dog run is as much fun as the ant farm you had as a kid, only the ants don't all slowly die and drag the bodies through the tubes to the most distant module that's their burying ground until there's only one ant left and it dies alone, and instead of homogenous trisegmented insects you've got the endless varieties of dogs. Don't miss the creative costumes of the Dog Run Halloween Parade, held at noon on the Sunday before Halloween. Tompkins Sq. Park, between 7th and 10th sts. and aves. A and B. ☎ **917/797-7073.** Subway: 6 train to Astor Place; F/V trains to Second Ave.

to 10am. It's free, but you should call in advance to register. All tours leave from the boathouse, just inside the Lincoln Road/ Ocean Avenue entrance.

☎ **718/287-3400.** www.prospectpark.org. Subway: B/Q/S to Prospect Park.

GO FISH

It's a fine line between standing like an idiot with a stick in your hands and going fishing, but kids love baiting up and casting in anyway. The city offers a few spots for gathering fodder for "the one that got away" tales.

Battery Park City FREE Drop a line in the Hudson and see if you can pull up any three-eyed specimens. (Actually, the river's been mending remarkably in recent years, thanks to antipollution measures.) Bait and equipment are loaned out in Wagner Park. Sessions run from 10am to 2pm on select Saturdays, and select Fridays at lunch 11:30am to 1:30am.

© 212/267-9700. www.bpcparks.org. Subway: 1/9 to Rector St.; 4/5 to Bowling Green.

Central Park `FREE` Like the good New Yorkers they are, some 50,000 fish pack uncomplainingly into the confines of the Harlem Meer. You can try your hand at catching a bass, catfish, or bluegill with equipment loaned by the Charles A. Dana Discovery Center. Bait, pole, and instructions are provided. Fish can be fondled, but they're not to be kept: It's catch and release. Open Tuesday to Sunday 10am to 4pm (last pole goes out at 3pm), mid-April to mid-October. `FINE PRINT` Valid photo ID is required.

Inside Central Park at 110th St., between Fifth and Lenox aves. © 212/860-1370. www.centralparknyc.org. Subway: 2/3 to Central Park North.

Hudson River Park `FREE` There's no dilemma whether to fish or cut bait, as the Big City Fishing program takes care of the latter for you. Experienced anglers are on hand to offer advice, and the rods are free to borrow. Reel fun can be found at piers 25 (TriBeCa), 45 (Greenwich Village), and 66a (Chelsea.) Noon to 5pm on summer weekends and Tuesday to Sunday in July and August.

Pier 25, the Hudson at No. Moore St. © 212/533-PARK. www.hudsonriver park.org. Subway: 1/9 to Franklin St. Pier 45, the Hudson at Christopher St.; 1/9 to Christopher St. Pier 66a, the Hudson at 26th St.; C/E to 23rd St.

EXPLORING DOWNTOWN

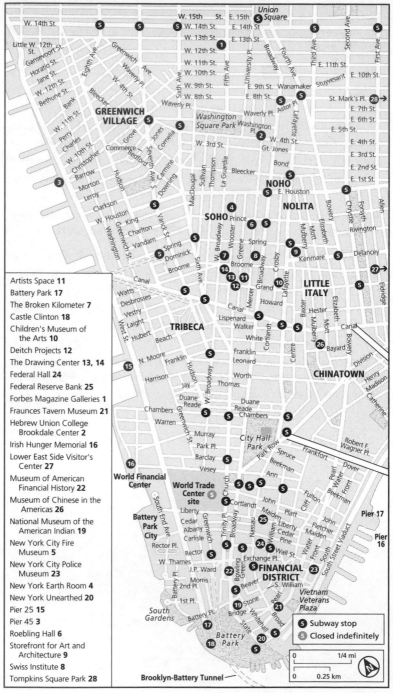

Artists Space **11**
Battery Park **17**
The Broken Kilometer **7**
Castle Clinton **18**
Children's Museum of
the Arts **10**
Deitch Projects **12**
The Drawing Center **13, 14**
Federal Hall **24**
Federal Reserve Bank **25**
Forbes Magazine Galleries **1**
Fraunces Tavern Museum **21**
Hebrew Union College
Brookdale Center **2**
Irish Hunger Memorial **16**
Lower East Side Visitor's
Center **27**
Museum of American
Financial History **22**
Museum of Chinese in the
Americas **26**
National Museum of the
American Indian **19**
New York City Fire
Museum **5**
New York City Police
Museum **23**
New York Earth Room **4**
New York Unearthed **20**
Pier 25 **15**
Pier 45 **3**
Roebling Hall **6**
Storefront for Art and
Architecture **9**
Swiss Institute **8**
Tompkins Square Park **28**

EXPLORING UPTOWN

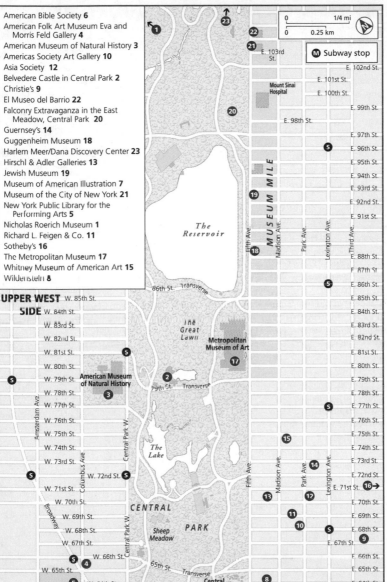

0   1/4 mi

0   0.25 km

M Subway stop

UPPER WEST SIDE

The Reservoir

MUSEUM MILE

Mount Sinai Hospital

E. 103rd St.

E. 102nd St.

E. 101st St.

E. 100th St.

E. 99th St.

E. 98th St.

E. 97th St.

E. 96th St.

E. 95th St.

E. 94th St.

E. 93rd St.

E. 92nd St.

E. 91st St.

E. 88th St.

E. 87th St.

E. 86th St.

E. 85th St.

E. 84th St.

E. 83rd St.

E. 82nd St.

E. 81st St.

E. 80th St.

E. 79th St.

E. 78th St.

E. 77th St.

E. 76th St.

E. 75th St.

E. 74th St.

E. 73rd St.

E. 72nd St.

E. 71st St.

E. 70th St.

E. 69th St.

E. 68th St.

E. 67th St.

E. 66th St.

E. 65th St.

E. 64th St.

E. 63rd St.

E. 62nd St.

E. 61st St.

E. 60th St.

E. 59th St.

W. 85th St.

W. 84th St.

W. 83rd St.

W. 82nd St.

W. 81st St.

W. 80th St.

W. 79th St.

W. 78th St.

W. 77th St.

W. 76th St.

W. 75th St.

W. 74th St.

W. 73rd St.

W. 72nd St.

W. 71st St.

W. 70th St.

W. 69th St.

W. 68th St.

W. 67th St.

W. 66th St.

W. 65th St.

W. 64th St.

W. 63rd St.

W. 62nd St.

W. 61st St.

W. 60th St.

W. 59th St.

86th St. Transverse

79th St. Transverse

65th St. Transverse

The Great Lawn

Metropolitan Museum of Art

The Lake

CENTRAL PARK

Sheep Meadow

Central Park Zoo

Wollman Rink

American Museum of Natural History

Lincoln Center

Columbus Circle

Central Park South

Amsterdam Ave.

Columbus Ave.

Central Park W.

Broadway

Fifth Ave.

Madison Ave.

Park Ave.

Lexington Ave.

Third Ave.

EXPLORING CHELSEA, THE FLATIRON DISTRICT, GRAMERCY & MIDTOWN

UPPER EAST SIDE

E. 64th St.
E. 63rd St.
E. 62nd St.
E. 61st St.
36 Roosevelt Island Tram
E. 60th St.
Queensboro Bridge

Fifth Ave.
Madison Ave.

From Lower Level
York Ave.

Queens

E. 59th St.
E. 58th St.
E. 57th St.
E. 56th St.
E. 55th St.
E. 54th St.
E. 53rd St.
E. 52nd St.
E. 51st St.

To Upper Level

Sutton Pl.
Sutton Pl. South

Roosevelt Island

35 **34**
33

MIDTOWN EAST

32 **29**
31 **30**
28
27
26

E. 50th St.
Mitchell Place

Beekman Place

Rockefeller Center
25

E. 49th St.
E. 48th St.
E. 47th St.
E. 46th St.
E. 45th St.
E. 44th St.
E. 43rd St.
E. 42nd St.
E. 41st St.

Sixth Ave. (Ave. of the Americas)
Fifth Ave.
Madison Ave.
Vanderbilt Ave.
Park Ave.
Lexington Ave.
Third Ave.
First Ave.

United Nations

24

Grand Central Terminal
23

Bryant Park
22 New York Public Library

Queens Midtown Tunnel

MURRAY HILL

E. 40th St.
E. 39th St.
E. 38th St.

Queens-Midtown Tunnel

21

E 37th St.
E 36th St.

Tunnel Exit

Tunnel Entrance

East River

E. 35th St.

Empire State Bldg.

E. 34th St.
E. 33rd St.
E. 32nd St.
E. 31st St.
E. 30th St.
E. 29th St.
E. 28th St.
E. 27th St.
E. 26th St.
E. 25th St.
E. 24th St.
E. 23rd St.

Broadway
Fifth Ave.
Madison Ave.
Park Ave. S.
Lexington Ave.
Second Ave.
First Ave.

20

Madison Square Park

19

Peter Cooper Village

FLATIRON DISTRICT

E. 22nd St.
E. 21st St.
E. 20th St.
E. 19th St.
E. 18th St.
E. 17th St.
E. 16th St.
E. 15th St.
E. 14th St.
E. 13th St.

Sixth Ave. (Ave. of the Americas)
Broadway

Gramercy Park
GRAMERCY PARK

18

Union Square

16
17

Union Sq. W.
Fifth Ave.
Union Sq. E.
Irving Pl.

N.D. Perlman Pl.

Stuyvesant Town

Asser Levy Pl.
Ave. C

Upper Manhattan

Uptown

Midtown

Downtown

S Subway stop

PARK
Transverse
Central Park S.
The Pond

253

EXPLORING BROOKLYN

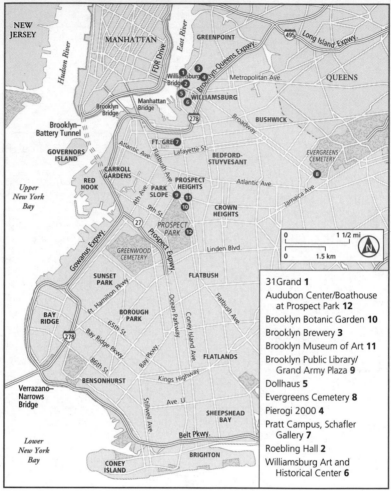

31Grand **1**

Audubon Center/Boathouse at Prospect Park **12**

Brooklyn Botanic Garden **10**

Brooklyn Brewery **3**

Brooklyn Museum of Art **11**

Brooklyn Public Library/ Grand Army Plaza **9**

Dollhaus **5**

Evergreens Cemetery **8**

Pierogi 2000 **4**

Pratt Campus, Schafler Gallery **7**

Roebling Hall **2**

Williamsburg Art and Historical Center **6**

EXPLORING QUEENS

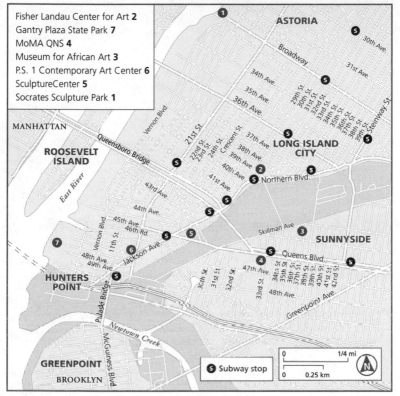

Fisher Landau Center for Art **2**
Gantry Plaza State Park **7**
MoMA QNS **4**
Museum for African Art **3**
P.S. 1 Contemporary Art Center **6**
SculptureCenter **5**
Socrates Sculpture Park **1**

ASTORIA

Broadway

30th Ave.

31st Ave.

34th Ave.

35th Ave.

36th Ave.

29th St.
30th St.
31st St.
32nd St.
33rd St.
34th St.
36th St.
37th St.
38th St.
39th St.

Steinway St.

MANHATTAN

Queensboro Bridge

Vernon Blvd.

21st St.

22nd St.
23rd St.
24th St.

Crescent St.

37th Ave.

38th Ave.

39th Ave.

40th Ave.

LONG ISLAND CITY

ROOSEVELT ISLAND

East River

43rd Ave.

41st Ave.

Northern Blvd.

44th Ave.

45th Ave.
46th Rd.

Skillman Ave.

SUNNYSIDE

Vernon Blvd.

11th St.

48th Ave.

49th Ave.

Jackson Ave.

47th Ave.

Queens Blvd.

34th St.
35th St.
36th St.
37th St.
38th St.
39th St.
40th St.
41st St.
42nd St.

HUNTERS POINT

30th St.
31st St.
32nd St.

33rd St.

48th Ave.

Greenpoint Ave.

Pulaski Bridge

McGuiness Blvd.

Newtown Creek

GREENPOINT

BROOKLYN

S Subway stop

0   1/4 mi

0   0.25 km

255

Built in 1920, Coney Island's iconic Wonder Wheel is the tallest Ferris wheel in the world—and it's a pretty cool ride, too. See p. 261 for more information.

FREE & DIRT CHEAP DAYS

hough New York is happy to gouge visitors for $40 bus tours and boat cruises, a person can scope out a lot of city for no money at all. It's hard to swing a cat in NYC without banging into a free daylong adventure or cheap date. The city's close quarters means you can hit a huge range of sites without putting excessive mileage on your soles. You don't even need to pack well—Gotham's corner stores are already storing your provisions for you.

Itinerary 1: A Day at Coney Island, Baby

Where	Coney Island, Brooklyn.
How to Get There	D/F/Q/W to Stillwell Avenue/Coney Island. The subway ride is about 40 minutes from downtown Manhattan. You can also use the B/Q trains at Brighton Beach.
How Long to Spend There	It's easy to amuse yourself along the boardwalk and environs for 2 or 3 hours. Anything longer probably requires a beach towel and a page-turner.
What to Bring	If you're planning on a dip, a bathing suit and towel are the obvious needs. There are public bathrooms, cabanas for changing, and showers for shedding saltwater. Even if you're going to keep to the streets, bring suntan lotion because there's plenty of light reflecting off the sand and sea.
Best Times to Go	Morning's calm is nice. Midday summer days can be brutal and hectic. Late afternoons the crowds start to disperse and the light is lovely.
Related Tip	The big holiday weekends bring in special events, but they also bring the biggest crowds. If you're not in the mood for the big crush, go on a weekday, or keep to the west, which is less populated. In the nonsummer months the amusement parks are closed, the boardwalk is almost empty, but the experience can be peaceful and replenishing.

After a few weeks or months of city living, trapped in the concrete canyons, it's easy to forget that New York City grew so far and fast because of its access to water. New York Harbor stays close to the public consciousness, but too many of us overlook the Atlantic Ocean, which is just a subway ride away. When you feel like traveling to a distant place but don't want to invest more than a couple of Metrocard swipes, Coney Island is hard to beat. In summer the area becomes a blue-collar resort, with salsa bands and volleyball games and screaming kids on the rides. As with all of Brooklyn, it's the furthest thing from monolithic. Tourists, hipsters, and elderly immigrant residents all intermingle on the beachfront benches. The area is low-budget and pretty rustic, which can be a very welcome relief from not just the oppression of modern corporate amusement parks, but also the non-frivolous, big-budget atmosphere of so much of the rest of the city.

① The Beach

The Atlantic up close is irresistible and the broad beaches here are a good spot to start a tour. Get good and hot in the sun and then go in for a dip.

ITINERARY 1: CONEY ISLAND, BABY

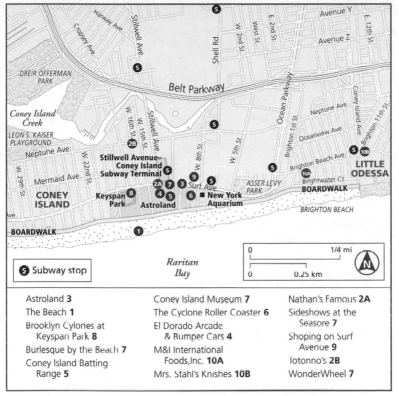

Astroland **3**

The Beach **1**

Brooklyn Cyclones at
Keyspan Park **8**

Burlesque by the Beach **7**

Coney Island Batting
Range **5**

Coney Island Museum **7**

The Cyclone Roller Coaster **6**

El Dorado Arcade
& Bumper Cars **4**

M&I International
Foods,Inc. **10A**

Mrs. Stahl's Knishes **10B**

Nathan's Famous **2A**

Sideshows at the
Seasore **7**

Shoping on Surf
Avenue **9**

Totonno's **2B**

WonderWheel **7**

The water is not the cleanest, but just follow the lead of the other souls out there bobbing in the waves. On a hot day it's particularly refreshing. A few blocks to the east the bodies thin out quickly and you can even find open stretches. If you're unwilling to track sand back in your shoes, a stroll along the boardwalk offers endless people-watching entertainment.

② Mealtime

There are almost limitless options for cheap beach food in Coney Island. Fried clams, fried dough, French fries, and soft-serve ice cream are among the highlights.

● On July 4th at high noon, big Americans and rail-thin Japanese fight it out in the annual Coney Island Hot Dog eating contest. For $2.44 a pop you can hold your own minicontest at **Nathan's Famous,** which still sells some million dogs a year at their busy stand.

● As good as a meal on a picnic table just off the beach is, it's worth noting that one of New York's best pizzas is just

Coney Island Costs

Free	
Sun, sand, and sea	$0
Dirt Cheap	
A day at the beach + 2 knishes	$3
Add-Ons for Spendthrift Millionaires	
Cyclone roller coaster or Wonder Wheel	$5
+ Half a pizza	$7
+ 28 pitches	$4
+ Sideshow	$5

a few blocks away. **Totonno's** is a casual, family run operation that serves up fresh pies (no slices). The fresh mozzarella, tangy sauce, and delicious thin crust haven't lost a step through eighty years of operation. Pies run about $14.

③ Astroland

Follow the sounds of electronic burbles and screaming kids up to this amusement park, where if you're feeling dirt cheap, the watching can be almost as much fun as participating. It's free to enter, and tickets for rides and games of chance range from $2 to $5.

④ The Bumper Cars

Another good spot for spectating is **El Dorado Arcade and Bumper Cars,** which is still holding out for that big disco comeback. Watch kids vent their sadistic urges under busy lights and mirrors to an infuriating refrain of "Bump, bump, bump your ass off."

⑤ The Batting Cages

The city's best mechanical pitchers hurl at the **Coney Island Batting Range,** a couple of blocks away. Swing away at deliveries that range from underhand to 95mph, $2 for 14 pitches. There's also mini-golf, bumper boats, go-karts, and a slick track.

⑥ The Legendary Cyclone

Technically part of Astroland but located across the street, the **Cyclone Roller Coaster** is the granddaddy of Coney Island amusements. Accelerating heart rates since 1927, it's the oldest and most-imitated roller coaster in the world. It's also a quota-starved insurance underwriter's nightmare, with engineering limited to a pulling chain and gravity, but still managing to get those rickety cars up to 60mph. The supporting rails and wooden boards look mighty untrustworthy, but of course that's the thrill (and in truth, the safety record here is excellent). Rides are $5 a pop ($4 for a reride) and for 1 minute and 50 seconds of action, so it's not exactly dirt cheap, though it's definitely memorable.

⑦ The Coney Island Museum & Sideshows

It's hard to imagine being over-charged for a museum that only costs 99¢, but the **Coney Island Museum** manages to pull it off. A handful of ratty artifacts fill the water-damaged second floor. To be fair, the museum is in the early stages of a capital campaign, but until a big stack of dollar bills have been collected, it's not worth the trip up the stairs.

Of more interest is **Sideshows by the Seashore,** run by the same people and located right around the corner. It's the nation's last 10-in-1 freak show;

The Coney Island Skyline

Parachute jumps were developed as military-training devices, but leave it to America to convert them to fun. **Coney Island's parachute jump** started out as a ride at the 1939 World's Fair in Queens before packing up for Brooklyn, where it served loyally until 1964. The skeletal form remaining has an unexpected elegance. It's now an official landmark and an enhancement to the local skyline, so much so that it's sometimes called the Eiffel Tower of Brooklyn.

The Eiffel Tower of Paris was the motivator for George Washington Gale Ferris, an engineer who took up the challenge for America to respond to the Frenchies' innovations in steel. The famous wheels still bear his name and Coney Island's version, 1920's **Wonder Wheel,** is the world's tallest at 150 feet. From the ground it looks like a gentle spin, but the reality can be somewhat stomach-churning. For panoramic views of the city and sea it's worth it. The $5 cost to ride, however, is a matter of individual budgetary discretion. Deno's Wonder Wheel. West 12th and the boardwalk, follow the signs. ℭ **718/372-2592.** www.wonderwheel.com. Weekends only in the off season, weather permitting. Memorial Day through Labor Day daily, 11:30am–11pm or midnight, weather permitting.

Make a Date

Coney Island after hours is even seedier than the daylight spectacle, but that doesn't impede on the potential for a great cheap date. The sight of the dark swells of the Atlantic and the cleared-out beach is pretty grand. The only thing that could improve on it is **free fireworks,** which come around 9:30pm every Friday night from late June to late August. After the fireworks if you've got money to burn, check out Sideshows by the Seashore's **Burlesque by the Beach.** Troupes from around the city come down to shake various body parts. Campy costumes and fire-eating round out the experience. Friday nights at 10pm; tickets are usually $10.

On Saturday nights, the same Sideshow folk unfold chairs in the **Coney Island Museum** so they can project campy films (see p. 49 in chapter 2). Coney Island-themed fare and other B-movie obsessions are the norm, and it's only $5. 1208 Surf Ave., 2nd floor. ℭ **718/372-5159.** www.indiefilmpage.com. Sat 8:30pm.

step right up to see fire-eating, illustrated men and women, albino serpent handling, and even beds of nails. The theater is small and run-down, with no air-conditioning, but there's 45 minutes of entertainment for only $5 adults, $3 kids 12 and under. If you're patient, you may hear the barker hustle up some empty seats at a discount, usually $3 for all ages. Weekend shows from Memorial Day to Labor Day, Fridays from 2 to 8pm, Saturday and Sunday from 1 to 11pm. Partial cast on Wednesday and Thursday afternoons.

⑧ Keyspan Stadium

The return of baseball to Brooklyn certainly hasn't diminished local pride, and tickets to Mets farmhands, the **Brooklyn Cyclones,** are hard to come by. Some standby seats are made available on game day outside the boardwalk stadium. Another option is to check in at the Stub Hub on the website, to see if anybody is selling. Seats are pretty cheap, for professional sports, $5 to $12.

⑨ Shopping Digression

If you're in need of cheap Russian furniture, you could do

worse than the showrooms on Surf Avenue, just east of the Cyclone roller coaster. More intriguing are the junk shops on the same block. There's a lot of literal junk for sale here—scraps of wiring and coat hangers—although there are also thrift-shop standbys like clothes and records. If you're in the market for a campy original print or painting, and if price is more important than quality, this is a great place to browse.

⑩ Bonus Round: Brighton Beach

If you want to leave America but have neglected to pack a passport, there is a close-by option. A quick trip east on the boardwalk will put you in the heart of **Little Odessa** in Brighton Beach. Between the strolling Russian émigrés, the cyrillic signs, and the clunky design on the sidewalk cafes, you'll be forgiven for thinking you've walked into a Black Sea resort town. The cafes are surprisingly pricey, but there's plenty of cheap street fare 1 block inland. Take a left and walk toward the El, which runs above Brighton Beach Avenue. This bustling street is dotted with caviar shops and street vendors.

For total immersion in a foreign land, check out the **M & I International supermarket.**

You can stock up for the trip home, or enjoy Russian pastries or smoked fish in the upstairs cafe. Prices are all outer-borough low.

Old-time Brooklynites grow as teary-eyed and nostalgic about memories of **Mrs. Stahl's Knishes** as they do about Ebbets Field. The key difference is that Mrs. Stahl's is still around and still baking delicious knishes of every conceivable flavor. A potato knish will only set you back $1.50.

Special Events

● In mid-July, the *Village Voice* sponsors the **Siren Music Festival** FREE, a massive rock concert. Some 150,000 indie fans show up to enjoy music on two stages from noon until 9pm. It's all free, no tickets necessary, just show up. Main stage: 10th Street at the boardwalk. Second stage: Stillwell Avenue at the boardwalk (© **212/475-3333;** www. villagevoice.com/siren).

● With body paint and beads, plus a few strategic scraps of fabric to keep things legal, the avatars of New York's retro-culture scene transform themselves into mermaids and Neptunes at the annual **Mermaid Parade** ☆ FREE. Classic cars join the procession as it works its way up Surf Avenue, dispersing when the participants dash down the beach to the ageless Atlantic. First Saturday after the summer solstice. Surf Avenue from West 15th to West 10th streets, D train to Coney Island/Stillwell Ave. www. coneyisland.com/mermaid. shtml. Take the W train to Coney Island/Stillwell Ave., and then walk toward the Atlantic. See also June in the "Calendar of Events," p. 18.

Itinerary 1 Index

Astroland   1000 Surf Ave., at the Corner of W. 10th St. ℂ 718/265-2100. www.astroland.com. Daily mid-June to early Sept noon-midnight, weather permitting. Weekends Apr-June 15, Sept-Oct noon-dusk, weather permitting.

Brooklyn Cylones at Keyspan Park   1904 Surf Ave., along the boardwalk. ℂ 718/449-8497. www.brooklyncyclones.com. Check the website for game schedule.

Coney Island Batting Range   3049 Stillwell Ave., near the boardwalk. ℂ 718/449-1200. www.coneyislandbattingrange.com. Daily 11am, noon for some rides.

Coney Island Museum   1208 Surf Ave., at W. 12th St. ℂ 718/372-5159. www.coneyisland.com.

Cyclone Roller Coaster   1000 Surf Ave., along W. 10th St. ℂ 718/372-0275. www.astroland.com.

El Dorado Arcade & Bumper Cars   1216 Surf Ave., between Henderson Walk and W. 12th St. No phone.

M&I International   237 Brighton Beach Ave., between Brighton 1st Place and Brighton 2nd St. ℂ 718/646-1225. Daily 8am-10pm.

Mrs. Stall's Knishes   1001 Brighton Beach Ave., at Coney Island Ave. ℂ 718/748-0210. Daily 9am-8am.

Nathan's Famous   1310 Surf Ave., at Stillwell Ave. ℂ 718/946-2202. www.nathansfamous.com. Mon-Thurs and Sun 8am-2am; Fri-Sat 8am-3am.

Sideshows by the Seashore   Surf Ave., at W. 12th St. ✆ 212/372-5159. www.coneyisland.com.

Totonno's   1524 Neptune Ave., between 16th and 17th sts. ✆ 718/372-8606. Wed–Sun noon–8pm.

Itinerary 2: From Brooklyn Bridge to DUMBO

How to Get There	To reach the Brooklyn Bridge, take the J/M/Z to Chambers Street or the 4/5/6 trains to Brooklyn Bridge-City Hall. Return from DUMBO on the F train at York Street, or walk about 15 minutes to Brooklyn Heights to catch the A/C train at High Street, or the 2/3 train at Clark Street.
How Long to Spend There	The walk across the bridge takes 30 minutes or so, and it's easy to spend an hour walking around on the Brooklyn side. Adding galleries, meals, and park time will stretch out the visit 2 or 3 hours.
Best Times to Go	A sunny afternoon is ideal, but it's all good. Late at night the bridge and DUMBO are close to deserted. It's more disconcerting than it is dangerous, but unless you're familiar with the area I recommend against it.
Tip	If you're interested in the galleries, check in advance to see which ones have exhibits up. Note that many galleries in DUMBO are only open on the weekends.

① The Bridge

The Brooklyn Bridge is one of New York's great treasures, and as such it's not a very well kept secret. Tourists, joggers, and commuters flood the planks on sunny days. The dizzying rigging, stunning views, and towering Gothic charm leave a person feeling like they're

Brooklyn Bridge/DUMBO Costs

Free	
Historic walk, art galleries, afternoon in the park	$0
Dirt Cheap	
Walk, art, park, plus an ice cream cone or hot chocolate	$2.50–$3
Add-Ons for Spendthrift Millionaires	
Brunch at Bubby's or Rice	$8.50–$10
Burrito and a beer at Pedro's	$8–$9

Crossings Over

New York's two other East Village crossings are more utilitarian approaches to Brooklyn, but they're excellent alternatives if you've already done the Brooklyn Bridge to death. The **Williamsburg Bridge** is newly refurbished, with walk- and bikeways to connect Brooklyn with the Lower East Side. The **Manhattan Bridge**'s pathway is narrow and the subway can be near deafening, but the views are unimpeachable. On the Manhattan end you get ancient tenements cutting razor-sharp lines through Chinatown; at midpoint you overlook the stunning full span of the Brooklyn Bridge, and on the far side you can spy on the parks of DUMBO.

within the sanctuary of an insided-out cathedral. The bridge's official romance with New York began in 1883, and from Walt Whitman through Hart Crane, the love has only grown. When you reach the first tower, stop for a while so you can admire the Manhattan views. The assorted plaques here are a mix of the ceremonial and the informative.

❷ The Brooklyn Side: DUMBO & Its Galleries

On the far side of the bridge, the pathway slants downward and divides. Going to the right takes you to Brooklyn Heights, and staying straight will put you beneath an overpass. Walk down the stairs, take a left, and head toward the water. Soon you'll find yourself among the cobblestones and broad-shouldered buildings that characterize **DUMBO.** DUMBO (Down Under the Manhattan Bridge Overpass) is a surprisingly well-preserved patch of old industrial New York. Artists have infiltrated, and their touches can be seen on and around many of the loft structures. For a closer look, check out some of the galleries. (Even if you hate the art, many of the galleries have killer views.)

● **Smack Mellon Studio** FREE A DUMBO classic. 56 Water St., at Front St. ✆ **718/834-8761.** www.smackmellon. org. Wed–Sun noon–6pm.

● **DUMBO Arts Center** FREE A 3,000-square-foot gallery. 30 Washington St., between

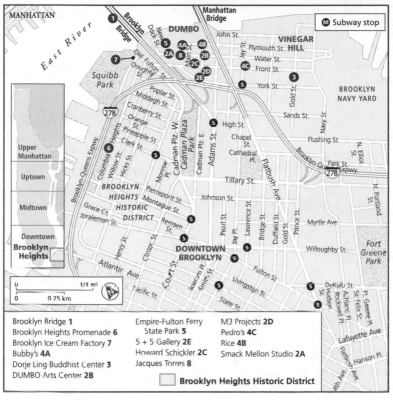

MANHATTAN

East River

Squibb Park

Upper Manhattan

Uptown

Midtown

Downtown
Brooklyn Heights

Brooklyn Bridge

DUMBO

Manhattan Bridge

Ⓜ Subway stop

John St.
Plymouth St. **HILL**
VINEGAR

Water St.
Front St.

York St.

BROOKLYN NAVY YARD

Sands St.

Flushing St.

Brooklyn-Queens Expwy

Tillary St.

BROOKLYN HEIGHTS HISTORIC DISTRICT

Johnson St.

Myrtle Ave.

Willoughby St.

Fort Greene Park

DOWNTOWN BROOKLYN

Atlantic Ave.

Pacific St.

State St.

Livingston St.

Fulton St.

DeKalb St.

Lafayette Ave.

1/4 mi
0   0.25 km

Brooklyn Bridge **1**
Brooklyn Heights Promenade **6**
Brooklyn Ice Cream Factory **7**
Bubby's **4A**
Dorje Ling Buddhist Center **3**
DUMBO Arts Center **2B**

Empire-Fulton Ferry State Park **5**
5 + 5 Gallery **2E**
Howard Schickler **2C**
Jacques Torres **8**

M3 Projects **2D**
Pedro's **4C**
Rice **4B**
Smack Mellon Studio **2A**

☐ **Brooklyn Heights Historic District**

Water and Plymouth sts. ℂ **718/694-0831.** www. dumboartscenter.org. Thurs–Mon noon–6pm.

- **Howard Schickler** FREE Space and astronomy specialists. 45 Main St., between Front and Water sts., #402. ℂ **212/431-6363.** www. schicklerart.com. Thurs–Fri 10am–5:30pm; Sat 11am–3pm.

- **M3 Projects** FREE 70 Washington St., between York and Front sts., Suite 700. ℂ **646/452-1300.** www.

mastelgallery.com. Sat–Sun, 1–6pm.

- **5 + 5 Gallery** FREE 70 Washington St., between York and Front sts., Suite 818. ℂ **718/624-6048.** www. fodde.com.

③ **A Moment of Zen & Vinegar Hill**

When you've had your fill of art, walk up Front Street (keeping the water to your left). When you reach Gold Street, peek through the yellow cement blocks on the corner.

The compound inside belongs to the **Dorje Ling Buddhist Center.** When Front Street dead-ends take a left and enter our favorite forgotten neighborhood in New York, Vinegar Hill. The well-preserved mid-

> ### But I Digress
>
> The entrance to the Brooklyn Bridge is just behind City Hall, which is just behind Chinatown, which is the cheapest place around to fuel up for a hearty walk. At dim sum brunches, carts full of dumplings and other delights are wheeled around the big banquet halls of Chinatown restaurants. It's easy to pack away a lot of food for no more than $10. My favorite spot is Chinatown's **Golden Unicorn,** with a lobby that on weekends looks like an office building during a fire drill. With four banquet hall floors, the wait for dumplings, pork-filled noodle crepes, and balls of shrimp and eggplant usually isn't too long, and on weekdays you can waltz right in. See the map on p. 108 in chapter 3. 18 E. Broadway, at Catherine St. ✆ **212/941-0911.** Daily 9am–10pm, dim sum until 4pm. Subway: J/M/N/Q/R/W/Z/6 to Canal St.

19th-century buildings are oddly juxtaposed with electric transformers. The neighborhood is only 4 square blocks, so it's a quick tour. Taking a right on Evans Street will bring you to a cul-de-sac, where you'll see an elegant white house behind a gate. Between 1806 and 1966 this is where the Navy Yard commandant hung his hat, while keeping watch over the outfitting of ships to fight everything from Barbary pirates to Nazis. The residence is now in private hands and the Navy Yard is closed to the public. If you're interested in the vine-smothered ruins of old naval housing, walk up Navy Street and turn left onto Nassau Street (it becomes Flushing Ave.), and then retrace your steps. Otherwise, double back down to Plymouth Street and walk south to DUMBO.

④ Mealtime

Two popular Manhattan joints have opened satellite locations in DUMBO, and both have cheap brunches on the weekends.

● With huge ceilings and plenty of surplus space, this location of TriBeCa legend **Bubby's** seems like it belongs in a less space-starved city. Prices are not exactly dirt cheap, but quality is high,

Make a Sweet Date

The **Brooklyn Bridge** at night is one of the most romantic spots in the city. You can take in the Manhattan skyline, plus the shimmering lights of Brooklyn, plus the mystery of the dark water below, plied by tugs and ferries. In the hours after dusk there's still plenty of foot traffic on the bridge so there's no menace, but it's much more secluded and sedate than at its rush hour and high noon peaks. If you've done a little planning, you can crank up the romance level a few notches by timing your visit with moonrise. The moon's location varies throughout the year, but generally it can be found creeping up over the Brooklyn skyline to the northeast. Check the paper or a weather website for the exact time of moonrise, and allow an extra 20 minutes or so for the satellite to clear the rooflines. If you're really organized, make the date for the full moon—it's the best free show the city's got.

After strolling along the bridge, cool down at the **Brooklyn Ice Cream Factory.** The ice cream here is as pleasurable as the view, well worth the $3 per cone. A little more inland, chocolatier extraordinaire **Jacques Torres** operates his factory out of DUMBO, where you can see the chocolate-making live for free. Though the chocolates themselves could never be confused with dirt cheap, once they take liquid form they become affordable. Winter brings the best hot chocolate in the city, and in summer special chilled drinks will cool you down for $2.50.

and you can get an omelet, pancakes, or sandwich for under $10. A selection of cocktails made with Bubby's own homemade sodas are only $3 each.

- Asian fusion fave **Rice** has brought Brooklyn its exotic grains, from Thai black to Bhutanese red. Starches are accompanied by curries, salads, and satays. Prices at brunch are $5.50 to $8.50, and at dinner most every dish is under $10.

- My personal favorite is **Pedro's.** Gigantic, tasty burritos are only $6. Wash it down with a $3 beer ($2 until happy hour ends at 7pm).

⑤ Park It

DUMBO offers twin spots for the cooling of jets, the **Empire–Fulton Ferry State Park** and Brooklyn Bridge Park. The former was the point of departure for the Manhattan ferry, which ran until 1924 despite competition from the Brooklyn Bridge. The northern park was a parking lot until it was decided that billion-dollar views of the city, the water, and the bridges, might be better appreciated by human beings than panel trucks. The boat traffic and skyline are both hypnotizing, and this is my favorite place to chill in the entire city.

⑥ Bonus Round: Brooklyn Heights

Just up the hill on the other side of the Brooklyn Bridge lies Brooklyn Heights. The neighborhood is staid, but the historic building stock is astounding. The fruit streets (Pineapple, Orange, and Cranberry, running east-west) are especially nice to stroll through. The **Brooklyn Promenade** along the Hudson has brilliant views of the Manhattan skyline.

Special Events

● Thursday nights in July and August walk over the Brooklyn Bridge and then reward yourself with a free flick. The **Brooklyn Bridge Park Summer Film Series** ☆ **FREE** projects in the shadow of the anchorage. (See p. 55 in "Entertainment" for a full review.)

● One weekend in mid-October (Fri–Sun) you can get the entire DUMBO arts scene at once. During the **d.u.m.b.o. art under the bridge festival** **FREE**, galleries and artists' studios open their doors. There's also live music, performances, and the streets are adorned with art installations. The DUMBO Art Center has a brochure with listings and a map (see "The Brooklyn Side," above, for more info).

● Every July, the **Brooklyn Waterfront Artists Coalition** curates an **outdoor sculpture show** **FREE** at Empire–Fulton Ferry State Park. It's my favorite time to visit, as the modern works are routinely excellent. The placement is even better, complimenting the natural contours of the park and the man-made wonders in the distance.

Itinerary 2 Index

Brooklyn Ice Cream Factory   Fulton Ferry Landing Pier, between Old Fulton and Water sts. ✆ 718/246-3963. Tues–Sun 1–10pm.

Brooklyn Waterfront Artists Coalition   ✆ 718/802-9254. www.bwac.org.

Bubby's   1 Main St., at Water St. ✆ 718/222-0666. www.bubbys.com. Kids eat free on Sun nights.

Dorje Ling Buddhist Center   98 Gold St., at Spruce St. ✆ 718/522-6253. www.jonang.org. Tues, Thurs, Sat 8:30am–9pm. Yoga and meditation classes offered throughout the week.

Jacques Torres   60 Water St., near Main St. ✆ 718/875-9772. www.mrchocolate.com. Mon–Sat 9am–7pm.

Pedro's   73 Jay St., at Front St. ✆ 718/625-0031.

Rice   81 Washington St., between Front and York sts., Brooklyn. ✆ 718/222-9880. www.riceny.com. Mon–Fri noon–11pm; brunch Sat–Sun noon–4pm.

Itinerary 3: Union Square & Environs

How to Get There	Take the L/N/Q/R/W/4/5/6 trains to 14th St./Union Square.
How Long to Spend There	The walking distances here are short and can be covered on foot in just a few minutes, but if you stop to linger over the exhibits, it can take a couple of hours.
Best Times to Go	Traffic flow is pretty constant, both for the park (crowded) and the exhibits (underused). Some of the latter are closed by 4pm. If you want to take advantage of the Greenmarket, make sure you're here on a Monday, Wednesday, Friday, or Saturday.

❶ Union Square

The park at Union Square opened in 1831, about the same time New York's smart set reached this elevation on their inexorable climb uptown. The elegant neighborhood was soon steeped in culture, with an influx of theaters and concert halls. Over the next few decades, the moneyed set moved on, and by World War I

Union Square Costs

Free	
3 exhibits, 2 museums, a tour, and a literary reading	$0
Dirt Cheap	
The exhibits, museums, tour, literary reading, plus a visit to a presidential birthplace	$3
Add-Ons for Spendthrift Millionaires	
Curry chicken and rice lunch	$5.25
Chicken burrito	$5.43
Chicken kabob sandwich	$4.75

the area was in decline. Union Square remained a popular location for labor rallies and protests, but the side streets got seedier and seedier. You can learn all about the neighborhood's history on a lively free walking tour given by the **Union Square BID** every Saturday afternoon at 2pm. Meet at the Lincoln Statue near the pavilion on the northern part of the park. When New York turned things around in the '80s, Union Square once again became the province of big spenders. Many of the city's trendiest and most expensive restaurants now fill the high-ceilinged spaces of cast-iron landmarks. The area is a popular shopping destination, which may contribute to general ignorance about the cluster of cultural gems available here.

② Center for Jewish History
Leaving Union Square, walk over to 15 West 16th St., between 5th and 6th avenues. The multifloor Center for Jewish History hosts several simultaneous exhibitions. Pass through the metal detector and get an admissions pass at the front desk. Displays range from photo shows to manuscripts to paintings, most documenting Jewish contributions to American society. Artifacts are well lit and exhibit notes are informative without running on too long. Everything is free except for the **Yeshiva University Museum** galleries, which require a separate fee. The center also offers free public tours on Tuesday and Thursday at 2pm.

③ Tibet House U.S. FREE
Go 1 block south to 15th Street, between Fifth and Sixth avenues. The faceless apartment house at 22 W. 15th St. is an unlikely place to find inspiring Tibetan art, but the second floor is home to a small collection of beautiful paintings, sculptures, and artifacts. The art is intricate and vibrant, and

ITINERARY 3: UNION SQUARE & ENVIRONS

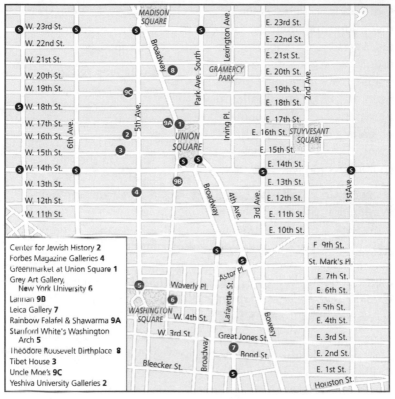

Center for Jewish History **2**
Forbes Magazine Galleries **4**
Greenmarket at Union Square **1**
Grey Art Gallery,
   New York University **6**
Lannan **9B**
Leica Gallery **7**
Rainbow Falafel & Shawarma **9A**
Stanford White's Washington
   Arch **5**
Theodore Roosevelt Birthplace **8**
Tibet House **3**
Uncle Moe's **9C**
Yeshiva University Galleries **2**

the quiet rooms encourage lingering study. A large gallery space hosts rotating shows with a Tibetan angle.

④ Forbes Magazine Galleries FREE

Walk 3 blocks south on Fifth Avenue to #62. Magazine magnate Malcolm Forbes' galleries here approximate what a 10-year-old boy with unlimited financial means would think to collect. Fortunately, a 10-year-old boy's enthusiasms radiate off the exhibits as well. Every time I visit I find myself

infected, caring more than I ever thought I could about model boats, toy soldiers, Monopoly boards, and trophies. For longer attention spans, the collection of presidential papers makes for engrossing reading.

⑤ Washington Square Park

A walk of 6 blocks south will lead you straight into Washington Square Park, a Village hub. After years of painstaking restoration, **Stanford White's Washington Arch** is positively glowing. Through this grand entrance you'll be able to find some form of free entertainment. Itinerant **street performers** often set up shop on the fountain, where they draw huge crowds. Along the fringes of the park neighborhood musicians are often noodling, or leading day-into-night singalongs. The park is a peerless spot for people-watching, too.

⑥ NYU Grey Galleries `FREE`
Washington Square is heavily trafficked by NYU students, who use the park as an informal quad. NYU owns many of the neighboring buildings, and it maintains galleries directly across the street from the park. The Grey Galleries show off every side of the visual arts, from painting to photo to

sculpture. There's a lot of space in the galleries and shows are fairly comprehensive.

⑦ Leica Gallery `FREE`
Cut over to Broadway and walk a couple of blocks down to #670. Legendary camera manufacturer Leica keeps a large gallery space on the fifth floor here. Usually two shows are going, a small one presenting one photographer in front and a larger selection of a different photographer in back. The range of styles is broad, covering different eras and mixing up black and white and color. When you're done, walk up Broadway 17 blocks, passing Union Square. Take a left on 20th Street to #28, which has a

Make a Date

It's hard to make a full-out meal from the **Greenmarket,** but it's easy to snack, or assemble a serendipitous minipicnic. In my own delicacy hierarchy, the apples are at the top. Dozens of plump varieties—not just the three or four flavorless waxed models of a supermarket—fill upstate farmers' tables. Baked goods are another specialty here, with both sweets and gourmet breads represented. Buy some artisanal cheese and you're in business. Picnic tables are available at the north end of the park.

If you're a careful planner, you can go right from your picnic to a free reading. The **Barnes & Noble** opposite the north end of Union Square is one of the city's best bookstores. Their reading series routinely attracts big names.

$3 admission charge that's well worth paying.

8 Theodore Roosevelt Birthplace

Theodore Roosevelt led an unlikely life. The asthmatic son of a prominent New York family, T. R. transformed himself into a symbol of fortitude, becoming a rancher, a soldier, a governor, and eventually the only New York City native elected president. Along the way he managed to write some 33 books, and the exhibitions in his childhood home can inspire a visitor to think they don't get enough done in a day. The original town house was demolished in 1916, but 3 years later friends and family built a replica on the site. Period pieces, the majority of which belonged to the Roosevelts, fill the stately rooms. A pair of galleries cover Roosevelt's conservationist achievements and memorabilia from his fascinating life. Take one of the informative hourly tours and you'll learn Eleanor Roosevelt's maiden name (it was Roosevelt), the origins of the teddy bear, and that T. R. survived losing his wife and mother on the same day. Admission is $3.

9 Mealtime

Besides the Greenmarket, you can find more substantial cheap eats all around Union Square. Three of my favorite spots in the city are nearby:

- At **Rainbow Falafel & Shawarma** ☆, the crispy falafel sandwich with marinated onions is just about perfect, and a steal at $3. There's no room to sit, but picnic opportunities abound in Union Square. See also the review on p. 171 in "Eating & Drinking."

- Republic is Union Square's most famous noodle shop, but I find the place to be overrated. Vastly superior is the Vietnamese cuisine at **Lannan.** Monster bowls of *pho* and hot-and-sour soup are under $6, and the majority of entrees are $7.75 or $8.75. I especially love the rice vermicelli dishes. The luncheon special from 11:30 to 4:30 is a mere $5.25, and dinner to go is only 70¢ more.

- New York seems destined to never have real Mission-style burritos, but **Uncle Moe's** serves up an array of California-Mexican standbys that are just as tasty. Burritos range from $5.43 to $7.55, depending on ingredients. A whole rotisserie chicken is only $10.27, and that comes with rice, beans, and corn tortillas. Everything tastes fresh here and there are plenty of tables to sit and enjoy.

Itinerary 3 Index

Barnes & Noble   33 E. 17th St., between Broadway and Park Ave. South. ✆ 212/253-0810. www.bn.com. Daily 10am-10pm.

Center for Jewish History   15 W. 16th St., between Fifth and Sixth aves. ✆ 212/294-8301. www.cjh.org. Reading Room and Genealogy Institute Mon-Thurs 9:30am-4:30pm; Fri by appt. All other galleries Mon-Thurs 9am-5pm; Fri 9am-2pm, Sun 11am-5pm.

Forbes Magazine Galleries   62 Fifth Ave., at 12th St. ✆ 212/206-5548. www.forbes.com/forbescollection. Tues-Wed and Fri-Sat 10am-4pm (hours can vary, call ahead).

Grey Art Gallery, New York University   100 Washington Sq. East, between Washington Sq. South and North. ✆ 212/598-6780. Tues and Thurs-Fri 11am-6pm; Wed 11am-8pm; Sat 11am-5pm. Suggested admission $3, not enforced.

Lannan   121 University Place, at 13th St. ✆ 212/420-1179. Daily 11:30am-midnight.

Leica Gallery   670 Broadway, Suite 500, between Bond and Great Jones sts. ✆ 212/777-3051. www.leica-camera.com/kultur/galerie/nyc/index_e.html. Tues-Fri 11am-6pm; Sat noon-6pm.

Quality Street Tours   ✆ 718/783-320. www.unionsquarenyc.com.

Rainbow Falafel & Shawarma   26 E. 17th St. ✆ 212/691-8641. Mon-Fri 11am-6pm.

Theodore Roosevelt Birthplace   28 E. 20th St., between Broadway and Park Ave. South. ✆ 212/260-1616. www.nps.gov/thrb. Admission $3 adults. Mon-Fri 9am-5pm (tours hourly 10am-4pm).

Tibet House   22 W. 15th St., between Fifth and Sixth aves., 2nd floor. ✆ 212/807-0563. www.tibethouse.org. Suggested admission $2, not enforced. Mon-Fri noon-5pm.

Uncle Moe's   14 W. 19th St., between Fifth and Sixth aves. ✆ 212/727-9400. Mon-Fri 11:30am-9:30pm; Sat noon-7pm.

Union Square BID   ✆ 212/460-1200. www.unionsquarenyc.com.

Itinerary 4: Crosstown Through the Crossroads of the World—From the U.N. to the Hudson

How to Get There	The nearest trains to the east are the 4/5/6/7 and Shuttle trains at Grand Central Station. The west side is close to the A/C/E and 1/2/3/9 trains.
How Long to Spend There	Just under 2 miles, this walk can take an hour with quick stop-offs, or over 2 hours with longer deviations.
Best Times to Go	The middle stretch bustles at all hours, just as the fringes are generally pretty calm. One great time is late afternoon. Looking back east from Ninth Avenue at dusk is an amazing experience, with all the lights and the area's brand-new skyscrapers adorning an already-decadent skyline.
Tips	Consider timing your walk so you can take advantage of a free or cheap event. Availability of tours, movies, dance, theater, and music are outlined below.

New York is intimidatingly large and complex and few tourists are assuaged when you explain that Manhattan at its broadest is only 13.5 miles long and 2.3 miles wide. Legendary 42nd Street is a perfect street for trying to come to terms with the city's range through a single, narrow slice. A walk along this schizophrenic cross-street brings you from the capital of the world at the United Nations, through the classic New York icons of Grand Central Station and the Public Library, into the European-style repose of Bryant Park, the tourist/lunatic asylum of garish Times Square, the cultural magnet of Theater Row, and finally out to industrial fringes along the Hudson. The whole trip is only 2 miles, but it spans the eras, cultures, and contrasts of New York City.

① Tudor City

Walk due east from the Lexington subway line and you'll experience a dramatic shift, as the hustle of the avenues gives way to the genteel village of Tudor City. Walk up the staircase on the south side of 42nd and admire the views of the **United Nations** and Long Island City, Queens. Tudor City

Greens, the little private park to your right, is a tranquil pocket for admiring late-'20s Tudor architecture contrasting with the glass behemoths of Midtown. When you're ready to move on, head west to Lexington Avenue.

② The Chrysler Building

Though the Chrysler Building only got to enjoy its status as

42nd Street Costs

Free	
Two parks, an art museum, a walking tour, and two exhibitions	$0
Dirt Cheap	
Parks, a mini art museum, a walking tour, two exhibitions, and two tacos	$4
Add-Ons for Spendthrift Millionaires	
Night at the theater	$5-$10
A beer and two hot dogs	$3.50

the world's tallest building for a few months (construction of the Empire State Building was hot on the Chrysler's heels), it holds a secure place in the hearts of architecture-loving New Yorkers. The stainless-steel Deco crown, with its jeweled notches, seems perpetually aglow, whether from sunlight or its own internal illumination. Designed by William Van Alen and completed in 1930, it's not much to look at up close, but you'll have some nice vistas when you get some distance. For a look at the lobby hang a right on Lexington and go through the revolving doors at 405, where you'll enter Art Deco overload. The groovy ceiling mural and glossy marble veneers create a Deco-cavern effect.

③ Grand Central

Grand Central Terminal in its new restoration is as inspiring as public buildings get. It cost $175 million to get the 1913 Beaux Arts landmark in this shape, but you can enjoy it all for free. In the main concourse look down to admire half an acre of gleaming Tennessee marble. Look up and you'll see what the constellations of a New York winter sky would look like, were the roof and the light pollution gone. Free art exhibits are often mounted in adjacent Vanderbilt Hall.

④ Whitney Sampler FREE

Philip Morris recently dropped its association-laden nom de smokes for the vaguely healthy-sounding and dot.commy "Altria," but the arts-friendly ground floor of its headquarters haven't changed. There's a tiny branch of the **Whitney Museum of Art** off to the side of a sculpture court. Usually living contemporary artists are highlighted. There isn't much square footage to wander through here, but it's not much of a time commitment either, and it's free. Also, free lunchtime gallery tours are offered Wednesday and Friday at 1pm, in

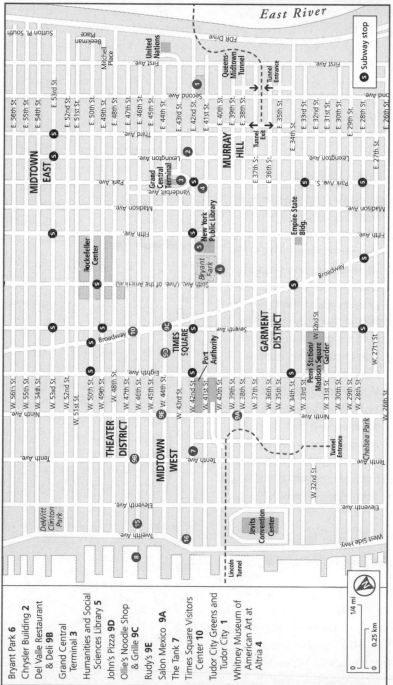

East River

Sutton Pl. South

Beekman Place

Mitchell Place

United Nations

FDR Drive

Queens-Midtown Tunnel

Tunnel Entrance

First Ave.

Second Ave.

Third Ave.

Lexington Ave.

Park Ave.

Madison Ave.

Fifth Ave.

Sixth Ave. (Ave. of the Americas)

First Ave.

2nd Ave.

MIDTOWN EAST

E. 56th St.
E. 55th St.
E. 54th St.
E. 53rd St.
E. 52nd St.
E. 51st St.
E. 50th St.
E. 49th St.
E. 48th St.
E. 47th St.
E. 46th St.
E. 45th St.
E. 44th St.
E. 43rd St.
E. 42nd St.
E. 41st St.
E. 40th St.
E. 39th St.
E. 38th St.

MURRAY HILL

Tunnel Exit
Tunnel Entrance

E. 37th St.
E. 36th St.
E. 35th St.
E. 34th St.
E. 33rd St.
E. 32nd St.
E. 31st St.
E. 30th St.
E. 29th St.
E. 28th St.
E. 27th St.
E. 26th St.

Grand Central Terminal

Vanderbilt Ave.

New York Public Library

Bryant Park

Empire State Bldg.

Rockefeller Center

Park Ave. S.

Lexington Ave.

Madison Ave.

Fifth Ave.

Broadway

Seventh Ave.

Times Square

Port Authority

Broadway

GARMENT DISTRICT

Penn Station/ Madison Square Garden

W. 32nd St.

W. 56th St.
W. 55th St.
W. 54th St.
W. 53rd St.
W. 52nd St.
W. 51st St.
W. 50th St.
W. 49th St.
W. 48th St.
W. 47th St.
W. 46th St.
W. 45th St.
W. 44th St.
W. 43rd St.
W. 42nd St.
W. 41st St.
W. 40th St.
W. 39th St.
W. 38th St.
W. 37th St.
W. 36th St.
W. 35th St.
W. 34th St.
W. 33rd St.
W. 31st St.
W. 30th St.
W. 29th St.
W. 28th St.
W. 27th St.
W. 26th St.

Ninth Ave.
Tenth Ave.
Eleventh Ave.
Twelfth Ave.

THEATER DISTRICT

MIDTOWN WEST

DeWitt Clinton Park

Ninth Ave.
Tenth Ave.
Eleventh Ave.

Chelsea Park

W. 32nd St.

Tunnel Entrance

Javits Convention Center

West Side Hwy.

Lincoln Tunnel

S Subway stop

0   1/4 mi
0   0.25 km

Bryant Park **6**

Chrysler Building **2**

Del Valle Restaurant & Deli **9B**

Grand Central Terminal **3**

Humanities and Social Sciences Library **5**

John's Pizza **9D**

Ollie's Noodle Shop & Grille **9C**

Rudy's **9E**

Salon Mexico **9A**

The Tank **7**

Times Square Visitors Center **10**

Tudor City Greens and Tudor Park

Whitney Museum of American Art at Altria **4**

addition to irregularly scheduled gallery talks. The Whitney's Performance on 42nd St. series brings dance and performance art to the space. Check the schedule, but shows usually start at 8pm, often on Wednesday nights.

But I Digress

For some quickie edification, when you're done with the Whitney, cut down Park to 41st Street. Embedded in the sidewalks on both sides of 41st between Park and Fifth avenues are plaques reminiscent of the Hollywood Walk of Fame, only with elegantly illustrated literary quotations instead of handprints of washed-up celebrities. But hey, that's the difference between New York and L.A. The quotes lead you to a nice vantage of the classical triangular façade of the New York Public Library.

⑤ Reading Between the Lions: The Library

Officially called the **Humanities and Social Sciences Library,** this 1911 icon features elegant Beaux Arts architecture, discreet landscaping, and famous steps. I love to people-watch here; the constant bustle is hypnotizing. When you

make it inside, you'll find the hushed interior just as impressive. Rotating exhibits show off rare editions from the collection. The thoughtful captions are a great reading experience on their own. As you leave, take a moment to admire the twin lion guards, *Fortitude* and *Patience*. These two traits will serve you well when you reach the Times Square segment of 42nd Street.

⑥ Bryant Park

Looking at the flourishing vegetation along the pebbled paths and Parisian folding chairs, it's hard to imagine that until the early '90s Bryant Park carried the nickname "Manhattan's longest urinal." Fully gentrified now, this Midtown jewel has a European charm and a schedule thick with freebies. Summer Mondays bring free films at dusk, and summer Thursday afternoons are equipped with live Broadway show tune samplers (see p. 42 and 54, respectively, for more information).

The Deuce

Once you cross over Sixth Avenue the crowds start to thicken. The intersections at Seventh Avenue and Broadway are among the most congested in the city. The stretch toward Eighth was known as the "Forty

FREE Grand Tours

There are five, count 'em *five*, free tours waiting to edify you on and around 42nd Street. On Wednesdays at half past noon, the **Municipal Art Society** offers a walking tour of the terminal. They ask for a $10 donation but there's no formal fee, just whatever you care to contribute. Meet at the information booth in the middle of the concourse, where you'll get great inside dope on America's commuter temple. The local BID, the **Grand Central Partnership,** runs a free tour on Fridays, also at half past noon. Meet in the Sculpture Court of the Whitney Museum at Altria. The **New York Public Library** shows itself off twice a day. Daily tours meet at 11am and again at 2pm beside the information desk in Astor Hall. When there's an exhibit mounted at Gottesman Hall, you can get a separate tour. Meeting times are 12:30 and 2:30pm daily at the entrance to the hall. If **Bryant Park's gardens** are more your speed, you can catch a free tour with a horticulturalist on selected Wednesdays at 12:30pm. Meet at the William Cullen Bryant statue on the east side in the park, between the cafe decks. Fifth and finally, the **Times Square BID** leads tours from its visitors center on Broadway between 46th and 47th streets. Tours go every Friday at noon. Of the five tours, this is the most bland, taking a mainstream approach to an overcommercialized stretch.

Deuce," or just "The Deuce." The refined theater scene thrived here in the early years of the 20th century. As the economy soured during the Depression, highbrow entertainment gave way to vaudeville. Vaudeville begat burlesque, and burlesque opened the door for garden-variety sleaze of every hue. There's still neon aplenty, but the peep shows have been replaced with sleaze of a corporate character. It doesn't seem to deter the tourist throngs, however.

⑦ A Play on Theater Row

As you get past the Port Authority Bus Terminal (7,200 buses and 200,000 passengers come through here on an average weekday), the streets calm down. Along "Theater Row" most of the stages are well above the dirt cheap threshold, though **The Tank** is a great spot for a low-budget night out (shows average about $7). Despite the lingering industrial structures, as you reach the far west the area starts to feel a little like a village again, an alternative universe to 42nd's opposite side in Tudor City.

8 The Hudson

Look up to the north and you'll see the *Intrepid* battleship, which is inexplicably floating in the Hudson at the end of 46th Street. The 40,000-ton *Intrepid* was once a city itself, with some 3,000 sailors on board. Now it's a museum with a substantial entrance fee ($14 for adults; battleship maintenance is apparently pretty steep when you're not taxpayer subsidized), but the decks can be circled and admired for free. At press time, Pier 84 was undergoing complete reconstruction. Eventually there'll be a community garden and lawn space, but for now you'll have to make do with picnic tables near the entrance to the Circle Line tours.

Before you move on, make sure to look back across Twelfth Avenue for views of the **Chinese Consulate Building.** At the end of 2 miles of attention-grabbing skyscrapers and neon signage, this building manages to be the oddest duck on the block.

9 Mealtime & Libations

As you make your way back, Hell's Kitchen has a burgeoning Mexican scene, and two great restaurants are just a few blocks off 42nd.

● **Salon Mexico** is more expensive than Del Valle below, but the portions are huge. A platter is $10, but it comes with rice, beans, and extraordinary sauces. The verde is my favorite, with mole a close second. On the cheaper side of the menu, the tasty sandwiches are only $5, and a veggie burrito is $6.50.

● **Del Valle Restaurant & Deli** ☆ is just as authentic, and the prices are even lower. Tacos, including the delicious carne asada, are just $2 a pop, and the densely packed burritos are all $5.95.

A couple of favorites for the pretheater crowd can be found on 44th Street between Seventh and Eighth avenues:

● At **Ollie's Noodle Shop & Grille,** huge bowls of soup and noodle dishes come in under $7. Most dinner entrees are under $10, and at lunch they're all $2 cheaper.

● **John's Pizza** makes real New York pizza and they sell it by the pie—no slices here. A large runs from $12 to $16, depending on the toppings.

● But why pay for a meal when you can eat for free? **Rudy's** knows a person can work up an appetite over a few pints. As a public service, this neighborhood dive distributes **free hot dogs.** Order a drink first, though. After all that walking, you've earned it.

Itinerary 4 Index

Del Valle Restaurant & Deli   655 10th Ave., between 46th and 47th sts. ℂ 212/262-5510.

Grand Central Partnership   ℂ 212/883-2420. www.grandcentral partnership.org.

H&H Bagels   639 W. 46th St., between Eleventh and Twelfth aves. ℂ 212/595-8000. www.hhbagels.com. Open 24 hr.

Humanities and Social Sciences Library   Fifth Ave. and 42nd St. ℂ 212/869-8089 exhibits and events, or 212/661-7220 library hours. www.nypl.org. Tues–Wed 11am–7:30pm; Thurs–Sat 10am–6pm.

John's Pizza   260 W. 44th St., between Seventh and Eighth aves. ℂ 212/391-7560.

Municipal Art Society   ℂ 212/935-3960. www.mas.org.

Ollie's Noodle Shop & Grille   200B W. 44th St., between Seventh and Eighth aves. ℂ 212/921-5988

Rudy's   627 Ninth Ave., at W. 44th St. ℂ 212/974-9169. Free hot dogs 1–10pm.

Salon Mexico   507 9th Ave., at W. 38th St. ℂ 212/868-7780.

The Tank   432 W. 42nd St., between Ninth and Tenth aves. ℂ 212/ 563-6269. www.thetanknyc.com.

Times Square Visitors Center   Free brochures and free Internet are the highlights at this tourist stop. 1560 Broadway, between 46th and 47th sts. ℂ 212/768-1560. www.timessquarebid.org.

Tudor City Greens   Daily 11am–7pm.

Whitney Museum of American Art at Altria   120 Park Ave., southwest corner at 42nd St., opposite Grand Central Terminal. ℂ 917/ 663-2453. www.whitney.org. Gallery Mon–Wed and Fri 11am–6pm;

Thurs 11am-7:30pm. Sculpture Court Mon-Sat 7:30am-9:30pm; Sun and holidays 11am-7pm. Extended hours for performances and lectures.

Itinerary 5: The Secrets of Lower Manhattan

Where	Lower Manhattan, skirting the East River, Hudson, and New York Harbor.
How to Get There	The area is very well covered by trains, J/M/Z trains to Broad Street and 2/3/4/5 trains to Wall Street are good places to start.
How Long to Spend There	A straight walk can be done in an hour. To get your fill of museums add 2 more hours, and a round-trip on the ferry clocks in at another hour.
Best Times to Go	The ferry's views of downtown and the Statue of Liberty are great at night, and incomparable at dusk.
Tips	On the weekends Lower Manhattan feels deserted, with tourists the only signs of life. Quiet streets in New York are a great luxury, but many of the museums and almost all of the stores and restaurants are closed. To really get a feel for the area hit it on a weekday.

The combination of too many tourists and too many uptight money-grubbers never makes for an inviting scene, but the Financial District gets a bad rap. New York City's post-Native American life began here, and the oddly shaped streets attest to the patterns of ancient, organic urban planning. New York is notorious for paving over its own history, but Lower Manhattan has some unlikely survivors. The area is densely packed and even a short walk can put a person in easy reach of a host of historical sites. Ignore the $9 trillion that changes hands down here every year at the New York Stock Exchange; there's a ton of freebies for the discerning seeker.

① Federal Hall National Memorial

This is not an especially popular memorial, probably because the really interesting stuff happened in predecessor structures on this site. Federal Hall was built in 1842 to serve as a customhouse and it's now a Park Service museum. Exhibits cover Washington's inauguration, the drafting of the Bill of Rights, and

ITINERARY 5: THE SECRETS OF LOWER MANHATTAN

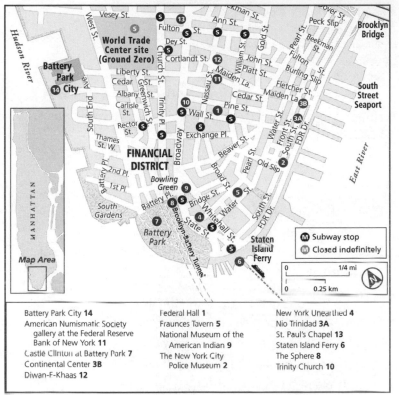

Battery Park City **14**
American Numismatic Society gallery at the Federal Reserve Bank of New York **11**
Castle Clinton at Battery Park **7**
Continental Center **3B**
Diwan-E-Khaas **12**

Federal Hall **1**
Fraunces Tavern **5**
National Museum of the American Indian **9**
The New York City Police Museum **2**

New York Unearthed **4**
Nio Trinidad **3A**
St. Paul's Chapel **13**
Staten Island Ferry **6**
The Sphere **8**
Trinity Church **10**

the first stirring of rebellion against British authority, all of which occurred right here. The building itself is a preeminent example of Greek Revival architecture, with an impressive rotunda behind the metal detector in the lobby. There are free guided tours, running on the hour during most of the day (call ahead for an exact schedule). The vertiginously steep stairs outside the building are a popular spot to spy on the chaos that surrounds the New York Stock Exchange.

② The Police Museum

The Police Museum is a recent addition to the area, housed in an odd fortresslike structure that for 6 decades was the First Precinct Station House. The exhibits can be a little uneven, and in places the museum is more of shrine than a source of information, but with three floors of galleries you're almost sure to find something of interest. I like the copper badges on the first floor (yes, that's where "cop" comes from), and the circa 1910–12 mug shots on

East River Walk Costs

Free	
Six museums, exhibits at two churches, and a round-trip ferry ride	$0
Dirt Cheap	
The museums, exhibits, ferry, and lunchtime concert	$2 (suggested donation)
Add-Ons for Spendthrift Millionaires	
Fraunces Tavern Museum	$3
Lunch	$6

the second floor. There is a suggested admission, but no one pays you much attention when you pass through the turnstile.

③ Meal Break

Nearby Front Street has several lunch vans to serve the worker bees from the adjoining financial and insurance offices.

- The best of the bunch is the **Nio Trinidad** truck, which parks at the corner of Front and Pine. For $7.50 you can get a fish or oxtail dinner, but my favorite is the Caribbean pancake called "roti." A veggie roti, pollinated with a delicious chickpea paste, is only $5. Only the very daring should ask for hot sauce. The area is dotted by benches and small parks, perfect for picnicking.

- In bad weather, head over to the **Continental Center** at 180 Maiden Lane, designed by I. M. Pei. The ground floor is public space, and free lunchtime recitals can often be found on the south side of the building.

On a nice day walk east to the river. Pier 11, at the end of Wall Street, has several spots for admiring the Brooklyn skyline as you nosh.

④ New York Unearthed

This tiny museum provides a quick sampler of urban archaeology. As you enter, dioramas show off items found during downtown building construction, moving backward from a 20th-century lunch counter to **American Indian relics.** Downstairs you can see more old shards in simulated cross sections of the city. You'll also be treated to the surreal sight of an actual conservationist in the middle of a glassed-in lab. Though there isn't much to this museum, everything is well presented. It's also a great stimulator for speculating on all the unknown treasures and trash entombed beneath our streets.

⑤ Fraunces Tavern

This is definitely an optional stop because it comes with an admission charge. Fraunces Tavern has impressive historical credentials—the building's origins date from 1719 and George Washington gave his farewell speech to his officers in the Long Room upstairs—but multiple fires and remodelings have made the current version something less than authentic. Your $3 entry ticket buys you a grainy 20-minute video and two floors of exhibits, including a re-creation of the Long Room and a flag gallery. Among the more interesting relics under glass is a lock of George's hair, which will be absolutely essential when it comes time to clone the father of our country. History buffs should definitely cough up for the tariff, but everyone else has my permission to keep moving.

⑥ Staten Island Ferry FREE

You're now very close to the poor man's Circle Line, the Staten Island Ferry (© 718/815-BOAT). This is one of my all-time favorite NYC freebies. From Manhattan to St. George and back again takes a little more than an hour, with inspiring views all the way. The brand-new terminal rises over the water at the end of Whitehall and State streets. Find a seat on the right-hand side of the boat as you enter. You'll have great vantages of the downtown skyline, including the somber gap marking Ground Zero. About halfway through the ride you'll spot Lady Liberty herself from the same western windows. Though there isn't much to do on the Staten Island side without a further bus or train ride, if you're really organized you can catch an inexpensive minor league baseball game (p. 95), just a few steps from the terminal.

⑦ Castle Clinton

Back on the Manhattan side, a few steps west from the ferry is **Battery Park**. The park is anchored by Castle Clinton, a Napoleonic-era fort. Although this battery has undergone several renovations—from theater hall to aquarium—the original 1811 walls are intact. If you walk in and look up, the modern skyline of downtown makes an interesting contrast through the open roof. There's a small stage on the east side that hosts free concerts on Thursday nights in summer, usually popular indie-rock bands.

⑧ The Sphere

As you exit Castle Clinton pass the Hope Garden and walk toward the modern art, which is part of a small and moving

9/11 memorial. **Fritz Koenig's sculpture, *The Sphere,*** stands behind an eternal flame lit on the first anniversary of the terrorist attacks. Koenig designed *The Sphere* as a symbol of world peace and for 30 years it adorned the plaza at the World Trade Center. The sculpture was salvaged from the rubble and placed here, where the shoreline would have been in 1625 New Amsterdam. Though battered and abused, *The Sphere* is surprisingly intact. There's a metaphor in there someplace, I hope.

⑨ National Museum of the American Indian

On the far side of *The Sphere* you'll hit a busy intersection that marks the end of Broadway. The small park across the street is Bowling Green, Manhattan's oldest public park. It was here or very close by that Peter Minuit, director general of New Netherland, traded the legendary $24 in beads with the native populations. Just a few feet away the Smithsonian maintains a museum dedicated to those Native populations. Most of the artifacts collected by New York banker George Gustav Heye are headed to a new home on the Mall in D.C., but rotating exhibits remain in three galleries. Native American

craftsmanship is unparalleled and the exhibits here are well lit and curated. Even if the walls were bare, the building itself, the former U.S. Custom House, would be worthy of a visit. It was completed in 1907 to the specifications of Beaux Arts master Cass Gilbert (he also did the nearby Woolworth Building), and the central rotunda by Raphael Guastavino is a structural marvel. Make sure you see it before the Native Americans reclaim their title to Manhattan and the eviction notices begin.

⑩ Trinity Church

Head north on Broadway and at the intersection of Wall you'll see Trinity Church. Trinity has been ministering Episcopal-style on this spot since 1698. The current Gothic Revival church was built in 1846 with a dark and somber interior. There's a small museum on-site. The churchyard is of more interest, with its ancient headstones somehow surviving in the shadow of Mammon. On Thursdays you can catch the **"Concerts at One"** program. (Mondays the series comes to St. Paul's Chapel; see below.) The suggested admission is $2, which in no way reflects the high caliber of the classical performers found here.

⓫ The Federal Reserve Bank of New York

Walk up 3 blocks on Broadway and you'll hit Liberty Street. A right turn and a 1-block walk will bring you to the Florentine Renaissance hulk of the Federal Reserve Bank (see p. 212 in chapter 6 for a full review). The American Numismatic Society keeps a gallery here, with a permanent exhibit on the history of money. You have to squint to see most of the coins, but the history behind them is fascinating. Among the cowrie shells and currency you'll find the only existing 1933 Double Eagle, a gold coin now worth some 400,000 times the value printed on its face.

⓬ Meal Break

Right around the corner is a small shop with fresh, delicious Indian food. **Diwan-E-Khaas** serves veggie entrees like rich palak paneer for only $4.99, and the chicken tikka masala is way undervalued at $5.90. Entrees include a choice of rice, nan, or roti.

⓭ St. Paul's Chapel

This satellite chapel of Trinity Church, completed in 1766, is the oldest continuously used public building in the city. The interior is cheerful and colorful, and even the 9/11 exhibits have an upbeat, healing tone.

On the north side of the chapel you can see the pew used by George Washington when New York was the official seat of the U.S. government and not just the de facto capital. Over the pew is a 1795 painting of the Great Seal, in one of its earliest renditions. The small churchyard behind the chapel is visually tranquil, although often the traffic and bustle of Church Street around Ground Zero prevent auditory serenity. Behind the headstones the void of the former World Trade Center site appears as an eerie prairie. This might be the best spot in NYC to put the long thread of the city's history into some sort of context.

⓮ Bonus Round: Battery Park City

A recent invention, Battery Park City is a complex of offices, hotels, and apartment buildings built on fill created by the excavation of the World Trade Center's foundation in the '60s. The city has never done a better job of landscaping and the walkways along the Hudson are ideal for strolling, or just sitting down to watch the river flow. **Vesey Street,** which runs along the north side of St. Paul's Chapel, will lead you past Ground Zero and straight down to the Hudson.

Itinerary 5 Index

American Numismatic Society gallery at the Federal Reserve Bank of New York   33 Liberty St., between William and Nassau sts. ✆ 212/234-3130. www.amnumsoc.org. Mon-Fri 10am-4pm.

Castle Clinton   In Battery Park. ✆ 212/344-7220. www.nps.gov/cacl. Daily 8:30am-5pm.

Continental Center   180 Maiden Lane, between Front and South sts. ✆ 212/799-5000, ext. 313, recital information.

Diwan-E-Khaas   53 Nassau St., between Maiden Lane and Liberty St. ✆ 212/571-7676. Mon-Fri 11am-8:30pm. **Two other locations nearby:** *26 S. William St.,* between Broad and William sts. ✆ 212/248-2361; *26 Cedar St.,* between William and Pearl sts. Closes at 3:30pm.

Federal Hall   26 Wall St., at Nassau St. ✆ 212/825-6888. www.nps.gov/feha. Mon-Fri 9am-5pm.

Fraunces Tavern   54 Pearl St., near Broad St. ✆ 212/425-1778. www.frauncestavernmuseum.org. Admission $3. Tues-Fri 10am-5pm; Thurs until 7pm; Sat 11am-5pm.

National Museum of the American Indian   1 Bowling Green, between State and Whitehall sts. ✆ 212/514-3700. www.americanindian.si.edu. Daily 10am-5pm, Thurs until 8pm.

The New York City Police Museum   100 Old Slip, between Water and South sts., 2 blocks south of Wall St. ✆ 212/480-3100. www.nycpolicemuseum.org. Suggested admission $5, not enforced. Tues-Sat 10am-5pm.

New York Unearthed   17 State St., enter off Pearl St. between Whitehall and State sts. ✆ 212/748-8628. www.southstreetseaportmuseum.org. Mon-Fri noon-5pm.

Nio Trinidad   ✆ 718/287-9848. Mon-Fri lunch hour.

St. Paul's Chapel   209 Broadway, at Fulton St. ✆ 212/233-4164. www.saintpaulschapel.org. Exhibit Mon-Sat 10am-6pm; Sun 9am-4pm. Concerts at 1pm Mon. Concert hot line ✆ 212/602-0747.

Trinity Church   74 Trinity Place, at Broadway and Wall St. ℂ 212/
602-0800. www.trinitywallstreet.org. Museum Mon–Fri 9am–
11:45am, 1–3:45pm; Sat and holidays 10am–3:45pm; Sun 1–3:45pm.
Guided tours Mon–Fri 2pm; Sun following the 11:15am service. Concerts at 1pm Thurs. Concert hot line ℂ 212/602-0747.

Get the skinny on destinations or events at information kiosks like this one, at the corner of Broadway and Park Row. See p. 293 for more information.

NYC BASICS

1 Information Centers

The city runs three info centers, with free maps and brochures as well as discount coupons for tourist-friendly fare.

New York City's Official Visitor Information Center 810 Seventh Ave., between 52nd and 53rd sts. © **212/484-1222.** Subway: B/D/E to Seventh Ave.; N/R/Q/W to 57th St.; 1/9 to 50th St. Mon–Fri 8:30am–6pm; Sat–Sun 9am–5pm; Thanksgiving, Christmas, and New Year's Day 9am–3pm; other holidays 9am–5pm.

City Hall Park Visitor Information Kiosk Broadway and Park Row. Mon–Fri 9am–6pm, Sat–Sun, holidays 10am–6pm. Subway: 2/3 to Park Place; R/W to City Hall; 4/5/6 to Brooklyn Bridge/City Hall; A/C/J/M/Z to Fulton St./Broadway Nassau.

Harlem Visitor Information Kiosk 163 W. 125th St., between Adam Clayton Powell Jr. Blvd. and Lenox Ave. Mon–Fri 9am–6pm; Sat–Sun 10am–6pm. Subway: 2/3 to 125th St.; A/C or B/D to 125th St.

Current Events

The city does a decent job of providing the latest scoop on goings-on around town. The **New York Convention & Visitors Bureau** has a 24-hour information hot line (© **800/NYC-VISIT** or 212/397-8222). For updated listings of music, theater, museum, and other events, check online at www.nycvisit.com. **NYC On Stage** (© **212/768-1818**) also has info on theater, music, and dance performances. The **City Parks Special Events Hotline** (© **212/360-3456**) provides a rundown on outdoor concerts and performances, and New York Roadrunner Club events.

Information at the Libraries   New York's public libraries are founts of information, and real live librarians are on hand to answer your brief factual questions (this service is of little utility for existential concerns). Bronx, Staten Island, and Manhattan residents can call © **212/340-0849** Mon–Sat 9am–6pm. In Brooklyn call © 718/230-2100, option 5, 10am–9pm Tues–Thurs, and 10am–6pm Fri–Sat. Queens InfoLine © 718/990-0714, Mon–Fri 10am–8:45pm.

2 Transportation

BY PLANE

New York City is served by three major airports: **LaGuardia Airport** (© **718/533-3400**), **John F. Kennedy (JFK) International Airport** (© **718/244-4444**), and **Newark International Airport** (© **973/961-6000**) in New Jersey. Newark often has the best cheap flight deals, and during high-traffic hours it can be the most accessible to and from Manhattan. For transportation information for all three airports call **Air-Ride** (© **800/247-7433**). The line is open 24 hours, with live operators Monday through Friday from 8am to 6pm. Similar information is online at **www.panynj.gov/airports**.

GETTING TO THE AIRPORTS
Cheap LaGuardia Transportation   The **M60 bus** ($2) serves all LaGuardia terminals, connecting to the Upper West Side of

Manhattan. The **Q33** and **Q48** also make LaGuardia runs. For the complete schedule call ✆ **718/330-1234** or log on to **www.mta. nyc.ny.us/nyct**.

Cheap JFK Transportation   The new **AirTrain JFK** is a little cumbersome if you have a lot of luggage, but it's a definite improvement over the old subway transfer system. The AirTrain costs $5 each way and connects terminals with the E/J/Z trains at Sutphin Boulevard/Archer Avenue, the LIRR at Jamaica Station, and the A train at Howard Beach. For the latter, make sure you catch an A to Far Rockaway, not to Lefferts Boulevard. The train runs 24/7. ✆ **877/JFK-AIRTRAIN.** www.panynj.gov.

Cheap Newark Transportation   The **AirTrain Newark** (✆ **888/EWR-INFO**) is a smooth ride, but it's a little pricey at $11.55 one-way. The cheapest trip is to take the **Path train** from Manhattan to Newark ($1.50). At Newark Penn Station you can catch the **62 bus,** which makes several stops but will get you to the airport for only $1.10. ✆ **800/772-2222.** www.njtransit.com.

BY BUS

As symbols of cheap interstate travel, Greyhound buses will live on in country songs. In the hearts of Eastern Seaboard adventurers, however, the Greyhound has been displaced by **Chinatown buses.** A round-trip to Washington, D.C., is only $35, and the slightly longer trip to Boston is an unbelievable $20. The difference between any two companies isn't dramatic; I choose based on who's got the most convenient schedule for me on any given trip. You can buy a ticket online or you can just show up at the departure point and let eager touts jostle each other for your business. The buses are full size and every driver I've ever had has been a professional.

Fung Wah Bus Service   This bus line travels between Boston's Chinatown (68 Beach St.) and New York's Chinatown (139 Canal St., between Chrystie St. and the Bowery). A one-way ticket is $10. ✆ **212/925-8889.** www.fungwahbus.com.

New Century Travel, Inc.   For the DC to NY and NY to Philly routes, this company runs a full schedule. The run to DC's Chinatown (513 H St. NW) is $20 one-way and $35 round-trip, and Philly (55 N. 11th St.) is $12 each way. ✆ **917/443-3986.** www. 2000coach.com.

The Atlantic City Bus

If you can't resist the call of the slots, **Gray Line** runs cheap trips to A.C. A 12-hour round-trip jaunt costs $30 on Fridays, Saturdays, and Sundays, and $25 on Wednesdays and Thursdays. It's only $15 on Mondays and Tuesdays. These fares get even cheaper when you factor in the complimentary $15 to $20 in chips and/or meal vouchers that many casinos will offer you as a come-on. (Then again, these prices get dramatically more expensive when an unlucky roll of the dice sucks up a quick $100.) Check your favorite casino's website for the current special offers. 777 Eighth Ave., between 47th and 48th sts. ℂ **212/397-2600.** www.graylinenewyork.com. Subway: C/E to 50th St.

Washington Deluxe If DC and New York's Chinatowns aren't convenient for you, this bus company makes pickups in assorted NYC locations (Brooklyn, Lower East Side, and Penn Station), and drops off at 1015 15th St. NW and at 441 New Jersey Ave. NW in DC. $20 for one-way and $35 round trip. ℂ **866/BUSNYDC.** www.washny.com.

BY (RENTAL) CAR

New York's unfriendliness to the private automobile extends to rental rates, which are in the fast lane. You can't do much better than $60 a day in Manhattan, and that only covers a compact car rented from a nonnational agency. The website www.carrental express.com will allow you to comparison shop for the best rate online. The closest rentals with normal prices (what people in the rest of the country pay) can be found at Newark Airport. Weekly rates start at around $30 a day for a compact, once all the taxes and fees have been factored in. A search on www.travelocity.com will allow you to compare. (Newark is admittedly not the most convenient location, but it's not so bad when you consider that you can train out there, avoiding the vehicular backups at the bridges and tunnels.) Some of the rental companies balk at renting to drivers with Manhattan addresses—check the fine print in the rental contract when you book online. Budget, for example, will want to run a full credit check. Also beware of Payless, which is located far from the terminal and slaps on big fees if you want to take the car out of New Jersey. For quick trips, **Zipcar** is a good alternative, with cars scattered around the city. It costs $25 to initiate an account, and then it's 40¢ a mile plus $8 to $16 an hour, depending on the day and location, though there's tax on top of that. The maximum 24-hour rate is $65, with 125 free miles and 18¢ a mile after that. © **866/4-ZIPCAR.** www.zipcar.com.

GETTING AROUND TOWN

UNDERGROUND

The MTA cooked its books to put the screws to subway and bus riders—$2 is now the price of a single ride. Until straphangers are called upon for our next bloodletting, there are a couple of discounts. When you spend $15 or more on a **MetroCard,** you get a 10% bonus. For 24 hours of heavy commuting you can get a Fun-Pass—all-you-can-ride for $7. Unlimited rides are also available in 7 day ($21) and 30 day ($70) formats. Children under 44 inches tall ride free. © **718/330-1234.** www.mta.nyc.ny.us.

ON WATER

Ferries Despite 2003's tragic accident, the **Staten Island Ferry** FREE is as safe a mode of travel as you'll find in New York. It's also hard to beat for scenic, with great Statue of Liberty, Ellis Island, and Governor's Island views (see p. 287 in chapter 7). The boat runs 24/7, leaving from the new terminal at Whitehall, on the southeastern tip of Manhattan. On the far side you can enjoy the scattered distractions of St. George, Staten Island, or you can follow the boat-loading sign and circle back across the harbor. Other ferry services and the New York Water Taxi also offer great views, but when you factor in ticket prices, they're not such great deals. © **718/815-BOAT.** www.ci.nyc.ny.us/html/dot. Boats leave every 20 to 30 minutes. Weekdays, less frequently off-peak and weekend hours. Subway: R/W to Whitehall St.; 4/5 to Bowling Green; 1/9 to South Ferry (ride in one of the first five cars).

3 Money Matters

FREE ATMS

The obvious way to avoid ATM surcharges is to only use your own bank's machines (assuming your bank doesn't gauge you for withdrawing your own money). Of course, high-stakes poker games and sample sales can put you in a spot without the luxury of a nearby home-bank ATM. In those instances, **Washington Mutual ATMs** may help. Their machines are free even for non-members. (Their online ATM locator is http://clients.mapquest.com/wamu/mqlocator?link=findusmain.) The lowest surcharge among non-bank mini ATMs is 99¢, at ATM Axis machines. They can usually be found inside New York's most popular chain (nope, not Starbucks—Duane Reade). Most everybody else will hit you up for $1.50, but watch out for HSBC, which takes $1.75, and of course, the deli ATMs, which will gouge you for $2.

4 NYC's Free & Dirt Cheap Resources

Disability Services   Alexander Wood of **Big Apple Greeters** (✆ **212/669-8159**) advises disabled visitors on how to get around the city. A few elevators aside, the subway system is largely inaccessible to the disabled, but 95% of the city's buses are equipped to carry wheelchairs.

Emergencies   ✆ **911** is, of course, the number for emergency police, fire, and ambulance service. For nonemergencies and just about any city government function you can think of, call ✆ **311.** Other emergency numbers include the **AIDS Hotline** (✆ 212/807-6655), **Animal Bites** (✆ 212/676-2483), **Poison Control** (✆ 212/340-4494), **Suicide Prevention** (✆ 718/389-9608), **Traveler's Aid** (✆ 212/758-0763), and **Victim Services Hotline** (✆ 212/577-7777).

Gay & Lesbian Resources   Being fabulous is a full-time job, but New York's LGBT community manages to find a few spare hours to stay well organized. The **Lesbian, Gay, Bisexual & Transgender Community Center** (208 W. 13th St., between Seventh and Eighth aves.; ✆ **212/620-7310;** www.gaycenter.org) is the meeting place for more than 400 organizations. Most of the online calendar lists events with charges, but there are a few freebies, in addition to the free lending library and archive. Other good places to look include the free weeklies *HX* (www.hx.com), *New York Blade* (www.nyblade.com), *Next* (www.nextnyc.com), *Gay City News* (www.gaycitynews.com), and the *Village Voice* (www.villagevoice.com). You can find copies stacked up in bars, clubs, stores, and sidewalk boxes throughout town. If you don't want to risk getting a little ink on your fingertips, the websites are also good sources of information. **Gay and Lesbian National Hotline** (© **212/989-0999;** www. glnh.org), offers peer counseling and information on upcoming events. Open Monday through Friday 4 to 8pm, Saturday noon to 5pm. **Gay Men's Health Crisis Hotline** (© **800-AIDSNYC**) provides information and support on HIV- and AIDS-related issues. The hot line is open Monday through Friday from 10am to 9pm, and Saturdays from noon until 3pm.

Internet Access   For free internet access, I suggest heading to **Three Jewels Refuge and Free Internet Café** ☆ in the East Village (211 E. 5th St., between Second and Third aves.; 6 to Astor Place; N/R/W to 8th St.; © **212/475-6650;** see complete review on p. 161 in chapter 4).

Moving   On city streetlamps, "Man with a Van" signs are ubiquitous. This is a good way to go for small moves. For the online version of these streetlamps, log on to **www.citimove.com**.

FREE The Wi-Fi Wave: Wireless Access Across the City

The city is rapidly going wireless. Our Wi-Fi zones are constantly expanding, already enveloping Bryant Park, Union Square, City Hall Park, the South Street Seaport, and the Columbia campus, among other places. Several hotels have gotten onboard, as have retailers like McDonalds and Starbucks. If you have access to an East Village rooftop or top floor facing south, you're also wired for free, courtesy of **www. evill.net**. Check **www.nycwireless.net** for the latest sites.

Many **public libraries** are Wi-Fi friendly, in addition to providing free Internet. Check online for more information, or your nearest branch (www.nypl.org in the Bronx, Manhattan, and Staten Island; otherwise www.queenslibrary.org or www. brooklynpubliclibrary.org). Many cafes offer Internet access, but only one provides it for free: **Three Jewels Refuge and Free Internet Café** (see above).

No-Pay Restrooms Open to the Public

For comprehensive information, you can take advantage of the efforts of people with way too much time on their hands by logging on to www.thebathroomdiaries.com or www.addyourown.com and browsing the lists of public facilities.

Many city parks have comfort stations, though they're usually not the cleanest. One excellent exception is **Bryant Park,** which has clean facilities in the northeast corner of the park along 42nd, between Fifth and Sixth avenues.

Transit hubs are good bets. The downstairs Dining Concourse at Grand Central recently added a second set of facilities on the west end. Until everyone else figures it out, they're not nearly as crowded. Penn Station has public restrooms on the Main Concourse near the ticket windows. Port Authority is not nearly as scary as it used to be, and there are bathrooms all over the terminal. The main restrooms, on the Main Concourse of the South Wing and on the second floor between the North Wing and the South Wing, are clean enough and heavily trafficked by commuters.

Movers bid against each other so you get decent prices, and movees critique the jobs so you know which companies to avoid.

Post Offices   The **Main Post Office,** at 8th Avenue and 33rd Street (✆ **212/967-8585**), is open 24 hours a day, 7 days a week. Call the **Postal Answer Line** (✆ **212/330-4000**) for other information.

Cheap(er) Telephone Services   Several small companies have come into the New York phone market, saving consumers hundreds of dollars a year versus the rates for AT&T and Verizon. The Man is threatening to give the Baby Bells their monopolies back, however, so we may not be able to enjoy **Vartec Telecom** (www.vartec.com) and its ilk for long. Vartec's customer service is almost comically disorganized, but the monthly rates are

Bookstores with cafes are almost always equipped with public restrooms. **Barnes & Noble** has seven Manhattan stores with decent facilities: Chelsea (675 6th Ave., at 21st St.), Union Square (33 E. 17th St., between Broadway and Park Ave. South), Astor Place (4 Astor Place, between Broadway and Lafayette St.), Midtown East (160 E. 54th St., between Third Ave. and Lexington Ave.), Lincoln Center (1972 Broadway, between 66th St. and 67th St.), the Upper West Side (2289 Broadway, at 82nd St.), and the Upper East Side (240 E. 86th St., at Second Ave.). All four locations of **Borders** have public restrooms: Wall Street (100 Broadway, at Pine St.), Kips Bay (550 Second Ave., at 32nd St.), Midtown East (461 Park Ave., at 57th St.), and Midtown West (10 Columbus Circle, Broadway at 59th St.).

Other stores worth noting are department stores and retailers like **Old Navy, Kmart**, and **Bed, Bath & Beyond**. Large, heavily trafficked tourist hotels are also great options. Times Square is a particularly unfriendly area for bathrooms, but the **New York Mariott Marquis** (1535 Broadway, at 46th St.) has nice facilities in its eighth-floor lobby.

great: $24.99 for basic, up to $49.95 for unlimited service. Note, however, that the Man slaps on up to $20 in additional taxes and surcharges every month. If you're already paying for broadband, you can get around the gummint by signing up with a company like **Vonage** (www.vonage.com). Monthly rates are low: $14.99 for basic (500 free min. of local and long distance), up to $29.99 for all-you-can-yak. Taxes are only 3% plus a $1.50 line charge. Broadband is rapidly improving in audio quality, and in many cases, you can keep your existing number (or choose from any area code in the country—just to keep 'em guessing). If you're only interested in long-distance savings, compare rates online at **www.lowermybills.com**. (The site offers rate comparisons on everything from cellphones to insurance to mortgages.)

INDEX